PROJECT PLANNING, SCHEDULING & CONTROL

REVISED EDITION

A Hands-On Guide to Bringing Projects In On Time and On Budget

James P. Lewis

McGraw-Hill
New York San Francisco Washington, D.C. Auckland Bogotá
Caracas Lisbon London Madrid Mexico City Milan
Montreal New Delhi San Juan Singapore
Sydney Tokyo Toronto

McGraw-Hill

A Division of The **McGraw·Hill** *Companies*

© 1995, James P. Lewis

ISBN 1-55738-869-5

Printed in the United States of America

BB

9 0

Designed and typeset by A-R Editions, Inc.

This book is dedicated to

My family:
Moffett P. Lewis
Alice Lewis
Hazel Stroud
Ann Atwell

and to the memory of

Norman L. J. Smith

CONTENTS

LIST OF FIGURES

PREFACE

The first edition of this book came out in 1991. Since then, I have been gratified by the response, in terms of total sales, and by all of the phone calls, letters, and faxes from people who have bought the book and found it to be helpful in managing their projects. It was my objective to write a book that was truly *practical*, that would be used by people actually managing projects, as opposed to a book full of theory, yet lacking in practical suggestions for actually managing. The results indicate that I achieved that target. In addition, I have found that the book is being used in college courses at both the graduate and undergraduate levels, which suggests that many academic programs are moving toward more practical curricula. I take that as an extremely positive sign.

Years ago, when I was trying to learn how to manage, I found that most books were *descriptive* rather than *prescriptive* in nature. I struggled for a long time trying to learn the "how-to" of managing, and hopefully this book will save you some of that wasted time. However, the book is not just a lot of "If you do this, then everything will work fine" kinds of statements. I have tried to capture both the *how* as well as the *why* of managing projects. Perhaps that comes from my empathy with children who always want to know *why*? Why do you do it that way, Daddy? they ask. And they don't like being told, "Go ask your mother." So I have tried to explain *why* I think a certain approach is proper in managing projects, then have explained *how* you carry out the steps.

To cover the *how*, I developed a flow chart showing every step in the process. That flow chart has been a tremendous help to people (they tell me) in walking step-by-step through their projects. That does not mean that negotiating the steps is *easy*— but it is one thing to be struggling with the question of "what do

I do now?" simultaneously with "how do I do it?" The flow chart removes doubt about what do I do next, and leaves you free to determine the "how."

It is fashionable today to write books on managing projects in terms of specific disciplines. Thus we have Data Processing Project Management, Construction Project Management, Engineering Project Management, and so on. The implication is that the method of managing varies as the discipline changes, and that simply is not true. Two plus two is four, whether applied to farming, engineering, rocket science, or medicine. The same is true for the tools of project management—they can be used in managing *any* kind of project. I have tried to write this book so that the examples are varied, in the hope that readers from any discipline can relate to the material.

Since 1991, I have entered the international market, and have conducted seminars in Singapore, Kualua Lumpur, Jakarta, Bangkok, India, and London for approximately 6,000 individuals. I have also done a significant amount of consulting to organizations to help them make project management "work." In the process, I have learned even more about the practice, and have incorporated that learning in this second edition.

Very early in my career, I found that I solved technical problems easily—if only I could resolve my *people* problems. For that reason, I think it is important to stress that project management is really *people management,* and I have presented ways of dealing with the people issues that must be applied in order to make the tools work.

I would like to thank all of my students, clients, and colleagues, who have shared their ideas with me over the past years. I especially appreciate the many discussions I had with my friend and colleague, Norm Smith, which have contributed to my understanding of the art and practice of project management. Norm passed away in November of 1994, and I have greatly missed those discussions.

Thanks to my editors at Irwin Professional Publishing, Pamela van Giessen, Kevin Thornton, and others who contributed substantially to the project and I value their help.

Finally, I can say from experience that a good team can always accomplish more than any individual working alone. My wife, Lea Ann, has contributed countless hours to developing illustrations to turn the lifeless printed page into something more attractive, interesting, and informative. She could not write the book alone, and I could not illustrate it. Together, I think we have made it greater than the sum of its parts. The technical term for the outcome is "synergy." It is what you get with good teamwork, and without it, no project can succeed.

May you have success and good teamwork in your own projects.

James P. Lewis
Vinton, Virginia

Abbreviations Used in This Book

ACWP	Actual Cost of Work Performed
AOA	Activity-on-Arrow
AON	Activity-on-Node
BAC	Budget at Completion
BCWP	Budgeted Cost of Work Performed
BCWS	Budgeted Cost of Work Scheduled
CPI	Cost Performance Index
CPM	Critical Path Method
CSSR	Cost-Schedule Status Report
C/SCSC	Cost/Schedule Control Systems Criteria
DIF	Data Interchange Format
EAC	Estimate at Completion
EEO	Equal Employment Opportunity
EF	Early Finish
ES	Early Start
FF	Finish-to-Finish
JIT	Just in Time
LF	Late Finish
LRC	Linear Responsibility Chart
LS	Late Start
MIS	Management Information System
NTSB	National Transportation Safety Board
PC	Personal Computer
PERT	Performance Evaluation and Review Technique
PMI	Project Management Institute
QFD	Quality Function Deployment
SPI	Schedule Performance Index
SS	Start-to-Start

AN OVERVIEW
OF PROJECT MANAGEMENT

About 2650 B.C. Imhotep built the step pyramid for the pharaoh Zoser at Sakkara, in Egypt. About 150 years later and 2,200 miles away, the ancestors of the British people began building huge stone circles throughout the British Isles. The best known of these is Stonehenge.

Another 2,500 years passed, and the Mayas had become a recognizable political group in Central America. They peppered the barren landscape of the Yucatán Peninsula with magnificent temples at Chichén Itzá, Sayil, Uxmal, and other sites.

The builders of these remarkable structures were the world's first project managers. They had no computers to assist them, no PERT (Performance Evaluation & Review Technique) or CPM (Critical Path Method) scheduling tools, and in some cases

not even paper on which to draw plans. Yet they managed some exceptionally complex projects, using the simplest of tools.

Managing projects, then, dates back at least 4,500 years, yet the role of project manager is only recently becoming recognized as a discipline in its own right. Universities are beginning to offer courses in project management, and several now offer a Master of Project Management degree as an option to the conventional M.B.A. In addition, with the development of scheduling software that runs on personal computers, interest in project management is growing at a rapid rate.

WHAT IS A PROJECT?

There are all kinds of projects. There are projects to develop new products, to develop a marketing plan, to build a large office building, to remodel a home, to landscape one's lawn, to develop a new vaccine, and so on. The possibilities are almost endless, making project management a nearly universal discipline. The most commonly accepted definition of a project is shown in the box.

> **A project is a one-time job that has definite starting and ending points, clearly defined objectives, scope, and (usually) a budget.**

The key words are *one-time, definite starting and ending points, budget,* and *objectives/scope.* Through these, a project is differentiated from repetitive activities such as production, order processing, and so on.

Even for such seemingly repetitive activities as building a number of homes using the same design, the terrain will be different for each, the weather will vary, and the work group will probably change, so each construction job will be unique. It is the uniqueness of each project that makes special demands on project managers and simultaneously makes project management an exciting discipline.

START

FINISH
*

A PROJECT IS A ONE-TIME JOB

Note also the part of the definition that says a project has a definite ending point. Some projects never seem to end. This is because the parties involved have failed to properly define what will constitute *finished*. Worse yet, they may have failed to define exactly what was to be done to begin with, thus allowing the project to grow, taking on a life of its own.

A second definition of a project that has merit is offered by Dr. J. M. Juran, the quality expert. A project is a problem scheduled for solution. This means that a project is always conducted to solve a problem for the organization. The importance of this definition lies in forcing us to recognize that we are solving problems.

> **A project is a problem scheduled for solution.**
> *— Dr. J. M. Juran*

Note, however, that there are two connotations to the word *problem*. One is that something is messed up. That is not the definition we are using here. For our purposes, a problem is a gap between where you are and where you want to be, and there are obstacles that prevent easy movement to close the gap. For example, you would like to develop a new product. If you could wave a magic wand and have the product appear, you would have no problem, only a desired result. The obstacles that prevent easy movement to close the gap are many: the need to fully define requirements, solve design problems, manufacture the product, and so on. Finding ways to deal with these obstacles constitutes problem solving.

However, it is not the solving of problems that seems to present the major difficulty for most of us. We are often good problem *solvers*, but poor problem *definers*. We have been taught for years to solve problems, but seldom have we been taught to properly define them. And, since the way a problem is defined determines the approaches used to solve it, a project team needs to spend time at the beginning working up a clear definition of the problem being solved. Often we find that project teams want to *get on with it*, and wind up solving the wrong problem. This will be discussed later in more detail.

What Is Project Management?

First, it might be good to say what project management *is not*. It is not just scheduling. With the growth in popularity of personal-computer-based scheduling software, many people think that if they simply buy the software and apply it, they will be doing sound project management. Then they find that they really do not know how to apply the software.

As a matter of fact, this is putting the "cart before the horse," since it is very difficult to know how to fully utilize the software unless you first have a good grasp of how to manage projects and exactly what you are going to do with the software. I could buy a superb accounting software package and be unable to use it, as I know very little about accounting practice.

For many years it has been customary to say that project management is the planning, scheduling, and controlling of project activities to achieve *performance, cost,* and *time* objectives, for a given *scope* of work, while using resources efficiently and effectively. These have been referred to as PCT objectives. They are also commonly called *good, fast,* and *cheap.* These more colorful terms capture the essence of what a project manager must achieve, as shown in Figure 1.1.

The last sentence of the definition is really loaded! The three objectives must be met *while using resources efficiently and effectively.* This is a key point in project management, and one that is too often overlooked. Every organization has limited resources, and unless the project manager can deal successfully

FIGURE 1.1
GOOD, FAST, CHEAP—PICK TWO!

with the resource allocation problem, she will not be successful. Experience shows that in many environments failure to manage resources properly is one of the most common causes of project failure. Methods of allocating resources will be covered in more detail in the scheduling section of this book.

The relationship among the four variables is given by the following equation:

$$C = f(P,T,S)$$

In words, the equation says, "Cost is a function of Performance, Time, and Scope." Ideally, a real equation could be written prescribing the actual relationships precisely. In practice, we never know that precise relationship. We have to estimate times and costs.

Now, for an equation containing four variables, how many can you dictate? Naturally, the answer is three. You cannot dictate all four of them. They simply won't go together (in all likelihood). Once you pick three of them, the fourth one will be whatever the equation says it will be. It is okay to estimate the fourth variable and let the estimate be a *target*, but we recognize that it will probably not come out exactly as targeted, since all of the variables on which it is based are themselves estimates.

In spite of that understanding, we still find senior managers trying to dictate all of the variables. One of the ten most common causes of project failure is that senior managers refuse to accept reality. In many cases, it is that a project is going to cost more than some preconceived notion they have. I heard about a project manager who told his company it would cost $60 million to do a job. He was told he would have to do it for only $30 million. When the job came in at $62 million, he was fired (scapegoated). Yet he was within 3 percent of his original estimate!

It is interesting to examine the relationship between cost and time alone. This is shown in Figure 1.2. Note that there is some optimum duration for the project, at which costs are a minimum. As the duration is extended, costs rise because of inefficiency. As the duration is reduced (we say the project is being *crashed*), costs rise because you generally have to apply premium labor rates to reduce time, and you also reach a point of diminishing returns. In addition, there is a duration below which you cannot go. No matter how many resources are applied, the project duration cannot be further reduced.

THE PROJECT MANAGEMENT BODY OF KNOWLEDGE

Project Management Institute (PMI), which is the professional association for project managers, has identified eight areas of knowledge that a project manager needs to have some familiarity with in order to be effective. In order to be certified by PMI as a *Project Management Professional*, an individual must pass an examination that covers all eight of these areas. The eight areas are defined as follows:

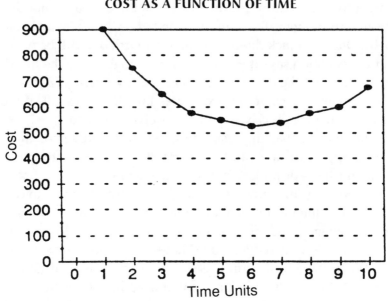

FIGURE 1.2
COST AS A FUNCTION OF TIME

- *Schedule/Time Management:* Managing the project to meet time objectives. This usually involves the use of Critical Path Method and/or Gantt schedules.
- *Cost Management:* The methods used to keep a project within its budget.
- *Quality Management:* The tools and techniques of Total Quality Management and related disciplines are applied to projects to ensure that work is done properly.
- *Human Resources:* Managing the human aspect of projects involves dealing with the behavior of contributors as well as the administrative component, which includes pay and benefits, government compliance with EEO requirements, and so on.
- *Contract/Procurement:* The project manager must be able to deal with the acquisition of materials and supplies. In addition, it may be necessary to administer contracts when outside contractors perform part of the work on a project.

- *Communications:* This involves having the proper skills to communicate to the right people at the right time, using the appropriate process. Sometimes written communications are appropriate, and at other times only face-to-face communication should be used.

- *Scope Management:* The scope of a project is the magnitude of the work being done. Scope changes that are uncontrolled usually result in cost and schedule overruns. Project managers must know how to manage the scope of a job to avoid such consequences.

- *Risk Management:* Murphy's much-quoted law says that "Whatever can go wrong will go wrong." This is certainly true in projects, and failure to manage risks can lead to disasters.

To cover all eight of these areas in detail would require a book much larger than this one, so some of the topics will be abbreviated. However, all except contracting will be covered in some detail.

THE PROJECT LIFE CYCLE

While the nature of projects will vary somewhat with the content of the work being done, there are a number of similarities that are independent of content. Most projects have a life cycle that consists of four to six phases. When six phases are involved, they are called *Concept, Definition & Planning, Design, Development or Construction, Application,* and *Post-Completion.* No matter how many phases are involved, the following points apply:

a. The character of the program changes in each life-cycle phase (see Figure 1.4).

b. The uncertainty regarding the ultimate time and cost diminishes as each phase is completed.

Unfortunately, too many projects go through a life cycle that looks like the one illustrated in Figure 1.3. One of the primary causes of this failure is a *ready-fire-aim* approach, in which the push is to "get on with it," with too little attention being paid to just what it is that should be done.

As Juran's definition suggests, project management is really *problem solving on a large scale,* and the first step in all problem solving is to make sure the problem is defined correctly. Otherwise, one is likely to develop the *right solution* to the *wrong problem!*

As can be concluded from examining Figure 1.3, definition of requirements came after the project turned into a nightmare, and this failure to define requirements at the beginning is exactly what caused the nightmare in the first place. Figure 1.4 illustrates the life cycles as they should be in the typical project.

THE LIFE-CYCLE PHASES

Concept Phase

The *concept phase* of a project is the point at which someone identifies a need that must be met. It can be for a new product or service, including buildings or renovations, a move from one location to another, a new banking service, advertising campaign, research program, and so on. At the concept phase, there is a very fuzzy definition of the problem to be solved. In fact, note that a *feasibility study* may have to be conducted in order to clarify the definition of the project before proceeding to the next phase.

Definition and Planning Phase

It is the *definition and planning phase* of the project that is intended to tie down exactly what is to be done. A problem statement is developed, which is meant to concretely define the problem to be solved. This is, of course, the ideal way of doing it. There are some projects in which the project definition will continue to evolve as work progresses, simply because neither the customer nor the project team is able to fully define what the customer needs.

In any case, once a suitable definition has been written, objectives are developed, strategies for achieving them are

FIGURE 1.3
INCORRECT LIFE CYCLE

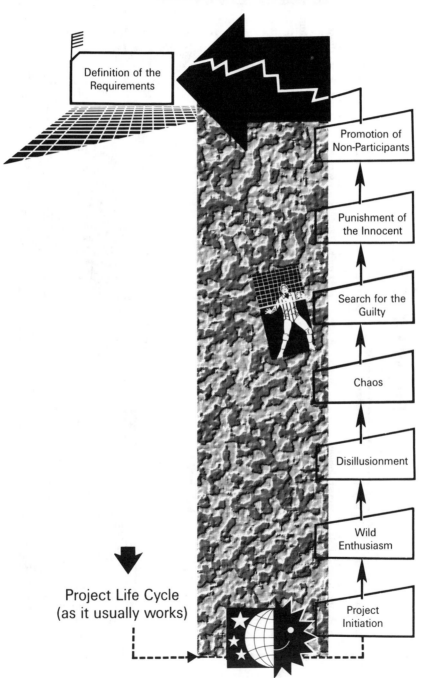

Definition of the Requirements

Promotion of Non-Participants

Punishment of the Innocent

Search for the Guilty

Chaos

Disillusionment

Wild Enthusiasm

Project Initiation

Project Life Cycle (as it usually works)

Figure 1.4
CORRECT LIFE CYCLE

Project Life Cycle

Concept	Definition	Design	Development or Construction	Application	Post-Completion
• Marketing input • Investigation of technology, feasibility studies, etc. • Survey of competition	• Specify objectives • Establish PCT targets • Quality Assurance procedures • Set up control system • Establish project organization • Set up project notebook	• Architectural, engineering • Design reviews • Assessment reports • Revise cost & performance targets	• First units • Begin sales campaigns • Quality control procedures	• Install and field test • Begin de-staffing • Advertising begins • De-bug and redesign	• Final de-staffing • Post-mortem analysis • Final reports • Closeout

selected, and detailed working plans are constructed to ensure that those objectives are achieved.

During this stage, an organization is established by identifying those individuals who will participate in the project, deciding to whom they will report, and defining the limits of their authority, responsibility, and accountability. Note also that a control system is developed, quality assurance procedures are set up (if they do not already exist), and detailed planning is completed.

When the plan is finished, it is placed in a *project notebook*, which then serves as the controlling document throughout the life of the project. The notebook is a very useful organizing device for project management, and may actually be a number of ring binders for very large projects.

Design Phase

The *design* phase may not exist (as in a construction project) or may be combined with the development phase. If it does exist, note that there is provision for revising cost and performance targets. Although this idea is "heresy" to some managers,

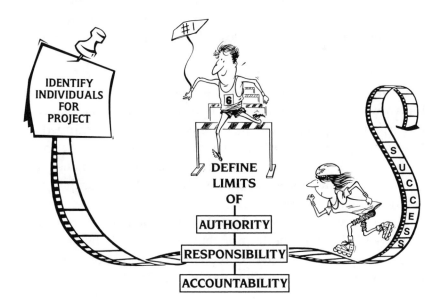

like it or not, one often finds during design of new products or services that original cost, schedule, or performance targets cannot be met.

Winston Churchill once remarked that we must have the right to be smarter today than we were yesterday. Because no one can forecast with 20/20 vision, changes to original targets must be made as new information becomes available.

A few years ago there was controversy in Congress about the fate of the B-2 bomber, and one congressman declared that he wanted it to "cost what they say it will cost." Yet this program spanned a decade, and it is certain that no one, including this outraged congressman, could accurately forecast the cost of such a complex project over that extended time frame.

Development or Construction Phase

The *development or construction phase* is the point at which completed products and services can be tested to see if they meet all performance targets. In the case of new product development, sales campaigns usually begin here. The danger, of course, is that if any serious glitches are discovered in the product after the sales campaign is launched, the organization may be placed in the very difficult position of not being able to meet promised deliveries, which can result in loss of goodwill from customers.

Application Phase

Application of the product or service can also yield some unhappy results if problems are discovered; therefore, it is important that products be field-tested before being shipped to customers. Software development companies usually ask some of their customers to beta-test their products so that glitches can be uncovered and corrected before any advertising campaign is begun to the general public.

Horror stories abound, however, of some major companies that have fallen into the trap of shipping products before thorough testing was completed, only to incur considerable expenses repairing or replacing defective product later.

Post-Completion Phase

The *post-completion phase* sounds contradictory at first glance. If the project is complete, how can this be a phase? In fact, this phase is *aborted* in many projects. Note that it involves a *postmortem* analysis of the project. The project manager should look back at the project and ask what was done well and what was not. Those things that were done well should be repeated in future projects, and conversely, problems that occurred should be avoided. If the postmortem is not done, it is likely that the mistakes of yesterday will be repeated.

One suggestion about postmortems: they should be done at each major milestone in the project, so that you can take advantage of what you learn for the current project as well as for future ones. Generally these are called project *audits*, a kinder-sounding term than *postmortem*.

THE PROJECT MANAGEMENT SYSTEM

In order to manage projects successfully, certain key elements must be in place in the organization. In systems terminology, those elements together constitute a project management system, and each element in turn is a subsystem itself. Since all systems consist of *inputs, outputs,* and some *process* for transforming those inputs into outputs, the same can be said for each component of a project management system.

The project management system consists of seven components, or subsystems, as shown in the diagram in Figure 1.5.

Human System

The *human system* is shown as the base of the pyramid for a very simple reason: it is perhaps the most difficult aspect of managing projects. The so-called *people-skills* underpin everything else. In fact, *none of the tools of project management are of any value if you can't get people to use them.*

For this reason, project managers need very good interpersonal, or human-relations skills. These include the ability to provide proper leadership for team members; the ability to negotiate with customers, team members, and other managers for needed performance, resources, and so on; skills in building a team; good communication skills; an understanding of how to handle decisions in a project team; and a knowledge of how to motivate team members when necessary. Since engineers, programmers, scientists, and other technically oriented individuals often lack people-skills, they may require training before they can successfully manage projects. In fact, one of the major reasons why technical people fail as managers is their inability to deal effectively with people.

By all means, if you detest the *people-problems* that managers must deal with, you should ask yourself honestly whether you really want to manage projects. If you don't like dealing with "people" issues, managing projects will be a pain, rather than fun.

FIGURE 1.5

THE COMPONENTS OF A PROJECT MANAGEMENT SYSTEM

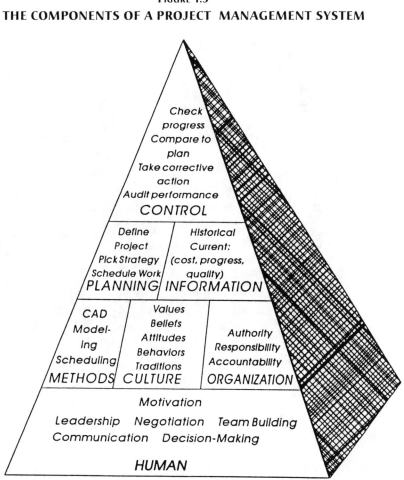

IF YOU DON'T LIKE DEALING WITH **PEOPLE ISSUES**

MANAGING PROJECTS WILL BE A **PAIN**

Culture System

Part of being able to deal with people also involves understanding cultural issues. The *culture* of an organization is the combined effect of the values, beliefs, attitudes, traditions, and behaviors of its members. The culture of the organization is essentially defined when someone says, "We don't do it that way around here." To violate the cultural expectations of powerful members of an organization is to invite trouble.

If an organization has been practicing "seat-of-the-pants" project management, then adopting a formal, disciplined system requires a change in the culture of the organization. The major change is that projects must be properly *planned,* and the initial response will often be that it takes too much time and ties up too many resources.

In addition, in market-driven organizations, the sales staff can no longer make delivery commitments to customers without first consulting the development group. This, too, will raise objections. Salespeople may argue that they need to meet the customer's delivery requirements in order to make sales. There is certainly no argument with such a statement.

However, my experience with organizations that operate this way is that such deadlines are often not met, simply because they were unrealistic to begin with, or they are met through the application of premium labor (overtime rates), so that it is doubtful that the company made any profit on the job. Further, customers often have more flexibility on their required dates than salespeople want to admit. Suffice it to say that successful project management requires *cooperation* among all the groups involved, and provides the tools whereby *realistic* delivery dates can be determined in advance of commitments to customers.

It is also worth noting that the introduction of formal project management is often resisted because people see nothing in it for themselves. In fact, all they see are the "costs" involved. To gain acceptance of the discipline, members of the organization must see that there is some benefit to themselves, rather than a penalty. Unfortunately, it is the time required to plan a project that is seen as a penalty. It takes time and experience to see that the planning done up front translates into fewer headaches later on.

As a final note about culture, in countries that are becoming more culturally diverse, it may be cultural differences that wreck a project. A manager told me that he had a drafter from a country where authoritarian management is still the norm. The manager was trying to be more participative with his people, so one day he asked the drafter for input on an issue. The man vehemently exclaimed, "Don't give me that participative crap! If you want me to do something, just tell me!" The perplexed manager asked what he should do. I told him to deal with the drafter in an authoritarian way for now. That is what he expects. To do otherwise is to lose his respect. Then the manager can slowly move toward more participation over time. The rule is: You must deal with people *where they are*—not where you *want them to be.*

Organization System

In order to coordinate the efforts of people, an *organization* is established that must define the limits of authority, responsibility, and accountability of participants. In the section on control, this issue will be discussed in depth, but here it is worth pointing out that if members of the project team have *no* authority, then they will feel no responsibility for their actions, and the project manager will have to make all decisions. As Bill Oncken has written, the result is that the project manager will find herself with monkeys on her back all the time.[1]

Methods System

Every project makes use of certain *techniques and methodologies* to get the work done. These might include certain technology, computer-aided design, PERT and CPM scheduling, costing models, and so on. Clearly, if proper methods are not employed in a project, objectives may be hard to achieve.

Planning System

Even though human skills underpin the model, the *planning* system is perhaps the most important. That is because if a poor plan is developed, it may be impossible to execute the project successfully no matter how effective a manager's human skills may be. As was stated previously, there is often a tendency to adopt a *ready-fire-aim* approach, which is to just *do something,* regardless of whether it is right or not.

People are often so task-oriented that they believe that everyone must be doing something task-related or they are *wasting time.* Planning is seen as not producing results, and so is considered a waste of time. A well-known company started a large development project some years ago, which involved nearly 2,000 engineers. The chief engineer decided to get them all into an auditorium for two weeks to do some preliminary planning. The accounting department got wind of this, did some quick math, and came up with an expenditure of around $8 million. Their response: *You're going to spend eight million dollars planning the project, and we're not going to get anything for it!* This is not unique to that company, but is a typical attitude toward planning.

In the Project Planning section of this book, concrete evidence will be presented to show why such an attitude is unacceptable, and why it leads to problems in managing projects.

Information System

The *information* system gathers the data that must be available so that a project manager knows whether a project is on target or not. However, that information must be *timely*, and one of the problems some organizations have is that the data on project status is gathered, fed into a mainframe computer, then batch processed and distributed at such large time intervals as to make the information useless for control. This is discussed further in the Project Control section of this book.

Control System

Control of a project is one of the major responsibilities of a project manager. Indeed, the primary purpose of managing is to control the application of scarce resources to achieve desired organization objectives. To do so, the manager must use data on project status to determine where the project is with respect to the plan, and initiate corrective action if there is a significant discrepancy. Note that a monitoring system alone is not a control system.

CONCURRENT PROJECT MANAGEMENT

For years projects have been run in a *throw-it-over-the-wall* fashion. In product development, for example, the marketing department identifies a vague customer need, writes an equally vague specification, and throws it over the wall to engineering. The engineering group then designs the product and throws the drawings over the wall to manufacturing.

Manufacturing takes one look at the drawings, has cardiac arrest, throws the drawings back over the wall to engineering, saying, "We can't make this thing!" Engineering gets indignant. Screaming and counter-screaming take place. Back over the wall the drawings go (with some grudging revisions).

The product is made and shipped. The customer uses it for a while, decides it doesn't meet the requirement and returns it. Or it breaks. The repair people can't fix it. No wonder. It was never designed to be repaired. (Several models of cars exist that require that the engine be pulled in order to get to the rear spark plug. Wouldn't owning one of those be a joy!)

This practice is not unique to product development projects. It seems to plague many kinds of jobs, including software development, construction, and so on.

To counter these problems, a practice has emerged in product development called *concurrent engineering*. While the term *engineering* does not apply to all projects, the concepts of concurrent engineering do. For that reason, I prefer to use the term *concurrent project management*.

The best definition of concurrent engineering that I know about is from Report R-338 (Winner, *et al.*, 1988) published by the Institute for Defense Analysis, entitled *The Role of Concurrent Engineering in Weapons Acquisition*. I have modified their definition, and present the following as a definition of concurrent project management:

> *Concurrent project management is a systematic approach to the integrated, concurrent design of products and their related processes, including manufacture and support. This approach is intended to cause the developers, from the outset, to consider all elements of the product life cycle from conception through disposal, including cost, quality, schedule, and user requirements.*
>
> *Concurrent project management is characterized by focus on the customer's requirements and priorities, a conviction that quality*

is the result of improving a process, and a philosophy that improvement of the processes of design, production, and support is a never ending responsibility of the entire enterprise.

Note that the word *product* should be understood to mean whatever the project team produces, whether it is a product, a service, or a document. Further note that *customer* is used in its broadest possible sense to include both external and internal users of the team's output.

A MODEL FOR MANAGING PROJECTS

If you are new to managing projects, the first question you might ask is, "Where do I start? In what order do I do things?" To answer those questions, I have developed a flow chart as a model for managing projects. It is based on best practice of organizations throughout the U.S., and can be used as the basis for managing any kind of project. It makes no difference whether it is an information system, product design, construction, or other kind of project—the basic steps are the same for all.

The model is shown in Figure 1.6. Each step in the process is numbered, and the remainder of this book describes what happens in each step in detail. The following discussion will summarize the steps briefly, using the step numbers as shown in the figure. Note the bold boxes containing numbers that appear beside each step in the model. The numbers inside the boxes refer to the chapter or chapters in this book that cover that step in more detail. Thus, the model serves as a quick cross-reference to the book.

THE STEPS IN MANAGING A PROJECT

The steps in the model are as follows:

- *Step 1.* A general concept for the project is developed. "We need something." "Wouldn't it be nice if . . ."

> **P**itfall: Accepting the concept as a formal problem definition.

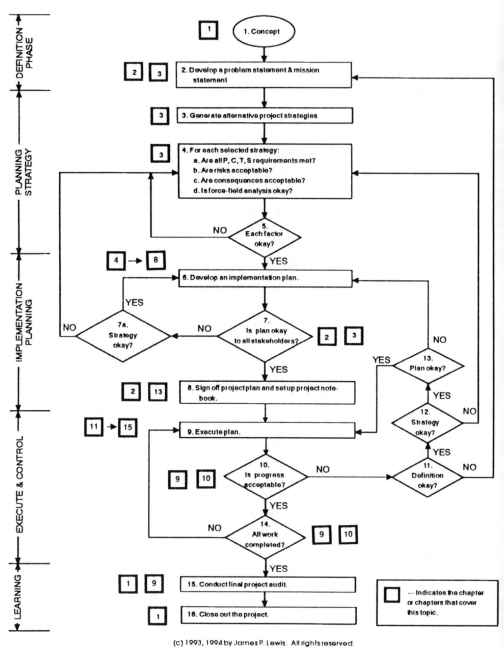

FIGURE 1.6
A GENERAL MODEL OF PROJECT MANAGEMENT

(c) 1993, 1994 by James P. Lewis. All rights reserved.

- *Step 2.* A problem definition is developed, which states the purpose of doing the work. Care should be taken not to define the problem in terms of symptoms. A project mission statement should be written in this step.

> **N**ot knowing the question, it was easy for him to give the answer.
> *Dag Hammerskjöld*

- *Step 3.* Strategies for conducting the project work are listed in a brainstorming manner. All approaches that might be valid should be stated.

> **P**itfall: Considering only one approach to be valid.

- *Steps 4 & 5.* Strategies are assessed. Is the approach feasible? What risks are involved? Are there unintended consequences? Can we live with them? Is the approach acceptable in this organization's culture? Which strategy is judged best of those available?

> **P**itfall: Assuming that any approach will work and that nothing will go wrong.

- *Step 6.* A detailed action plan is developed. This plan will develop tactics and logistics. This step itself consists of eight substeps. These will be presented following the overview of the general model. The following chapters will discuss how the plan is constructed.

> **P**itfall: Not planning in enough detail. Adopting a *ready-fire-aim* approach.

- *Steps 7, 7a, & 8.* The plan is reviewed by all stakeholders and signed, signifying that it is considered acceptable and feasible.

> **P**itfall: Failing to have the plan reviewed before implementation.

- *Steps 9, 10, & 14.* The project is executed and results are monitored. If the desired outcome is not being achieved, control procedures are exercised. Is the fault with the definition (step 11)? Is project strategy correct (step 12)? Is the plan okay (step 13)? It may be necessary to replan.

> **P**itfalls: Failure to monitor and take corrective action when required. Continuing to work to a plan that is unsound.

- *Step 15.* When all project work is complete, a final postmortem should be conducted. What was done well? What could have been done better?

> "**T**is a poor sort of memory, that only works backwards," the Queen remarked.
>
> *Lewis Carroll*
> ALICE'S ADVENTURES
> IN WONDERLAND

- *Step 16.* The project is closed out and final reports filed for future reference. The project notebook containing *all* reports and documentation is placed in a central file for use by managers in planning subsequent projects.

STEP SIX EXPLODED

As was stated above, Step 6 in the model actually consists of eight substeps, as shown in Figure 1.7. Since these substeps are self-explanatory, no further detail will be given here. Rather, they will be dealt with in the chapters that follow.

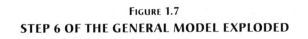

FIGURE 1.7

STEP 6 OF THE GENERAL MODEL EXPLODED

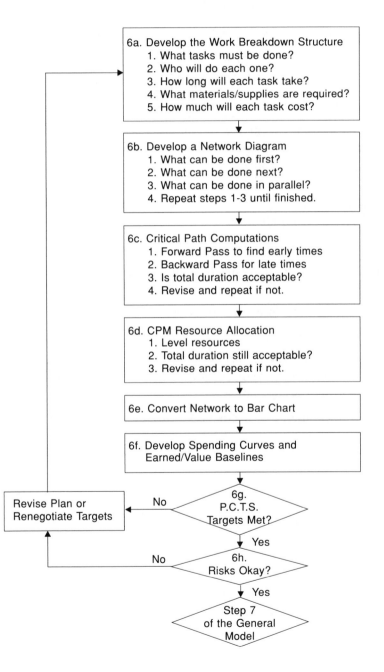

ANSWERS ARE IN APPENDIX B

QUESTIONS FOR REVIEW

1. Give at least one definition of what a project is.

2. What probable impact will an increase in project scope have?

3. Why do project costs initially decline as project duration increases, then begin to rise again?

4. What are the benefits of concurrent project management?

5. Specify at least two points in a project life cycle where inadequate management may cause problems, and describe the problems.

KEY POINTS *from Chapter 1*

- A project is a one-time job, rather than a repetitive process.
- Only three of the variables in the cost equation can be dictated.
- A project team must be built over time.
- Failure to define a problem correctly may lead to failure.
- A postmortem or audit should be conducted at each major milestone in the project, with a final one being done once the project is completed.
- A project manager needs good human-relations skills to get the job done.

Reference

1. See William Oncken, *Managing Management Time*. Englewood Cliffs, NJ: Prentice-Hall, 1984.

Chapter 2

AN INTRODUCTION TO PROJECT PLANNING

Suppose the CEO of a company in Raleigh, North Carolina, called in one of her people and said, "We have a real emergency situation in Shelbyville, Tennessee. I want you to get out there right away and fix it. You know, of course, that you'll have to drive the service van, because it has all the equipment that you'll need to work on the problem."

> **P**lans are worthless, but planning is everything.
>
> *President Dwight Eisenhower*
> *November 17, 1957*

"Got it. I'll get going right away," says the service person.

With that, he rushes out of the CEO's office, back to his desk, starts frantically packing his briefcase, and running around like a chicken with its head cut off.

"What's happening," one of his coworkers asks.

"Got to get to Shelbyville, Tennessee, in a hurry," says the serviceman.

"You been there before?"

"No, never."

"How you going to go—Interstate 40?"

"Don't know."

"Don't you have a map?"

"Nope. Don't have time to worry about a map just now. Just got to get there."

Clearly, this person is headed for trouble. If he really has to get to Shelbyville in the fastest time, he definitely needs a map, since he has never been there before.

You might say, "He really is stupid. No one would do that." Or you might say that my scenario is unrealistic. Yet there are project managers who run projects in the same way all of the time. They have no plan (map) and will tell you they don't have time to make one. Is it any wonder they wind up lost out in the boonies (figuratively speaking, of course)?

Everyone knows that one of the key functions that managers perform is planning. Yet experience also shows that many managers either do very little or no planning, or that the plans they do put together are sadly inadequate.

Needless to say, the results are often disastrous. Case after case has been cited in the literature.[1] Nevertheless, managers don't seem to learn the lessons taught by those case studies.

Working without a plan is, of course, the *ready-fire-aim* approach mentioned in Chapter 1. What is not understood by many managers is that they are not in control when they use this approach, even though they will readily agree that being in control is one of the primary requirements of a manager.

Perhaps they have lost sight of what is meant by management control. Control consists of comparing where you are with where you are supposed to be, then taking action to correct for any deviation from target.

Since the way you know where you are supposed to be is by reference to

> **Con • trol**: Comparing where you are with where you are supposed to be, then taking action to correct for any deviation from target.

a plan, then without a plan, there is nothing to track progress against. Therefore, if you have no plan, you have no control. Planning and control are Siamese twins: they are inseparable.

> **I**f you have no plan, control is impossible!

As the serviceman said in the scenario above, one of the most frequent reasons for not planning is summed up by the statement, "I don't have time to plan." Actually, the more critical your time constraints, the less you can afford to *not* plan. During World War II, high-speed production of military aircraft, ships, and other equipment was absolutely essential.[2] Boeing was producing B-17 bombers as fast as they could, and other companies were scrambling to reduce production times. One example was Ford Motor Company and the B-24.

Before the war, Ford had built airplanes, the Trimotor being one of the best known. However, Henry Ford had abandoned the building of airplanes and concentrated entirely on cars. When the government approached him and asked him to build bombers for the war effort, he was not terribly excited about the prospect, but finally yielded to the pressure.

He assigned his car makers to the project. A plant was constructed on the site of a former apple orchard, at Willow Run, Michigan. By the time they achieved peak capacity, they were turning out a B-24 every 58 minutes!

A similar feat was accomplished by Henry Kaiser, who was asked to build Liberty ships. He knew nothing about shipbuilding, but he was a *planner.* He sat down and asked himself, "How do you go about building a ship?" Once he had it worked out, the shipyard was able to turn out a ship every five or six days, and at one point they actually managed to produce one in 48 hours!

This was all done by careful planning of subassemblies. Ford invented wiring harnesses that would snap into place, so that the harnesses did not have to be created inside the airplane, where space was at a premium and it was hard to work.

I know some readers will argue that this is all fine for well-defined projects like ship- and airplane-building. The same isn't possible for research. People are always telling me, "You can't plan a research project." However, if you don't plan a research project, you are unlikely to make much progress.

MISTAKES IN PLANNING

Even when managers plan, there are at least two common mistakes made. One is to not involve in the planning process the people who must implement the plan. This is done either by the manager who plans unilaterally or by the organization that makes use of a planning group. Either way, there is likely to be difficulty with implementation because of inaccurate estimates, overlooked work, or lack of commitment on the part of the people who must execute the plan.

A manager who plans someone else's work without soliciting any input from them is likely to expect the person to do the work in less time than is possible. This seems to be a common error, probably caused by the fact that the manager is using a self-based estimate. It may very well be that the manager could do the job in the estimated time, but that will not necessarily be true for the individual assigned to do it.

Further, managers often fail to consider that the person for whom they are planning is not working full-time on the project activity, so that the total elapsed time required to do the job is considerably greater than the time allowed.

Why open issues are so important.

Issues management is the least understood management tool, but probably the most important. Issues are matters in dispute or where there's uncertainty. An issue remains open when the team doesn't have the knowledge or authority to resolve it by a decision. Because an issue is only resolved by a decision, it is important to identify who will decide each issue. And in order to get a decision, you often have action items to assemble and present information.

I like to put issues right into the project plan as they arise, and show by dependencies what work will be held up unless the issue is decided. If there are a large number of open issues, the team will become paralyzed because too much is up for grabs. Work may have to be redone, depending on how an issue is decided, so there's naturally less urgency to get it done. My rule of thumb is that a project is in serious trouble if there are more than two open issues per man-year of work effort.

Tom Conlon

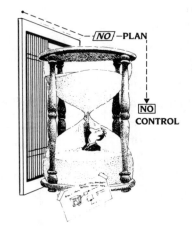

The net result of giving someone a plan for which they had no input is that they will often react by saying, "There's no way I can do it that fast." With that reaction, the plan is doomed to failure at the outset.

The second mistake made in planning is the "ready-fire-aim" mistake. This is done because people don't think they have time to plan the project. They simply must get on with it. This is a serious trap. In fact, the more critical your time line, the more important a plan becomes. Consider, for example, trying to do the evening network news broadcast. The staff has about 20 minutes for news. Can you imagine what a disaster it would be if they tried to do the broadcast without a good plan? They actually spend more time planning the program than it takes to execute it.

WHAT IS PLANNING?

Planning is answering the following general questions:

- What must be done? This question deals with objectives and magnitude or scope of work.

- How should it be done? Answering this question leads to the selection of project *strategy*.

- Who should do it? Roles and responsibilities can be assigned by answering this question.

- By when must it be done? Scheduling is accomplished with this one.

- How much will it cost? The budget is developed.

- How good does it have to be? Quality levels are determined.

- What performance is required? Performance specifications are generated.

THE PROJECT NOTEBOOK

In Chapter 1, I said that a project notebook is an excellent device for documenting and controlling a project. Ideally, a complete, written project plan should be prepared prior to the time work is started. Realistically, the work may be started before the plan is complete, but the plan should still be put together as quickly as possible, before the work has progressed very far.

> **E**lectronic document management
>
> While a notebook is useful, Lotus Notes permits the use of shared files on a local area network. Team members can send each other electronic mail and they can call up the project schedule, progress reports, and other documents to help manage the project more effectively.
>
> *Tom Conlon*

The plan should define the objectives of the project, the approach to be taken, and the commitments being assumed by the manager and key contributors.

The plan should cover the following general topics. This list can, in fact, be considered a *table of contents* for the project plan. It should be housed in a notebook (or notebooks, for large projects), and copies should be distributed to key members of the project team. Electronic media are now coming into their own, and may eventually make hard-copy notebooks less desirable. (See comments above by Tom Conlon.)

- *Assumptions:* All assumptions that have been used to develop the plan should be documented clearly. Otherwise, estimates and other aspects of the plan are difficult to understand.

> **A**ssumptions
>
> It is a good idea to document the assumptions to be used in developing a plan and get agreement that they are valid *before creating* the plan! Otherwise, if there is disagreement about the assumptions, the plan can hardly be valid.
>
> *Tom Ryba*

- *A problem statement:* This is a definition of the problem to be solved by the project. As has been stated in Chapter 1, without a sound definition of the problem, one is likely to waste valuable resources by developing the right solution to the wrong problem. Techniques for defining problems follow in this chapter.

- *Project mission statement:* This is a summary of the overall goal and purpose of the project, identifying the client and outlining the general approach to be followed in doing the work. A more specific detail of the approach to be followed is also contained in the plan (see below). Details on how to develop a mission statement are presented in Chapter 3. The formal procedure is appropriate for large projects, while an informal approach is acceptable for small ones. Having *no* mission statement is unacceptable for *any* size project.

- *Project strategy:* The mission statement provides only the most cursory statement of the approach to project work. A more specific statement is needed, so that other people in the organization can decide if the proposed approach fits in with the strategies preferred by management. Are we only going to manage subcontractors? What technical methods will be employed? Is a make-or-buy situation involved? Etc.

- *Statement of project scope:* This is a statement of what *will* and *will not* be done in the project. It establishes boundaries, so that the customer knows what she will get when the project is completed. See comments following this listing on controlling for *scope creep.* (Chapter 2)

- *Project objectives:* These include technical, profit, performance,quality,and other targets. Major project objectives should be in writing, to avoid misunderstandings of team members and to provide focus throughout the life of the project. There are forms in Chapter 3 to be used in writing objectives and conducting a SWOT analysis. (See Chapter 3.)

- *Quality Function Deployment (QFD) analysis:* QFD or some other means of translating customer needs into solutions should be part of the plan—see Juran (1989), Akao (1990), or Dimancescu (1992) for details on how to do QFD. (See also Chapter 3.)

> ## Scope
>
> Scope defines the boundaries of a project so that people know what (and who) is included and what's excluded from consideration. In defining scope, I try to find what and who will be impacted (significantly affected) by a project. Consider: Organizations impacted—which groups, sites, jobs may have their work or workload impacted—even if the people won't be users of the products of the project. (You may create surplus office space that needs to be disposed of. Or nonusers may need to be retrained as groups of users are reorganized.) Other projects impacted: Does your project interfere with another project? Change another team's assumptions or timetable? If so, members of your team may spend time coordinating with other teams.
>
> *Tom Conlon*

- *Contractual requirements:* List all deliverable items—including reports, prototypes, documentation. In projects that require significant reporting (such as military projects) failure to account for the cost to prepare such documentation can result in a cost penalty to the project. It is a good idea to have a deliverable at each major project milestone so that progress can be assessed easily.

- *Exit criteria:* Each milestone should have criteria established that will be used to determine if the preceding phase of work is actually finished. (Chapter 3. Also, see Dimancescu, 1992.)

- *End-item specifications:* These would include engineering specifications, software functional specifications, building codes, government regulations, and marketing performance specifications that position a product against its competition. Where regulations and other specifications exist in published form, it may be satisfactory to simply cite these. However, internal specs should always be included in the notebook. Quality Function Deployment can be used to develop specs that translate customer requirements into design and production criteria.

- *Work breakdown structure (WBS):* This is the heart of the plan, and serves to tie everything together. It provides a way of estimating resource requirements, total project budget, and work scheduling. It also provides an excellent visual display of total project scope. Finally, it can be used as a point-of-reference against which to track progress. Development of work breakdown structures will be covered in Chapter 4.

- *Schedules:* The plan must include major milestones, together with detailed task schedules, that will be used by people doing the work. Major milestones are dates at which key portions of the project work should be completed, and should involve a *deliverable* whenever possible. By requiring something tangible at a milestone, it is easier to evaluate whether the milestone was actually met as required. In addition to milestones, task schedules are the detailed schedules that show how various milestones are going to be achieved.

- *Required resources:* Resources include people, equipment, facilities, and materials. Because every organization has limited resources, success in managing projects depends on the efficient and effective use of those resources.

As for human resources, these are best displayed using loading diagrams, which show how many people of a given skill category are being used at any given time. (Or they show how many hours per day a specific individual is to work on the project.) Loading diagrams are used by functional groups to determine if adequate support is available for all projects and if not, whether to work overtime, or seek permanent or temporary staff to provide the required support. Chapter 7 offers more detail on resource management.

- *Control system:* How will progress be measured and reported? To whom will reports be distributed? How often will measurements be required? If changes are required to the project, how will they be handled and who will pay for them?

- *Major contributors:* These will usually be leaders of functional groups. What are the limits of authority, responsibility, and accountability of various contributors? One device for showing the level of involvement of contributors is the Linear Responsibility Chart, which is presented in Chapter 4.

- *Risk areas:* In planning a project, it is helpful to ask, "What could go wrong?" By identifying risks, steps can be taken to deal with them actively rather than reactively. Examples of risks would include financial limitations, penalties for nonperformance, subcontractor default, work stoppages, technical exposures, and other possible problems. See Chapter 3 on conducting a SWOT and risk analysis.

- *Statements of work (SOWs):* These are optional for most projects. They may be required of government contractors.

SIGN-OFF OF THE PLAN

When the plan is complete, it is submitted to *stakeholders* for approval. Anyone who has a vested interest in the project is a stakeholder. Typical stakeholders include functional managers, managers of project managers, the customer, financial officers of the company, subcontractors, and so on.

Customers are always stakeholders. They include both external and internal customers. For example, the marketing department and the manufacturing group can each be considered customers of a product design group.

stake · hold · er: anyone who has a vested interest in the project. This includes customers, project team members, senior managers, and so on.

Each stakeholder signs the plan, attesting that *as far as his or her area of concern goes, the plan seems to be feasible and appears to address those concerns properly.* For example, a functional manager would sign signifying that he or she feels confident that the number of support people required to get the job done will be available when required, and that they will be able to handle the technical requirements of the job.

Once the plan has been approved, it gives the project manager authority to execute and control his or her project to completion. Significant changes in approach or other revisions to the plan that are made after initial approval must be communicated to stakeholders and approved.

Getting the plan signed off should be done in a meeting. It should not be done by circulating copies of the notebook through company mail and asking people to read and sign it. Under those conditions, they will often fail to read carefully, and when they are later required to "deliver" on their part of the project, they will be unable to do so.

During the sign-off meeting, the project manager should highlight key areas of the project that could be problems and encourage all members of the group to ask "embarrassing" questions about *any* area of the plan. Better that those questions be asked during the meeting than later.

If possible, the meeting should be held in advance of the start date of the project to allow changes to be made to the plan if necessary. However, as was mentioned previously, the project may be started before the plan can be completed and signed off.

The purpose of getting a plan approved is to *ensure that it is realistic and feasible,* not to use it as a club to "beat up" on people if there are problems!

THE PLAN[3]

In the beginning was the plan, and then the specification.

And the plan was without form, and the specification was void.

And darkness was upon the faces of the implementors;

And they spoke unto their manager, saying: *"It is a crock of cow manure, and it stinketh."*

And their manager went to the second level manager, and he spake unto him, saying: *"It is a crock of excrement, and none may abide the odor thereof."*

And the second level manager went to the third level, and he spake unto him saying: *"It is a container of excrement, and it is very strong, such that none may abide before it."*

And the third level went to the division manager, and
he spake unto him, saying: *"It is a vessel of fertilizer, and none may
abide its strength."*

And the division manager went to the assistant vice-president,
and he spake unto him, saying: *"It contains that which aids plant
growth, and it is very strong."*

And the assistant vice-president went to the vice-president,
and he spake unto him, saying: *"It promoteth growth and
it is very powerful."*

And the vice-president went before the president and spake
unto him, saying: *"This powerful new product will promote growth
of the company."*

And the president looked upon the product and
saw that *"It was good!"*

THE FIRST STEP IN PLANNING: DEVELOPING A PROBLEM STATEMENT

As was mentioned in Chapter 1, project management is problem solving on a large scale, and that is the first step in the planning process. Until a satisfactory definition has been developed, steps for doing the work cannot be devised, since the definition determines the proper approach to take. For example, the question, "What is the best way to put a person

> **prob · lem:** a gap between where you are and where you want to be, that is confronted by an obstacle that prevents easy movement to close the gap.

> **H**ow a problem is defined determines the solution possibilities.

on the moon?" is very general and allows many possible strategies to be considered. The question, "How can we build a rocket to put someone on the moon?" however, is more narrowly focused and yields more limited answers.

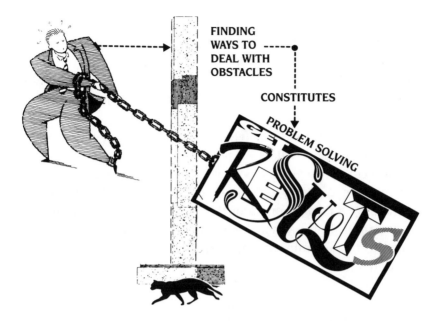

Note the definition of a problem, as stated above. It is a gap between where you are and where you want to be, and an obstacle (or obstacles) prevents easy movement to close the gap. If you have no obstacles to get around or overcome, you don't have a problem, you only have a desired goal. Finding ways to overcome or get around obstacles is what constitutes problem solving.

OPEN- AND CLOSE-ENDED PROBLEMS

There are two kinds of problems. They are called open-ended and close-ended. An open-ended problem is one that has no single correct answer, and that has boundaries that can be challenged. A close-ended problem does have a single answer. Which category is biggest? You guessed it! There are far more open-ended problems than close-ended ones. Yet, most of our training is in how to solve close-ended problems.

Because our educational system teaches us to find the *one right answer* to problems presented, we leave school believing that all problems are close-ended, and many of us are thereafter unwilling or reluctant to challenge boundaries of real-world problems, even though most such problems are open-ended. Roger von Oech (1983, 1986) suggests that one way out of this dilemma is to always insist on finding the *second right answer!*

Most projects will involve the solution of open-ended problems. That is, there will be no *single approach* to apply in solving the problem. However, a few projects might be thought of as fitting into the category of close-ended problems. For example, overhauling a power generator that has developed a fault might be thought of in this way. Once a diagnosis has determined the defect in the generator, the approach to repair the unit is fairly well-defined.

Figure 2.1
RECOGNIZING OPEN-ENDED PROBLEMS

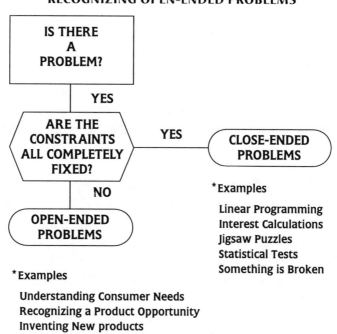

(adapted from Rickards: see reading list)

However, when there is doubt as to what kind of problem exists, Figure 2.1 should help you determine whether the problem is open- or close-ended.

AN AID FOR DEFINING PROBLEMS

Once you have determined if the problem is open- or close-ended, you have to develop a formal problem statement (or definition). To help you arrive at a sound problem definition (or redefinition, if you have decided the initial statement is inadequate), refer to the questions in Table 2.1.[4]

TABLE 2.1
PROBLEM DEFINITION AIDS

1. Write down a general description of the problem under consideration.
2. Now complete the following statements about the problem. If you cannot think of anything to write for a particular statement, move on to the next one.
   a. There is usually more than one way of looking at problems. You could also define this one as . . .
   b. But the main point of the problem is . . .
   c. What I would really like to do is . . .
   d. If I could break all laws of reality (physical, social, etc.) I would try to solve it by . . .
   e. The problem, put another way, could be likened to . . .
   f. Another, even stranger, way of looking at it might be . . .
3. Now return to your original definition (step 1). Write down whether any of the redefinitions have helped you see the problem in a different way.

AN EXAMPLE

To show how all of the project management tools fit together, we will use a sample project. As you can imagine, it is very difficult to find a project that everyone can understand. During the past two years, I have been using one that has been very successful, though not 100 percent perfect. We will assume that the company for which we work is Global Publishing, and our project is to develop a book for them. The book will be about the island of Bali, which is located near the island of Java in Indonesia. Bali was made famous years ago when *National Geographic* magazine did an article on the firewalking ceremony that is held there.

This project will include the writing and preparation of copy for printing, but not the actual production of final books themselves. The copy (called *camera-ready copy*) will be turned over to the printer. That will constitute the end of the project for our purposes.

We will assume that this book is addressed to a general audience, rather than a specialized one such as historians or scholars. It is to tell about the history, customs, religion, and other details of the past and present inhabitants of the island, and is to be profusely illustrated with color photographs of the temples and other points of interest.

The problem that we are trying to solve, then, is to fill a gap in the market. Our problem statement might read as follows:

> **There is no currently existing, up-to-date book on the island of Bali and its people, written for a general audience.**

Our mission will be to produce that book, and in the following chapter, we will develop a mission statement to that effect.

PHASED PLANNING

It is generally not possible to plan a long-duration project or a research project in great detail, because, as was stated previously, no project manager has 20/20 foresight. In research projects, there are conditional branches: based on the outcome of this phase, where do we go from here? Similarly, in many conventional projects, decisions are made following completion of one phase of project work that impact subsequent work. Attempting to plan a long-term project in great detail only leads to the fruitless attempt to meet a completion date that was set before the full requirements of the system were known.

Phased planning is a realistic approach that permits the project manager to plan only to the level of detail that is known at the time. Using this approach, the output of each phase of a project includes two planning documents: a Phase Plan and a Project Plan. The phase plan is prepared at the task or work package level (see the section in Chapter 4 on Work Breakdown Structures for a definition of the terms *task* and *work package*) and provides the detailed work that will be done in the next phase of the project.

Phased planning, in its broadest sense, may not be acceptable in some environments. It is often necessary to impose a deadline on a project before it starts. The customer needs to be in the building by a certain date. The book is to be published and released at the time a movie comes out, in the hope that the book will "piggyback" on the anticipated success of the movie. (The author of *Karate for Kids* did just this to piggyback on the movie *The Karate Kid*.)

However, even when the deadline is imposed, phased planning is still a useful approach. In fact, it bears out the first rule that must be learned in project planning:

> **The first rule of project planning is to be prepared to *replan!* No project manager has 20/20 foresight.**

PROJECT PLANNING STEPS

The model for managing projects shows the steps in flowchart form. The steps in planning a project are listed below, together with the documents that are generated at that step. Note that the steps refer to the numbers in the flowchart (not all flowchart steps are listed).

Step 2: Define the problem to be solved by the project (Problem Statement). Develop a mission statement for the project (Mission Statement).

Step 3: List alternative strategies for doing the work (Strategy Listing).

Step 4: Select the best strategy for the project (Statement of Project Strategy; SWOT Analysis; Risk Analysis; Force-Field Analysis; Consequence Analysis).

Step 6: (a) Develop a detailed implementation plan. Begin with the Work Breakdown Structure (WBS).

(b) Using the WBS, estimate activity durations, resource requirements, and costs (as appropriate for your environment); (Budget; Linear Responsibility Chart; Activity Durations).

(c) Prepare the project master schedule (PERT/CPM diagrams and/or Gantt charts).

(d) Decide on the project organization structure—whether matrix or hierarchical (if you can choose).

(e) Set up the project notebook.

Step 8: Get the plan signed off by all project stakeholders. A sample sign-off form is shown in Figure 2.2.

FIGURE 2.2
A PROJECT PLAN APPROVAL FORM

Project Plan Approval		
Project Description	Project Code	Date
From	Department	

Your signature below indicates that you agree with the plan submitted,
so far as your interests are concerned.

	Approving Individual	Signature	Date
Functional Managers			
Directors			
Others			
Comments			

QUESTIONS FOR REVIEW

1. *What is a basic definition of control?*

2. *What does project planning have to do with project control?*

3. *What is planning in its essence?*

4. *What does a signature to a project plan mean?*

5. *When would phased planning be appropriate?*

6. *What should you do if a key member of the project team refuses to sign off the project plan?*

KEY POINTS *from Chapter 2*

- If you have no plan, control is impossible!
- The people who must execute a plan should be involved in its preparation.
- Use a project notebook to fully document a project.
- The project plan should be signed off by stakeholders in a meeting, not through the mail.
- When significant changes to the plan are required, they are signed off by affected stakeholders.
- A stakeholder is anyone who has a vested interest in the project.
- Watch out for scope creep!
- Conduct a SWOT analysis during the planning stage.
- Define the problem to be solved before developing an implementation plan.
- Phased planning recognizes that planners do not have 20/20 foresight.
- Follow the project management flowchart.

References

1. Heal, David. *"How to Screw Up."* Management Today (September 1987) pp. 77–79.
2. I am greatly indebted to my colleague, Russell Ostrem, a military historian, for the research he provided me on this topic.
3. Source unknown.
4. Adapted from Rickards (see reading list).

Chapter 3

DEFINING YOUR MISSION AND DEVELOPING PROJECT STRATEGY

THE IMPORTANCE OF THE MISSION STATEMENT

In Chapter 2, I presented methods of developing a problem statement. This is called for in Box 2 of the general model (flowchart) presented in Chapter 1. Once a problem statement has been written, a mission statement can be developed for the project. Both steps are contained in Box 2 of the model.

In his book, *The Northbound Train*, Karl Albrecht emphasizes the importance of mission statements. He writes,

> *In twenty years of working with organizations of almost every imaginable type, I've seen relatively few really powerful and meaningful corporate statements of vision, mission, or philosophy. Most are either vague, puffy, and meaningless, or dull, prosaic, and uninspiring. A very few actually have the power to move people.*[1]

The same could be said for projects. I recently received a call from a project manager in one of my client companies. "I've just spent two hours on a conference call with the parties to this project," he said, "and I concluded that we don't agree on what we're really trying to do. Can you help us?"

We got the entire team together, about 15 people, and it took only a few minutes to confirm his conclusion. They did not agree on what they were really trying to do.

It would be one thing if this were an isolated instance, but I find it to be very commonplace. When a project is in trouble, the first thing I ask the project manager is, "Do all of your people agree on the project mission?"

They invariably tell me that they do.

Then I ask the team members, "What is the team's mission?"

> [Alice said] "Would you tell me, please, which way I ought to go from here?"
>
> "That depends a good deal on where you want to get to," said the Cat.
>
> "I don't know where…" said Alice.
>
> "Then it doesn't matter which way you go," said the Cat.
>
> *Lewis Carroll*
> *ALICE'S ADVENTURES*
> *IN WONDERLAND*

You know the outcome. I get differing answers from each person or some vague answer that cannot possibly provide a sense of direction for them.

In case you think I am only dealing with simpletons, let me correct that assumption: most of these people are very well educated. Some have doctorates. Many have M.B.A. degrees. As Albrecht says, very few organizations seem able to develop a meaningful vision, mission, or sense of purpose. In today's world, that leads to disaster.

Perhaps it is because, as Albrecht says, mission statements are of such poor quality that people hold them in low regard. Nevertheless, a mission statement is invaluable when

> If you don't know where you're going, how will you know when you get there?

properly used. The key word is *used*. This seems obvious, yet many organizations seem to forget the mission statement after it is written. Perhaps it is because they go into the fire-fighting mode and forget their mission. Like the old joke, they have forgotten that the objective was to drain the swamp, because they have been too busy fighting the alligators.

In any case, the mission statement should be used to set goals and objectives, to make decisions, and to provide the goods and services the organization has determined it should be providing to meet the needs of customers. In short, any time a question must be answered, people should ask, "How do we answer that question (or take that step) in such a way that it supports the attainment of our mission?"

THE MISSION IDENTIFICATION PROCESS

A mission statement should answer three questions:

1. What do we do?
2. For whom do we do it?
3. How do we go about it?

Before these questions can be answered, it is useful for the team to work through a formal process in which they answer a number of questions. Table 3.1 lists the questions that should be answered before attempting to write the mission statement. Since this process takes a day or more, for short-duration projects it may be necessary to simply answer the three questions without going through the process.

The last step in the table is to actually write the mission statement. All of the previous steps have simply been aimed at helping the team understand what is involved in the project. The final step consists of the sequence shown in Figure 3.1.

Note that the process of writing a mission statement involves identifying stakeholders, among whom are your *customers*, and that you are supposed to list what customers want from you. This is a major undertaking in most cases. Suppose, as an example, that you were teaching grade-school children and

TABLE 3.1
DEVELOPING A MISSION STATEMENT

STEPS TO FOLLOW	COMMENTS
Identify the team's *internal* and *external* environment	Easy for teams in a department. Harder for cross-functional teams. Keep it brief.
List of all of the team's *stakeholders*.	A stakeholder is *anyone* who has a vested interest in what the team is doing—customers, suppliers, senior management, etc.
Highlight the team's *customers* from within the list of stakeholders just generated.	A customer is a *user* of the team's output.
Check the three most important stakeholders —at least one of them should be the team's major customer.	This step will generate much discussion and debate. Do not cut this off prematurely.
Make a list of those things your three most important stakeholders want from the team.	The objective is to ensure that you satisfy the customer's needs! Don't *guess*—find out!
When the team has finished its job, how will members know they were successful? List those *criteria for success* which will be used to judge the team's performance.	Criteria can be soft or "hard." Budgets, schedule, quality might be measured. Learning, satisfaction, and other criteria are soft. They can be as important as the hard measures.
What critical events might occur in the future that could affect the team's success either positively or negatively.	Examples: a merger, hostile takeover, recession, change in technology, population change.
Now write the mission and purpose statement.	Follow the steps in the model presented next.

FIGURE 3.1
THE STEPS IN WRITING A MISSION STATEMENT

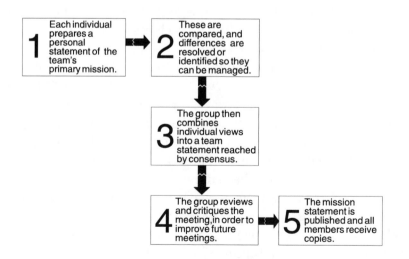

you asked them what they wanted from the school. You know the answers you would get.

More recesses. Less homework. Shorter school days.

Would satisfying these wants be appropriate? Of course not. Your job as teacher would be to *translate* the students' needs into coursework that will meet those needs.

This translation is always part of the job. However, it is too often done without really understanding the customers' needs. We sometimes resort to giving the customers what we *think* they should have, rather than what they really need.

One of the tools for analyzing customer needs and translating them into product or service offerings is called *Quality Function Deployment (QFD)*. This is, in my opinion, a pretty intimidating name. A more simple term that is sometimes used is *House of Quality*. While it is outside the scope of this book to cover QFD analysis in depth, an example will be presented to illustrate the process. See the following references for more detail: Juran (1989), Akao (1990), Dimancescu (1992), Wheelwright and Clark (1992).

Let's suppose we surveyed 50 potential readers of this book on project management. We ask them what they want from a book, and identify the following factors. The book should be: *practical, complete, understandable, a good reference, easy to use,* and *good value for its cost.* We also ask each respondent to rate each factor in terms of its importance.

The next step is to think about the features of a book and identify the following as relevant: *length, writing style, illustrations, page layout,* and *indexing.* There are other features that could be listed, such as binding (hardback or softcover), color versus black-and-white, and so on. This hypothetical example is meant to be illustrative rather than exhaustive.

Once all of this has been done, we draw a matrix as shown in Figure 3.2. When there is a positive correlation between a feature and a customer want, we place a + in the cell. If the correlation is very strong, we use two + signs. If the correlation is inverse, that is, if a feature would detract from satisfying a customer need, we use a minus (–) or double minus (– –). If there is no correlation between a feature and a customer need, we can leave the cell empty or place a zero inside. At the top of the matrix, we look at the correlations that exist between the features of the book themselves.

The idea behind this analysis is simple: we want to give the customer everything that is important to him or her, but we do not want to provide anything that is unimportant. To fail to provide important features and to provide things that are unimportant is to produce a product or service that misses the mark completely.

FIGURE 3.2
A HYPOTHETICAL QFD ANALYSIS
FOR A PROJECT MANAGEMENT BOOK

Features

		Text	Flow Charts	Index
Needs	Quality Information	++	++	0
	Practical Procedures	++	+	0
	Ease of Access	+	+	++

+ = correlation
++ = very strong correlation
0 = no correlation

AN EXAMPLE OF A MISSION STATEMENT

As I said in Chapter 2, we will illustrate the various tools of project management by using the Bali book project as an example. Following is an example of a mission statement for that project.

> **Our mission is to develop a well-illustrated book on the island of Bali, detailing its history, the customs and religion of its past and present inhabitants. The book will be for a general audience. It will be developed by Global Publishing staff, through the use of staff researchers, photographers, and other personnel. The writing will be contracted to freelance writers.**

Note that this statement answers the three questions:

1. What? Write a book about Bali.
2. For whom? A general audience—the primary customer. (Global is a customer also.)
3. How? By contracting the writing and doing other tasks internally.

STRATEGIC PLANNING IN PROJECT MANAGEMENT

Once the project team has a clear understanding of their mission, the next step (step 3 in the model) is to develop a strategy for getting there. Note that step 3 calls for developing *alternative* strategies. This is because there are almost always several ways to achieve a mission, and you want to pick the one that seems best. This step is similar to a standard problem-solving approach, in which you brainstorm a list of alternative ways of solving the problem. The similarity is not accidental. Remember Juran's definition of a project: A project is a problem scheduled for solution.

Strategic Planning Defined

The word *strategy* comes originally from military terminology. The *Oxford English Dictionary* offers the following:

> **strategy:** the art of projecting and directing the larger military movements and operations of a campaign. The mode of executing tactics.
>
> **tactics:** the art of handling forces in battle or in the immediate presence of the enemy.

In colloquial terminology, we sometimes call strategy a "game plan," an overall approach to achieve our major objectives. The important point here is that strategy can only be decided upon once an organization's mission and objectives have been determined. All planning is done to meet objectives, and strategy is only the broad outline of the plan.

As examples of strategy, we have JIT, concurrent or simultaneous engineering, and self-directed work teams as ways of achieving business objectives.

Another example of strategy was just related to me recently. During World War II, Avondale Shipyards devised a new way of building ships. For centuries, shipbuilders have followed a basic approach, which is to build the ship in the position that it ultimately occupies when placed in the water. That is, the keel is on the ground and the decks are above. That construction method is fine for wooden boats, but when steel is employed, welding in the keel area is difficult, plus the steel plate tends to deform slightly, leading to quality problems.

Avondale decided to build the ship upside down. Naturally, they had to devise a way of turning the ship over once the assembly was complete up to the decks, and they did. This strategy was so much more efficient than traditional approaches that Avondale had a significant competitive advantage over shipyards that employed the old method.

In developing project strategy, two fundamental questions must be answered by the project team:

- What are we going to do?
- How are we going to do it?

Timing is very important. If strategic planning is done too soon, it may be so vague (because of lack of sufficient definition) as to be useless. If it is too late, decisions may have been made already that will limit possible alternatives. In the model presented in Chapter 1, the step to develop alternative strategies for implementing the project follows the definition phase. To keep the overall model simple, strategic planning is shown as a single activity or step. This step, however, must be broken down into some substeps. Figure 3.3 illustrates those substeps.

THE STRATEGIC PLANNING MODEL

The substeps in the strategic planning model are not in any particular sequence. In fact, they are to some degree interactive, so that the information derived from one analysis might require going back to another step and digging out more information. Two of the components in the strategic planning model are contained in the model for developing a mission statement, presented above. These are the identification of the expectations of major inside and outside interests, which are called stakeholders in the mission-development model. This means that, if a mission statement has been developed in accordance with the model, stakeholder expectations have already been identified. Also, for a project team, some of those stakeholders listed in the strategic planning model may be relevant while others may not.

Conducting the database analysis is limited in some organizations by a lack of good historical data. In that case, the analysis depends on the memories of individuals, and is subject to all of the biases and inaccuracies to which human beings are prone. Those limitations should be noted in making use of remembered data.

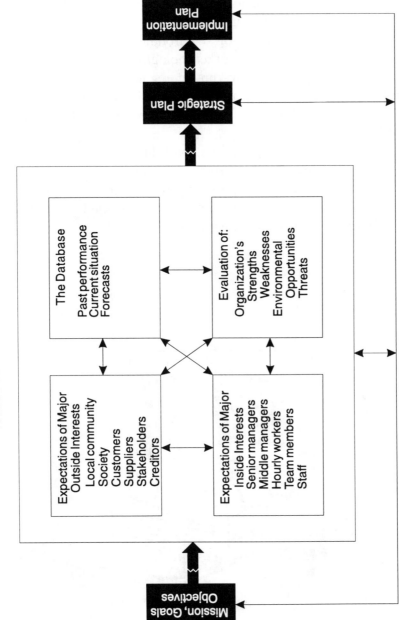

FIGURE 3.3

A MODEL FOR STRATEGIC PLANNING

The Database
Past performance
Current situation
Forecasts

Evaluation of:
Organization's
  Strengths
  Weaknesses
Environmental
  Opportunities
  Threats

Expectations of Major
Outside Interests
  Local community
  Society
  Customers
  Suppliers
  Stakeholders
  Creditors

Expectations of Major
Inside Interests
  Senior managers
  Middle managers
  Hourly workers
  Team members
  Staff

Mission, Goals
Objectives

Strategic Plan

Implementation
Plan

Analysis of the current situation should be easier, assuming that the project team members have access to vital information on the business, its competitors, and so on.

Forecasts are based on environmental scanning. They should include examination of technological developments, economic trends, pending government regulations, social trends, and so on. Naturally, forecasting is very difficult, and is limited by what information is available on competitors and other key entities.

Finally, we have the evaluation of the environment and the company for some specific variables. This evaluation is generally called a SWOT analysis. It prescribes that the team examine the company's *Strengths* and *Weaknesses* as well as the *Opportunities* and *Threats* presented by the environment.

Just when you thought it was SAFE, you realize you need more technical support.

CONDUCTING THE ANALYSES

Environmental Factors

The major environmental factors that may affect a project are economic, technological, governmental or legal, geographic, and social. The economic variable can affect a project in many ways. During a recession companies tend to run "leaner" than in more prosperous times, making resources more scarce and conflicts among projects almost inevitable. When the project spans national borders, currency fluctuations can be a significant factor. In addition, the economy in both the host country and the home country will be a consideration.

Technological changes can be the most difficult to forecast and deal with. There may be no advance warning of a new development, and failure to incorporate that development into a new product might seriously affect its marketability.

E.F. Schumacher (1989) has observed that Westerners are inclined to do all projects with the highest technology available, when that might not be the best approach for projects in developing nations. He suggests that employing the right level of technology is important for the project to be judged a real success.

Projects are increasingly affected by government regulations and legal issues. Product liability suits in the United States have grown to such an extent that companies are very cautious in their handling of new products, construction, and so on.

Geographic factors certainly play a part in how some projects are run. Many companies are now global, and co-location of project participants is impossible. Fortunately, with modern communications technology, they are able to achieve what is called *virtual co-location,* whereby members of the team "meet" as often as necessary through teleconferencing. Naturally, geography also affects strategy in construction projects in terms of terrain, material resources available, and so on. The other influence is human resource availability. I recently saw the construction of a large Shell refinery in Bintulu, Sarawak. Ten years ago,

Bintulu was a small fishing village of about 6,000. Now almost 60,000 people live there—naturally, most of them are imported.

Social factors are sometimes overlooked, especially by technical people, in planning project strategy. The social factor includes an assessment of the values, beliefs, traditions, and attitudes of people—in short, the culture of the people who are stakeholders in the project. Religious and other significant holidays must be factored into project scheduling. In January people in the Far East celebrate the Chinese new year much more avidly than Westerners do our new year. Everything may come to a halt for a few days while people get ready and celebrate this important event.

By the same token, ignorance of the social *taboos* of a culture can create embarrassment and actual failures in projects.

IGNORANCE OF SOCIAL TABOOS

MAY CAUSE EMBARRASSMENT & AFFECT PROJECT SUCCESS

In looking at all of the environmental factors, one asks, do they represent an *opportunity* or a *threat* to the success of the project? Technological developments, for example, can be either, depending on circumstances.

Organizational Factors

Assessing an organization's strengths and weaknesses is a key element in strategic planning. Unfortunately, biases too often discredit the analysis. Managers are inclined to be optimistic about the strengths and a bit blind to the weaknesses of the organization. Nevertheless, the analysis must be done.

Factors to examine include expertise of personnel; labor relations; physical resources; experience with the kind of project being planned; company image; senior management attitudes; morale of employees; market position of the organization; tendencies to overdesign or miss target dates; commitment of the organization to supplying resources to the project as promised. Naturally, you want to capitalize on strengths and minimize the impact of weaknesses. Further, those identified environmental threats must be capable of being offset by the team's strengths, and a conscious effort should be made to take advantage of opportunities presented by the environment.

Expectations of Stakeholders

Expectations of senior managers can be a major influence on the success or failure of a project. When those expectations for project performance are unrealistic, the impact is almost always negative. One of the more common expectations is that *all* target dates will be met. Such expectations lead to conflict.

FORMULATING PROJECT STRATEGY

Once all of these factors have been identified and examined, the project team is ready to develop a number of alternative methods of project implementation. These methods must meet external threats and take advantage of opportunities. Usually strategy will be a combination of several elements.

Coxon (1983) lists 12 possible strategies for projects:

1. Construction oriented: an example of this would be the Avondale Shipyards approach to building ships.

2. Finance based: this might involve some creative way of funding a project, perhaps through the use of bonds or grants; it might also involve special attention to cash flow and cost-of-capital.

3. Governmental: this involves taking into account government requirements and working closely with appropriate agencies to ensure that no pitfalls will block progress.

4. Design: when certain design techniques have an advantage over others, this strategy may offer an advantage.

5. Client/contractor: this might include forming partnerships between client and contractor.

6. Technology: employing a cutting-edge technology might present certain risks, but offer greater competitive advantages. As mentioned previously, choosing the right level of technology might be important in developing countries.

7. Commissioning: if the commissioning aspects of the project are considered to be especially difficult or complex, then this strategy might be employed.

8. Cost, quality, or time: because these are interrelated, emphasizing one will be at the expense of impacting another. For example, when speed is of the utmost importance, and quality standards must be simultaneously maintained, then cost must increase. Nevertheless, if there is a significant market advantage to be gained through speed, the cost may well be offset by the profits made.

9. Resource: a resource strategy would be necessary when a particular resource is limited or abundant. For example, in Indonesia, Thailand, and other eastern countries, labor costs are so low that many construction projects are labor-intensive by Western standards.

10. Size: it may be that for certain kinds of projects, economies of scale are only obtained once the size of the job exceeds a certain level.

11. Contingency: this strategy goes only so far as planning what to do if certain things happen.

12. Passive: this is a situation in which the project manager decides (consciously or unconsciously) to have no strategy at all (paradoxical, since this is in itself a strategy). It might be appropriate when the future is believed to be very stable or, conversely, to be so chaotic that developing a strategy is virtually impossible. This is also called "flying by the seat of the pants."

SELECTING A PROJECT STRATEGY

In Step 4 of the project management model (the flow chart) we select from the available strategies the one that appears best for our project. In order to be viable, the strategy must pass four tests:

- Are all P, C, T, and S requirements met? That is, can we meet performance, cost, time and scope requirements? How do you know at this point? You estimate.

- Are risks acceptable? If you build a ship upside down, you risk dropping it when you try to turn it over. Is that risk small enough that you are willing to take it? If not, then this approach should be rejected. We will see how to conduct a risk analysis later in this chapter.

- Are consequences acceptable? It has been said that many of today's problems are the result (consequence) of yesterday's solutions. Environmental problems represent one such class of problems. We must ask, "Are there any unintended consequences of this strategy that will create new problems for us?" If so, we might reject this strategy.

- Is the force-field analysis okay? There are social forces that might affect the successful implementation of a certain strategy. Suppose, for example, that the president of Avondale Shipyard felt very strongly that building ships upside down was the most ridiculous thing ever suggested. Then it is doubtful that this approach would ever have been tried. An approach for conducting force-field analysis is presented later in this chapter.

CONDUCTING A SWOT ANALYSIS

Following are the questions asked in conducting a SWOT analysis. The form in Figure 3.4 should also help simplify the process. The questions that must be answered are:

- What **S**trengths do we have? How can we take advantage of them?

- What **W**eaknesses do we have? How can we minimize the impact of these?

- What **O**pportunities are there? How can we capitalize on them?

- What **T**hreats might prevent us from getting there? (Consider technical obstacles, competitive responses, values of people within your organization, and so on. Note that threats are not necessarily the same as *risks*.)

- For every obstacle identified, what can we do to overcome or get around it? (This helps you develop contingency plans.)

RISK ANALYSIS

The simplest way to do a risk analysis is to ask, "What could go wrong?" Note that a threat is usually something done by competitors or other people that might impact a project adversely. A risk, however, can happen through one's own actions. In practice, threats and risks might overlap. In any case, for every risk identified, it is useful to decide what might be done to deal with the situation. Again, this helps develop contingencies. A risk

FIGURE 3.4
A SWOT ANALYSIS FORM

SWOT Analysis Form		Goal/Objective under consideration:			
List Strengths	How Can You Best Take Advantage of These?		List Weaknesses	How Can You Minimize the Impact of These?	
What Opportunities does this Project Present?	How Can You Best Take Advantage of Them?		List Threats (Those Risks or Obstacles that Might Prevent Success)	How Can You Deal with Each Identified Threat?	

analysis with contingencies for the Bali book project is shown in Figure 3.5.

One caution is in order: No attempt should be made to identify *all* of the possible risks that might affect a project. To do so leads to a condition called *analysis paralysis.*

Sometimes the identification of a risk allows the project manager to take steps to prevent its occurrence. When that cannot be done, then a backup plan can be developed.

FIGURE 3.5
RISK ANALYSIS FOR THE BALI BOOK PROJECT

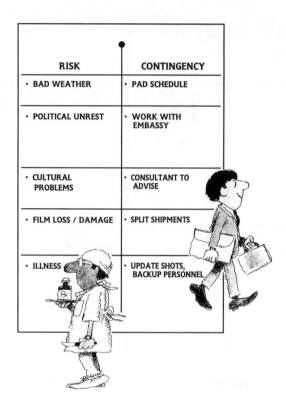

RISK	CONTINGENCY
• BAD WEATHER	• PAD SCHEDULE
• POLITICAL UNREST	• WORK WITH EMBASSY
• CULTURAL PROBLEMS	• CONSULTANT TO ADVISE
• FILM LOSS / DAMAGE	• SPLIT SHIPMENTS
• ILLNESS	• UPDATE SHOTS, BACKUP PERSONNEL

There are, naturally, situations in which *nothing* can be done to prevent or deal with a risk. In that case, the project must be managed in such a way that the probability of its occurrence is minimized.

THE FORCE-FIELD ANALYSIS

In every environment, there will be forces that assist in the achievement of project objectives, as well as those that inhibit progress. Usually we are concerned with forces that are the result of actions by people. For example, a key member of senior management simply does not approve of a particular approach that is advocated by the project manager. If that person's resistance is very strong, the project manager may have to follow a different approach, even though the desired strategy is deemed the best.

It is almost impossible to quantify forces in such an analysis, so I simply recommend that you focus on the negatives and try to find ways to deal with them. The most productive approach will be to find some way to *neutralize* negative forces. To try to overcome them simply leads to the strengthening of those very forces as a rule.

An example of a force-field analysis is shown in Figure 3.6.

IMPLEMENTATION OR TACTICAL PLANNING

Once appropriate strategy has been developed, an implementation plan must be produced that actually follows the strategy. The remaining chapters on planning deal with the implementation aspects of planning.

FIGURE 3.6
AN EXAMPLE OF A FORCE-FIELD ANALYSIS

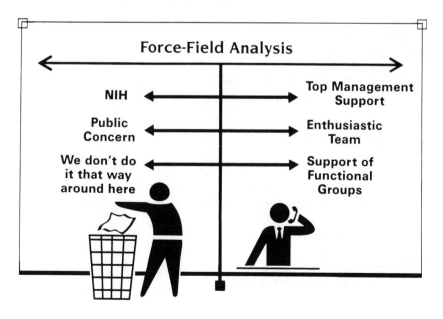

QUESTIONS FOR REVIEW

1. Why is a mission statement important for a project?

2. Who should participate in preparing a project mission statement?

3. What is the purpose of having exit criteria at a project milestone?

4. What is the difference between strategy and tactics?

5. Why is selecting a good strategy important?

6. Give examples of some practices that organizations employ as strategies.

7. What does SWOT stand for?

8. What is one danger of doing a risk analysis?

9. Why does the recommended approach for doing a risk analysis avoid the problem of creating morale problems in the team?

KEY POINTS *from Chapter 3*

- A mission statement should be developed for larger projects, before goals and objectives are established.
- A mission statement should be used as a guide to make decisions in the project.
- Satisfying the customer(s) of a project must be a primary concern.
- A SWOT analysis should be conducted as part of the planning process.

Reference

1. Albrecht, Karl. *The Northbound Train*, p. viii.

Chapter 4

DEVELOPING AN
IMPLEMENTATION PLAN

O nce you have devised a project strategy, as outlined in Chapter 3, you are ready to proceed to Step 6 in the General Model, in which you develop an implementation plan. As an example, if you are Avondale Shipyards, and you have decided to build boats upside down and turn them over, you have to work out the details of how that will be done. This will include designing the fixture on which the boat will be built, as well as all of the other details necessary to do the construction itself.

Until this point in a project is reached, you have generally only assigned a few core members to the project team and you have fleshed out only the broad details of the project. Now you can begin planning to a lower level of detail, and this will involve assigning more people to the team as a rule, estimating durations and costs for various tasks, and working up a schedule for the job. Once this is done, the plan is reviewed and signed off by stakeholders (Steps 7 and 8 of the Model). As an example of how that might work, let us continue with the Bali book project, introduced in Chapter 2.

THE UNIVERSAL PROBLEM

As I mentioned in Chapter 1, it is fairly common for a project manager to be told the scope of the project, the quality of work desired, the deadline, and the amount of money to be spent. In other words, all four variables of the cost equation are dictated.

However, let us assume that the general manager of Global Publishing tells us she wants to know how much the project will actually cost before she gives final approval to start. She has specified the scope, quality, and time (she wants it in time for the Frankfurt book fair, held in October of each year).

At this point, you can estimate cost by simply comparing this book to a similar one that was done recently. You compare the two projects and note that each contains about the same number of photographs, the same number of pages, and so on. However, the Bali book is going to require that you send a photographer, and possibly your writers, from Roanoke, Virginia, to Bali, which will be a significant expense compared to the other book, which required no such travel. You add money for travel. You take off some money for reprint permissions, which the Bali book is unlikely to have. You put in a bit for uncertainty. This gives you a *ballpark* estimate, to use the common term.

The problem with such estimates is that they may not be very accurate. When one project is truly like another, the comparison might yield accuracies of 10 to 15%. However, they can be as bad as +100% to -20%, when the similarities are poor.

To arrive at a better estimate and understanding of the work to be done, we need more detail. The tool of choice at this point is the Work Breakdown Structure (WBS), which can be used to define the work to be done.

USING THE WORK BREAKDOWN STRUCTURE

Trying to get a handle on a complex job is virtually impossible unless some way is found to conceptualize it. Studies have shown that the human mind is able to deal with about 7 ± 2 bits of information at one time. This limit can easily be reached very quickly for even small projects. To reduce the complexity, the tool of choice is the Work Breakdown Structure, as mentioned above.

Again, in terms of the General Model presented in Chapter 1, we are at Step 6. Further, Step 6 is the combination of eight sub-steps. These are shown again for your convenience in Figure 4.1. Note that developing a WBS is Step 6a, and this is done by answering the questions inside the box. Steps 6b through 6h are performed later, and they are discussed in subsequent chapters. For now, the focus is *only* on Step 6a.

If defining the project is the most important step in managing a project, developing the WBS is the next most important step in the planning process, since it provides a framework from which the following can be done:

- All tasks to be performed can be identified and resources allocated to them.
- Once resource levels have been allocated to tasks, estimates of task durations can be made.
- All costs and resource allocations can be totaled to develop the overall project budget.
- Task durations can then be used in developing a working schedule for the project.
- Performance can be tracked against these identified cost, schedule, and resource allocations.
- Assignment of responsibility for each element can be made.

An example of a WBS for doing a yard project is shown in Figure 4.2. This is not a very large project, but illustrates the idea. For many projects, a six level WBS will be adequate. For six levels, names can be assigned as shown in Figure 4.3.

The six-level structure is not the only possibility, of course. Organizations that do very large projects, such as construction of power-generating plants, may use a structure with 10 to 12 levels. A rule of thumb is that no more than 20 levels should be used, no matter how large the project.

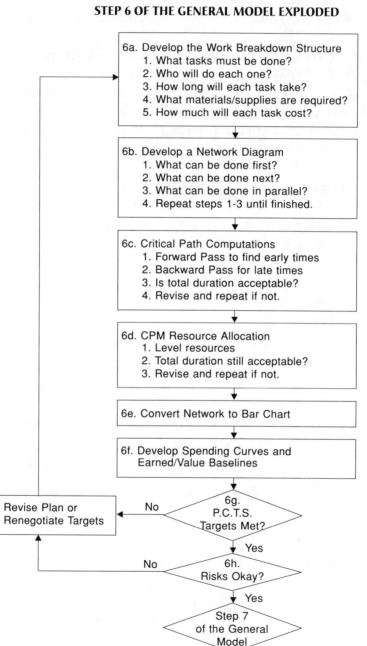

FIGURE 4.1
STEP 6 OF THE GENERAL MODEL EXPLODED

6a. Develop the Work Breakdown Structure
    1. What tasks must be done?
    2. Who will do each one?
    3. How long will each task take?
    4. What materials/supplies are required?
    5. How much will each task cost?

6b. Develop a Network Diagram
    1. What can be done first?
    2. What can be done next?
    3. What can be done in parallel?
    4. Repeat steps 1-3 until finished.

6c. Critical Path Computations
    1. Forward Pass to find early times
    2. Backward Pass for late times
    3. Is total duration acceptable?
    4. Revise and repeat if not.

6d. CPM Resource Allocation
    1. Level resources
    2. Total duration still acceptable?
    3. Revise and repeat if not.

6e. Convert Network to Bar Chart

6f. Develop Spending Curves and
    Earned/Value Baselines

Revise Plan or Renegotiate Targets   ← No   6g. P.C.T.S. Targets Met?

Yes

No   6h. Risks Okay?

Yes

Step 7 of the General Model

FIGURE 4.2
A WORK BREAKDOWN STRUCTURE FOR YARD PROJECT

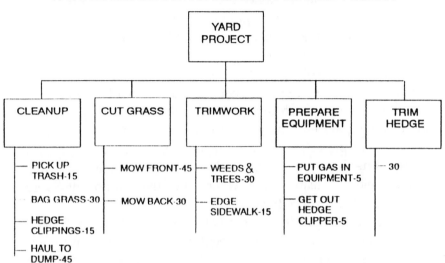

FIGURE 4.3
NAMES FOR WORK BREAKDOWN STRUCTURE LEVELS

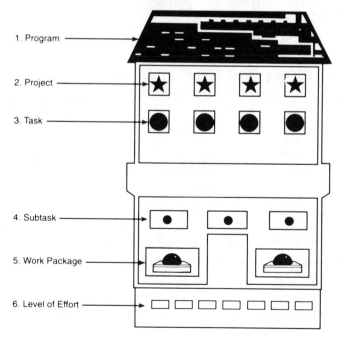

1. Program
2. Project
3. Task
4. Subtask
5. Work Package
6. Level of Effort

The six-level structure shown in Figure 4.3 begins at the program level. The difference between programs and projects is, then, simply a matter of magnitude. A manager who supervises a number of project managers would be called a *program manager*, based on this notation scheme.

An example of a program would be the development of the space shuttle. There were numerous projects involved in developing the shuttle. Such things as designing the heating and air-conditioning system, the guidance and navigation system, and so on, were projects in their own right. Many of those projects were done by contractors, and the program manager was responsible for ensuring that when all of the components were integrated, they worked in concert.

Figure 4.4 is a WBS for the Bali book project. I have broken the work down to reasonable detail. Some of them could obviously be subdivided some more. An example would be Staff Travel to Bali. We could break that down to Go to airport, Fly to Bali, Go to hotel, and so on. Naturally, it begins to get ridiculous. After all, our purpose is to plan and estimate to a level of detail that will permit us to get control over project work. Neither too much nor too little detail will help.

There is no easy way to answer the question, "How far should you break down the work?" However, there are two basic answers. First, you break down the work until you can do an estimate that is accurate enough for your purposes. If

> **R**ule: break down the work only as far as needed to develop an estimate to the required degree of accuracy.

you are doing a ballpark estimate in order to decide whether a project should be done at all, then you probably don't need to break the work down very far. On the other hand, if you are pricing out the job to the nearest 10%, then you will have to go down fairly far.

The second answer is given by considering the smallest units of time in which you plan to schedule the work. If you are

Figure 4.4

WORK BREAKDOWN STRUCTURE FOR BALI BOOK PROJECT

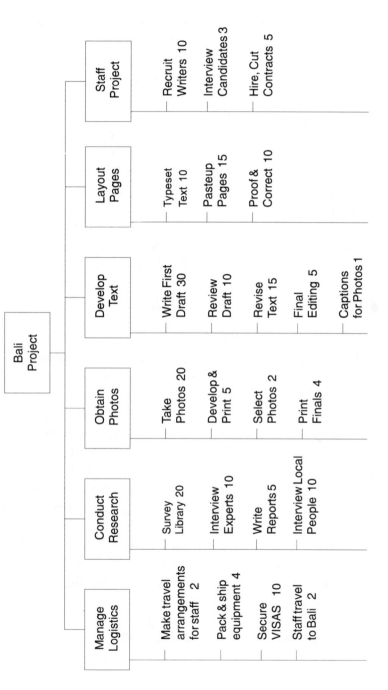

NOTE: Numbers beside tasks are durations in working days.

going to schedule to the nearest day, then when activities get down to the point where their times are in days, you stop. If you plan to schedule in hours, then break the work down into units that have durations in hourly increments. Those are the best rules that can be applied.

Keep in mind also that you should never plan in more detail than you can actually manage. If you are overhauling a power generator, and you can control work to the nearest hour, then you break the job down to that level. However, if you cannot do better than about a week, then that is the level you stop at.

We could think of the Bali book as a program or a project. If we call it a program, then the boxes at level two are projects. Certainly just the photography could be thought of as a project itself. However, I believe it is better to think of this as a single project, and reserve the term *program* for larger jobs.

DEVELOPING THE WBS

As a practical matter, the procedure for developing a WBS is fairly straightforward. You simply ask the question, "What will have to be done in order to accomplish . . . ?" I started with the finished book in mind (which you must do for any project) and imagined all of the things that would have to be done. The text must be written. It will have to be edited. Photographs will have to be taken, processed, and selected. Research will have to be conducted. We will have to get staff to Bali and back home.

In order to estimate task durations, I must assume that certain resources will be applied and find out from them how long the work will take. Figure 4.5 shows a listing of personnel assigned to the tasks listed in the WBS.

Eventually, we will have to work out the order in which every task will be performed. That aspect of the project will be discussed in the chapters on scheduling. (Note: You *do not* try to work out sequencing while doing a WBS. That is done only after all of the tasks have been identified.)

FIGURE 4.5

WORK BREAKDOWN STRUCTURE FOR BALI BOOK PROJECT, WITH RESOURCES ASSIGNED TO TASKS

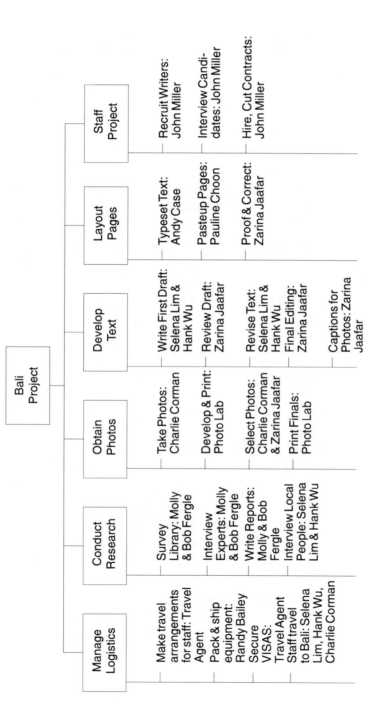

Note the comments made by my colleague, Tom Conlon, in the sidebar. I agree with the essence of his argument, but there are times when his suggestion is difficult to follow. For example, if you are servicing a car, and *change oil* is one of the tasks to perform, it is hard to specify a *thing* as a deliverable. An auto with fresh oil is about as close as you can come.

I would prefer to say that generally a WBS box contains both a *noun* and a *verb*. After all, we are breaking down *work*, which implies verbs. But the end result is to produce things in many cases. What I think is really significant about Tom's point is that it is so hard to determine *done*, unless you have tangible evidence. So what would be the tangible evidence that oil has been changed in a car? You would have some empty oil cans, a container of dirty oil that was drained from the car, the dipstick would indicate that the crankcase was full and the oil on the stick would be clean-looking. These are Dimancescu's *exit criteria*, mentioned in Chapter 3.

Understanding "done"

The Work Breakdown Structure (WBS) chart shows the project's *destination*, i.e., what "done" means. It does not address how to get there—the *route*—or the timing. That's the job of the project schedule.

I have found the most useful WBS to be a decomposition of the project in terms of end deliverable items. My WBS charts tend to be very physical, like a bill of materials or table of contents of a book. I ask, is each element labeled with a noun?

One advantage of a *thing*-oriented WBS is that it remains very stable over the life of the project in a way that activities never seem to be. And stable structures are important to team understanding and communication.

Another advantage of a *thing*-oriented WBS is that it is a much more reliable base for measuring progress. If you have 100 PCs to assemble and test, and 90 are done and working, you really are 90% done.

This important chart needs to be detailed to assure that nothing that may require calendar time, effort, or money is omitted.

Tom Conlon

ESTIMATING COSTS

In any case, as mentioned above, once a suitable level has been reached, estimates of activity durations can be developed, resources can be assigned, and cost estimates can be determined for the work. For example, if an activity will require 10 hours of work, and labor is expected to cost $12.00 per hour, the activity will cost $120.00 dollars. (See Figure 4.6.) If costs are developed for each work package, those that combine to make a subtask can be added up to obtain the subtask cost. These can then be combined to develop a task cost, and so on, until total project cost has been calculated. (See Figure 4.7.)

FIGURE 4.6
WORK PACKAGE ESTIMATE

	Time, days	Cost/day	Total
Obtain Photos			
Take Photos: Charlie Corman	20	$300	$6000
Develop & Print: Photo Lab	5	n/a	$300
Select Photos: Charlie Corman & Zarina Jaafar	2	$250	$500
Print Finals: Photo Lab	4	n/a	$500
		TOTAL:	$7300

Figure 4.7
USING A WBS TO DEVELOP TOTAL PROJECT COST

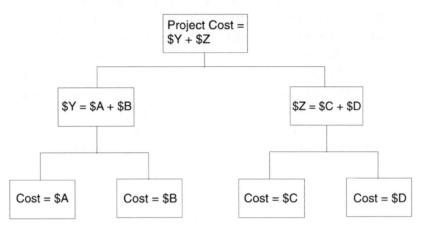

THE ESTIMATING PROBLEM

This all assumes, of course, that times can be estimated. We all know that is easier said than done. The question is, how does a project manager know how long it will take to do *anything?* The answer is, *from experience!* You have done it before. In our example, we have done a lot of books in the past. That work gives us a basis for estimating, but the uniqueness of this particular job might make the estimates somewhat *iffy.*

In any case, let us examine what we really mean by *experience* and its relationship to estimating activity durations. As an example, if you have been driving to the same workplace from the same home for several years, using the same route each time, you know about how long it takes to get to work. In large metropolitan areas, people report times like those shown in Table 4.1.

When asked, "What is your best estimate of how long it will take you to get to work tomorrow?" they usually respond with, "45 minutes." That is, they give the average driving time.

However, if you ask, "How long would you allow yourself to get to work if you absolutely had to get there on time?" they

TABLE 4.1

DRIVING TIMES FOR METROPOLITAN WORKERS

Average time	45 minutes
Shortest time	35 minutes
Longest time	60* minutes

assuming no blizzards, etc.

say, "one hour." So they allow themselves the upper limit, just in case they are faced with a wreck or whatever causes their time to go to the upper limit. That way, they will be sure to get to work on time, unless the situation is extreme and the time exceeds the one-hour upper limit.

In a project, much the same process is involved. If a task has been performed a large number of times, the average duration is known, given a certain level of human resources to do the work, and this average can be used as the basis for an estimate.

There is only one difficulty. If we assume for simplicity that the driving distribution is normal (it is not—it is almost always skewed), then from statistics, we know that an average duration has only a 50/50 likelihood of occurring (See Figure 4.8.).[1] That is, there is a 50% chance that it will take longer than the average duration and also a 50% chance that it could take less than the average. Having a 50% chance of success in completing one's work is not very comforting, especially if the stakes are high and the organization is determined to have the project completed by some predetermined date.

It is for this reason that people are inclined to pad their estimates. As the normal distribution curve in Figure 4.8 shows, there is an 84% probability that a duration one standard deviation above the mean can be met, 98% for two standard deviations, and 99.9% for three standard deviations. Thus, by

FIGURE 4.8
NORMAL DISTRIBUTION CURVE

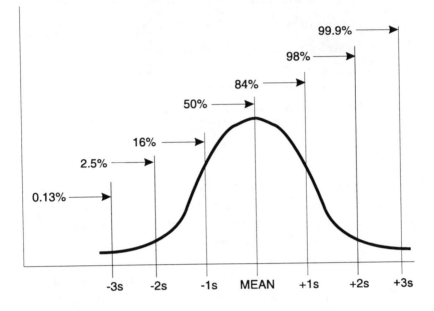

padding, the project manager can greatly increase the probability that the work can be completed in the estimated time.

Unfortunately, safety carries a price. While increasing the allowed time increases the probability of a successful scheduled completion, it also increases the budgeted cost of the project, and it is possible that such an increase will increase the total estimated project costs to the point that the job will most likely not be funded.

For this reason, one of the assumptions made in project estimating is that *average durations are used, unless specified otherwise*. The idea is that, for a project consisting of a large number of activities, some of the work will take longer than the average estimated duration, while other tasks will take less than the average, so that the total project completion time will gravitate toward the mean expected time for the critical path! Unfortunately, Murphy's Law seems to prevent such an occurrence.

While padding is certainly justified to reduce risk, my opinion is that it must be done aboveboard, on a task-by-task basis. Otherwise, the project manager might assume that every member of the team has provided average-duration estimates and then put some padding into the project at the top level, thus adding more "fat" to the pads that individuals have already put into their estimates, and the project is sure to be too expensive then.

This is one reason for not getting into game playing in an organization. It sometimes happens that a manager asks for an estimate, and when it is provided, the manager cuts the estimate by 10 or 15%, based on the belief that the estimate contains at least that much "fat." Note that the probability of achieving a time one standard deviation below the mean is only 16%, so cutting an estimate that was an average expected duration severely reduces the probability that the time can be met.

If the project manager gets burned because his estimates were averages and they were cut, then the next time he is asked for an estimate, he will indeed pad, since he expects that his estimate will be cut. This time, however, the manger cuts 20%, so the next time the project manager pads 25%, and so on. Such "games" are hardly productive.

The objective of all project planning should be to develop a plan that is *realistic*, so that managers can make decisions as to whether to do the work. The objective should not be to try to "get" the project manager when he is unable to meet unrealistic deadlines. (I understand that in some organizations game playing is so firmly entrenched that a project manager cannot change it unilaterally. It is, nevertheless, not the way to run an organization.)

It is instructive to consider the cause of variations in working times, using the driving example as a guide. Suppose we agree that the time it takes to drive to work varies widely because of unpredictable traffic-flow patterns. If we could eliminate those, then the variation in driving time could be greatly reduced.

Indeed, suppose there was absolutely no other traffic on the road besides the single driver. (Perhaps this can be accomplished by leaving very early in the morning, before other drivers get out on the road.) In that case, there should be no variation in driving time—right? Of course that is not true. Even though the variation would be reduced, no driver can maintain an exactly constant speed, or even the exact same variation at the same point in the road day after day.

For this reason, there will always be some variation in working times, caused by *factors outside the control* of the operator! It is therefore unrealistic to expect that anyone can estimate precisely how long a task will take to complete. (As someone has said, anyone who has 20/20 precision in forecasting should leave project management and invest in the stock market. The returns would be far greater than anyone could make managing projects.)

OTHER FACTORS IN ESTIMATING

An average expected duration for an activity can be developed only by assuming that the work will be nearly identical to work previously done and that the person(s) being assigned to the task will have a certain skill level. If a less-skilled person is assigned to the work, it can be expected to take longer, and conversely, a more-skilled person could probably do the job faster. Thus, adjustments must be made for experience or skill of the resource assigned to the task.

However, we also know that there is no direct correlation between experience and speed of doing work. It may not actually be true that the more experienced person can do the job faster than the person with less experience. And putting pressure on the individual will pay dividends only up to a point. I remember once when I was pressuring one of my project team members to get a job done faster, and he got fed up with the pressure. Finally, he said, "Putting two jockeys on one horse won't make him run any faster." And he was right.

Then there was a project manager who told me that when his boss doesn't like an estimate of how long it will take to perform a task, he tells him to *use a more productive person!* That was his solution to all scheduling problems (Figure 4.9).

Another factor is how much productive time the person will apply to the task each day. It is not uncommon in some organizations for people to spend an average of 25% of each day in meetings, on the phone, waiting for supplies, and other activities, all of which reduce the time available to spend on project work. Allowances must be made for such nonproject time.

In addition, if experience with a task is minimal, the expected duration might be adjusted upward, compared to the closest task for which experience exists. If virtually no experience can be used as a basis for estimating, then it might be

FIGURE 4.9
USE A MORE PRODUCTIVE PERSON

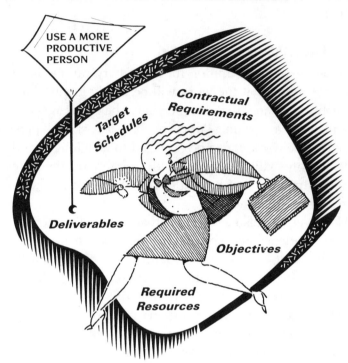

appropriate to use PERT techniques (see Chapter 8). Another possibility is to use DELPHI or some other estimating method. For an application of DELPHI method to project estimating, consult the book by Burrill and Ellsworth, cited in the reading list.

For construction projects, there are books available containing *means tables*, which list the average expected durations for typical construction activities, together with "fudge factors" to be used in adjusting those times to compensate for geographic location, weather, and so on.

For other types of projects, unfortunately, there are no means tables available, so historical data must be developed by keeping records on previous project work. This is, perhaps, one of the most important benefits of developing a standardized project management methodology—by doing the work in specified ways and by keeping records on actual working times, an organization can develop a database that can be used to greatly improve future project estimates.

ESTIMATING ACCURACY USING THE **WBS**

Earlier we saw that estimating project costs at the project level can yield budgets that have fairly large tolerances. Typical figures are −10% to +100%. If work is broken down to level six, those tolerances might be reduced to as little as ± 5% for very well-defined construction projects, or around ± 15% for others, such as research and development.

As an example of how uncertainty affects estimating tolerances, suppose you were asked how long it would take and how much it would cost to develop an AIDS vaccine. This work has been going on for a number of years already, with no end in sight.

The Safety Factor Paradox

Project managers often add a safety factor to make the initial estimate closer to the project's real (true) size. But here's what unfortunately happens: A bigger estimate often leads to faster staff buildup early in the project, which adds communication and maybe training overhead, leading to lower productivity. So while the safety factor works, i.e., the adjusted estimate is closer to the real size, the actual size (and cost) turns out to be higher! The pressure the team feels depends on their perception of the fat in the budget (estimate) and schedule. A bigger estimate may reduce pressure on the team, leading to more dallying around in the early stages.

Conclusion: A different estimate creates a different project! This phenomenon should also convince you to work harder to discover the hidden or undiscovered tasks early during planning.

Advice: You will have to trade off accuracy of your initial estimate verses actual project cost. Do add a safety factor for undiscovered (hidden) project tasks. But make sure your sponsor and steering committee understand what you're doing. Have them set aside a management reserve if returning to the well for more funding is a real problem.

Tom Conlon

USING THE WBS TO SHOW PROJECT SCOPE

One additional benefit of the Work Breakdown Structure is that it provides a visual representation of the total scope of the project. It is not uncommon for project managers to develop cost and duration estimates for a project, only to have someone ask, "How can it cost so much?" Having a WBS in hand, it becomes easier to show others the total magnitude and complexity of the work involved so that they can see first-hand why it costs so much.

LINEAR RESPONSIBILITY CHARTS

One rather common problem in larger projects is that people lose track of who is supposed to be working on what tasks. While the standard organization chart shows who reports to whom, it does not show relationships in a project. The linear responsibility chart is designed to do exactly that, and Figure 4.10 contains an example.

Linear Responsibility Chart
(also called Responsibility Assignment Matrix)
Hold a group session with people from performing organizations who can commit resources. Document agreements on overhead transparencies in real time. Later transfer to a spreadsheet.

This type of arrangement shows in one horizontal line all team members involved in a work function, and the nature of their involvement. The one vertical line shows all work in which a person is involved, together with the degree of his or her responsibility.

In the chart shown in Figure 4.10, Lea Ann has actual responsibility for three tasks and is providing support for another. She has responsibility for *Final layout of forms, Design package,* and *Production coordination.* She is providing support on *Design forms.* In this example, no code 3 levels have been used. These are generally used for special coordination requirements.

FIGURE 4.10

A LINEAR RESPONSIBILITY CHART

Linear Responsibility Chart

| Project: | Notebook for Proj. Mgrs. | Date Issued: | 01-Dec-90 | Sheet | 1 of | 1 |
| Manager: | Jim Lewis | Date Revised: | 15-May-95 | Filename: | LRCSAMP | |

Task Descriptions	Project Contributors									
	Lea Ann	Susi	Jim	Norm S.	Carolyn					
Design forms	2		1							
Final layout of forms	1	2								
Write guidelines for use			1	2						
Design package	1		2	2						
Develop sales plan			1	2	2					
Production coordination	1	2	2							

Codes: 1 = Actual Responsibility ‖ 2 = Support ‖ 3 = Must be notified ‖ Blank = Not involved

A blank cell in the matrix indicates that the person is not involved in the work package. Most importantly, *no horizontal line can contain but a single "1," since two people cannot have ultimate responsibility for getting a job done.*

A horizontal line can contain only a single **1**, since two people cannot have ultimate responsibility for getting a job done!

QUESTIONS FOR REVIEW

1. *What is the reason for using a WBS?*

2. *What is the probability of achieving an estimate based on the average time that it has previously taken to do something?*

3. *What causes the time required to perform a task to vary?*

4. *Why should time worked on a project be recorded daily?*

KEY POINTS *from Chapter 4*

- Estimates are based on experience, using the average expected time to perform a task.

- Padding is legitimate to reduce risk, but should be done *aboveboard*.

- An estimate is not a *fact!*

- Reduce time available for a person to work on a project to allow for meetings, breaks, and so on.

- The Work Breakdown Structure is used to develop estimates, assign personnel, track progress, and show scope of project work.

- Break work down only to the level needed to develop an estimate sufficiently accurate for the intended use.

- Time worked on the project should be recorded daily to avoid writing fiction!

- Use a linear responsibility chart to show who is responsible for various activities in a project.

Reference

1. The reader unfamiliar with statistics should consult a basic text, such as the one by Walpole, cited in the reading list, to see why this is true.

Chapter 5

DEVELOPING THE PROJECT SCHEDULE: GENERAL GUIDELINES

INTRODUCTION TO SCHEDULING TECHNIQUES[1]

When Imhotep built the pyramid for pharaoh Zoser, he undoubtedly had to do the work in a certain order, and deciding on the activity durations, assigning resources, and sequencing of work is

> **W**e can't leave the haphazard to chance!
>
> *N. F. Simpson*

the essence of scheduling. Estimating activity durations and assigning resources was covered in Chapter 4. These two steps are taken when the WBS is developed. This chapter will concentrate on developing the schedule itself.

Whether Imhotep was able to work out the sequence of steps required to build the pyramid using some sort of scheduling notation we don't know. However, it is inconceivable that he built such a huge structure with no forethought about order, and so we can assume that these early engineers must have developed some method of scheduling their projects.

Terms Used in This Chapter

The work breakdown structure presented in Chapter 4 assigns specific names to each level of work. For simplicity, in this chapter I will refer to any work being done as *a task* or *activity*.

THE PURPOSE OF SCHEDULING

A deadline is imposed on most projects today. If it is constructing a building or road, the client wants it finished by a certain date. If it is writing a book, the publisher wants to begin selling it at the beginning of the sales season. Software must be developed before the beginning of next month so that it can be used to do the company payroll.

In addition, the starting time for the project is often constrained by factors outside the project manager's control. Specifications or people or materials won't be available until a certain time. Thus the project cannot start until then. The result is that the work must be done within the boundaries of the constrained starting time and the imposed deadline. This is the classic problem of trying to put *ten pounds of trash in a five pound bag!* It is also *the* problem that every project manager must be able to solve.

An Example

Let us suppose that you operate a delivery service. A client in a distant city calls and asks if you can pick up some materials in two different cities and deliver them to her by 3:00 P.M. She says it is of the utmost importance that the parts be at her location by three o'clock. Failure on your part to deliver on time will cost her a very important contract with one of her clients. She offers you a bonus if you deliver by 3:00 P.M. but says if you are late she expects you to pay a large penalty to cover her losses. While the bonus is very attractive, the penalty is severe, and you want to see if you have a chance of making it on time before you agree to her terms. You tell her you will call back in a few minutes with your answer.

After you hang up the phone, you draw a diagram as shown in Figure 5.1. The general term for such a diagram is *network*. As we will see later, other designations are also used. The diagram in Figure 5.1 shows that one of your delivery staff will have to drive from your location to Town A, which is 20 miles away, pick up some materials, then drive 60 miles to the client's location. The other driver will have to drive to Town B, which is 30 miles away, make a pickup, then drive 80 miles to the client's location. Assuming that the drivers can average 50 miles per hour and that the pickups take zero time, it will take the number of minutes shown in Figure 5.2 to reach the destinations as shown. Note that, for simplicity, I am pretending that the pickups take zero time.

Note that the path from your location to Town A and on to the client's town is 80 miles total, whereas the one through Town B is 110 miles. This means that it will take the driver longer on one path than the other to reach the final destination. The total

FIGURE 5.1

ROUTES FROM VENDORTOWN TO CLIENTVILLE

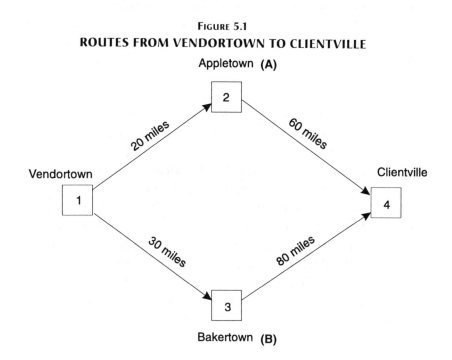

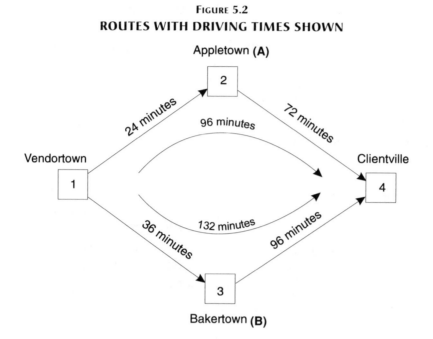

FIGURE 5.2
ROUTES WITH DRIVING TIMES SHOWN

time through Town B is 132 minutes (2 hours and 12 minutes), and through Town A it is 96 minutes (1 hour and 36 minutes).

You look at your watch and discover it is already 12:30 P.M.! You need to get the driver who goes through Town B on the road by 12:48 at the very latest in order to reach the client on time. The other driver, however, needs only 96 minutes to get to the client. That driver could leave 36 minutes after the first one and still arrive on time. (See Figure 5.2a.)

We say that the longest path is the *critical path.* If we back away from the deadline by 2 hours and 12 minutes, that path has no latitude whatsoever. The driver must average 50 miles per hour on the longest leg of the trip or arrive late. The other driver, however, has 36 minutes of latitude if he leaves at the same time as the first one. We say that the second driver has some *slack time,* or latitude. If his average driving speed falls a little under 50 miles per hour, he can still arrive on time, so long as he does not use up more than the 36 minutes of slack.

Remember, though, that there is a heavy penalty if the delivery is late. Also, consider the driving times. They are based on an average *estimated* driving time of 50 mph. What happens if there is an accident on the highway that ties up one of the drivers? Or suppose the delivery vehicle breaks down. If anything happens on the critical path, and we have waited until the last minute to leave for the client's location, then we will be late and have to pay the penalty.

This example shows the importance of knowing where in a project the critical path exists. For many reasons, we find that most projects do not start until they absolutely have to, which means that the critical path has no slack at all. In fact, the conventional way to find the critical

The *critical path* in a project is the longest series of activities, and determines the earliest date at which the work can be completed.

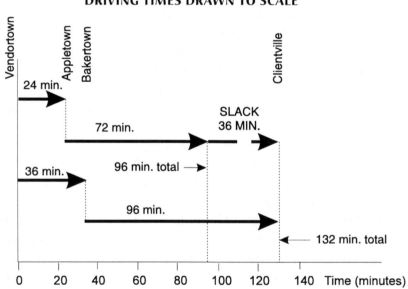

FIGURE 5.2A
DRIVING TIMES DRAWN TO SCALE

path in a project is to force one path to have no slack (or float, as it is sometimes called), and it will always be the longest path as well. We will see how this is done in the next chapter.

When the critical path is both the longest path and also has no slack, then the project manager must *do whatever is necessary* to see that activities on that path are achieved in the allocated times, or the project deadline will be missed. This usually means allocating more effort (resources) to the critical path to reduce its duration. However, there are times when adding resources won't help, as we will see in Chapter 7. In our example, the driver would have to pace himself to ensure that he averages 50 miles per hour.

Understanding the Schedule Diagram

In Figures 5.1 and 5.2 we used arrows to show the routes taken by two different drivers to get to the client's location. Since driving is an activity, we call the diagram an *activity-on-arrow* (AOA) diagram. The boxes are called *nodes,* and each node contains at least two *events.*[2] An event is a point in time at which something happens. It is *binary*—that is, it has either happened or has not. There is no in-between condition. An activity, on the other hand, can be partially completed.

Note that we are using the term *event* in a very special, restricted way. The English language often refers to functions that span time as events. For example, a ball game is called an event. The same is true for a party, meeting, and so on. In project scheduling, we restrict the word, as mentioned above.

Now, consider Figure 5.3. I have redrawn the driving diagram with capital letters beside each arrow to serve as a "name" or designation, and have numbered the nodes. Thus, we have activity A, between nodes 1 and 2, B between 1 and 3, and so on. We can also refer to these activities using their node numbers, so that we have activity A as activity 1-2, or activity$_{1,2}$. Any of these designations is okay to use.

For activity 1-3, node 1 represents its start and node 3 represents its finish. Also, we know that as soon as the driver

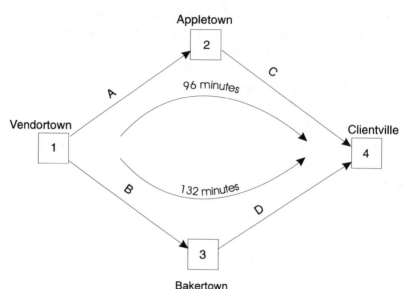

FIGURE 5.3
SCHEDULE WITH ARROWS "NAMED"

reaches Bakertown, he must leave for Clientville. There is no slack. This means that node 3 represents the finish of activity B and the beginning of activity D. Further, if we assume that it takes only a few seconds for the driver to pick up the materials to be delivered to the client, then activity D can begin *immediately* after activity B is finished.

Activity 2-4, however, does not have to begin immediately after activity 1-2 is completed. There is slack on this path (36 minutes). Thus, even though node 2 is the finish of activity A and the start of activity C, and we are saying that an event is binary, we see that node 2 actually represents two events that can happen at two points in time. In fact, it might be more meaningful if the diagram were drawn as shown in Figure 5.4. Now we have events 2a and 2b, with the dashed arrow representing the amount of delay (slack) that can take place from the time activity A is finished (event 2a) and the time activity C begins (event 2b). (We can say that node 2 has been *decomposed* into two components, events 2a and 2b.)

FIGURE 5.4

SCHEDULE WITH SLACK SHOWN AND NODE 2 EXPLODED

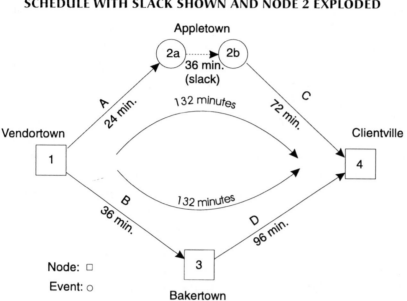

Now the interesting thing is, we could move the arrow representing slack ahead of activity A or behind activity C. That is, the slack can be applied anywhere along path 1-2-4. If it is moved ahead of activity A, this means that the activity could start 36 minutes after activity B has started and the driver could still arrive at Clientville on time.

Alternatively, if the slack is placed after activity C, then the driver can leave at the same time as the driver on path 1-3-4, arrive 36 minutes ahead of the deadline, and start home. Another possibility is that the drive from Vendortown to Appletown might take longer than 24 minutes. Remember, this was an estimated time assuming that the driver could average 50 mph. Since there is a 36-minute slack time available on this path, the driver does not have to be so concerned about maintaining that 50 mph average speed, as was mentioned above. Thus, we see the usefulness of slack.

More-Complex Schedules

The driving example used above is quite simple. There are only two paths. Naturally, you can hardly expect most projects to be so simple. To illustrate more-complex situations, suppose the driver on Path 1-3 of the preceding schedule wants to coordinate with the other driver once he reaches Bakertown. He wants to radio that driver to tell him it is okay to proceed on to Clientville. Whether it is okay to proceed depends on whether the driver in Bakertown has obtained all of the materials he needs. The supplier was supposed to get everything in before the driver arrived, but there was some doubt that every item would arrive on time. However, since the supplier in Appletown also carries similar items, if the Bakertown supplier is short anything, there is still a chance to get it from the Appletown vendor.

Now the driver to Appletown can only proceed to Clientville if two things have taken place: (1) he has reached Appletown and picked up his materials, and (2) he has received word by radio from the Bakertown driver that it is okay to proceed. Since the radio transmission takes only a few seconds, we will treat it as having zero duration. The resulting network diagram will then look like the one in Figure 5.5.

The dashed arrow connecting events 3 and 2 is called a *dummy*. It has zero duration, and shows nothing but a logic relationship. We can now think of Task 1-3 as representing "drive to Bakertown, pick up materials, and radio other driver." If these things have all been done, the driver in Appletown can proceed.

Note the effect that this dummy now has on the driver in Appletown. Originally, he could leave as soon as he reached Appletown. Now he must wait for a call from the other driver. Since it takes that driver 36 minutes to reach Bakertown, the earliest the second driver can leave Appletown is at $t = 36$ minutes, assuming both drivers left Vendortown at the same time. Originally, the driver could leave at the end of 24 minutes. This means he has lost 12 minutes of the slack that he had originally. Since he had 36 minutes altogether, this does not present a problem. (In the next chapter, we will do more elaborate calculations.)

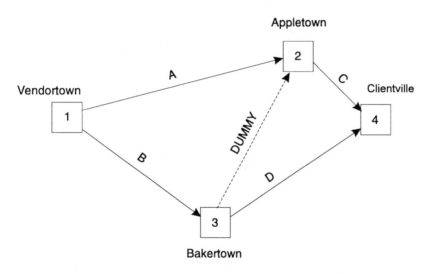

FIGURE 5.5
NETWORK WITH DUMMY ADDED

OTHER WAYS OF DRAWING NETWORK DIAGRAMS

In previous sections, we have drawn diagrams using arrows to show activities, boxes to show nodes, and circles to show events. This is called activity-on-arrow (AOA) notation. Another way to draw schedule diagrams is to use boxes (or nodes) as the activities, and connect them with arrows to show the sequence. This is called activity-on-node (AON) notation. Figure 5.6 is a diagram for the driving example using AON notation.

If all scheduling were to be done manually, it would be possible to select the notation that you personally like the best. However, since all schedules of any significance are, for practical reasons, done using computers, the choice of scheduling software will likely determine which graphical scheme you will use.

As I have mentioned previously, when drawing schedule diagrams, it is common practice to first do a WBS, then take the activities from the WBS. Either form of notation (activity-on-arrow or activity-on-node) can be used, and an activity can be a *level-of-effort*, a *work package*, or a *subtask*. Note that if you dia-

FIGURE 5.6
ACTIVITY-ON-NODE DIAGRAM FOR DRIVING EXAMPLE

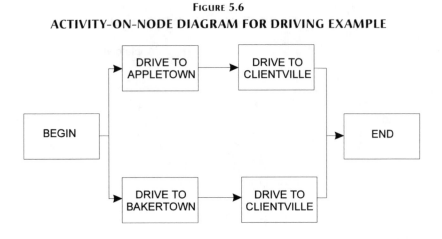

gram *level-of-effort* work, then you do not need to diagram the *work package* above, as the smaller tasks collectively make up the larger one. Later in this chapter, I will discuss what should be diagrammed from the WBS.

Although both AON and AOA diagrams arrive at the same schedule dates or times, there is one small advantage of AOA networks over AON diagrams. It is that the events can be numbered, as shown previously in the driving example, and the activities can be referred to in terms of their event numbers. Thus, activity 1-2 is activity A. This notation is called *i-j notation,* from mathematics. It makes data input to a computer somewhat easier than is true of activity-on-node networks, since the computer automatically knows how to link the activities by using the event numbers, whereas with activity-on-node networks, you have to tell the computer exactly how everything is linked. Figure 5.7 provides definitions of some of the more common network terms.

CONSTRUCTING MORE-COMPLEX ARROW DIAGRAMS

The previous edition of this book showed how to do network computations, but did not offer any suggestions on how to actually construct a diagram. In the four years that have passed since

Figure 5.7
DEFINITIONS OF TERMS USED IN NETWORKS

Definitions of Network Terms

Activity: An activity (task) is any portion of the project that requires time or resources; it has a measured beginning and ending. Activities can include paperwork, labor, negotiations, machinery operations, purchased-part lead times, and so on. When an activity represents purchased-part lead times or license wating periods, it is inserted into the schedule to reflect that subsequent work can only be done after that lead time has passed. Such lead times might be the acquisition of parts or materials, the curing of concrete, and so on. Using WBS terminology, an activity could be a *subtask,* a *work package,* or a *level-of-effort,* as was mentioned above. It all depends on the level of detail desired in scheduling.

Critical: An activity or event that must be achieved by a certain time, having no latitude (slack or float) whatsoever.

Critical Path: The *critical path* is the longest path through a network and determines the earliest completion of project work.

Dummy Activity: An arrow that denotes nothing but a dependency of one activity upon another is a dummy activity, and carries a zero duration. Dummies are usually represented by dashed-line arrows (although solid arrows are sometimes used).

Events: Beginning and ending points of activities are known as events. An event is a specific point in time. Events are commonly denoted graphically by a numbered circle.

Node: A point in a network diagram where arrows converge or exit.

Milestone: An event that represents a point in a project of special significance. Usually it is the completion of a major phase of the work and often a project review will be conducted at that time.

Network: Networks are called arrow diagrams. They provide a graphical representation of a project plan showing the relationships of the activities.

I wrote the first edition, I have found that constructing the diagram presents a major obstacle for many of my seminar participants, so I will try to offer some guidelines. If you already feel comfortable drawing diagrams, you can skip this section and go directly to the following section, entitled Common Pitfalls to Avoid.

In order to deal with something very simple to diagram, I have selected preparing a meal as an example. It is very hard to find activities than anyone can relate to, and this one is no exception. However, I believe that anyone can follow it, so it is about as good as any choice can be.

To begin with, I have constructed a WBS (Figure 5.8) to detail all of the things that might go into preparing a meal for your family and some guests. Note that in doing so, I am reflecting some conditions that will not exist everywhere. I assume that the ingredients for this meal will be purchased from a store. If you live on a farm, you might very well have grown them yourself. That being the case, certain tasks that I have listed would not be in your WBS for the same job.

This illustrates an important point. There is no single WBS that would represent a given job, nor is there a single schedule. Almost all real-world problems have many solutions. Yet one of the common experiences that I have with groups is that they get into *heavy* arguments about the *right way* to do a project. This is very counterproductive, and gets groups bogged down. My suggestion is to do a schedule that is at least *feasible,* and then refine it. There is only one way in which you can say that a diagram is

FIGURE 5.8
A WBS TO COOK AND SERVE A MEAL

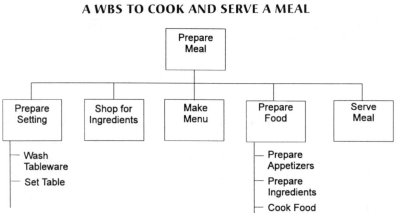

wrong, and that is if logic is absolutely violated. As an example, if you were diagramming the writing of this book and you showed proofreading the copy happening before the text is written, you have violated logic.

For simplicity, Figure 5.8 shows only the main tasks that would be involved in preparing a meal. Clearly, many subtasks would exist. To develop a CPM diagram for this project, I ask myself which task can be done first or, alternatively, which task *must* be done first. It seems clear that I must prepare a menu before I can do anything else. Then I can go to the grocery and purchase the ingredients. Once that is done, the raw ingredients can be prepared for cooking. The actual cooking comes next. Finally, the meal can be served. Note that I have ignored several tasks, because I recognize that they can be done in parallel with the tasks that I have just listed.

That is, they can be done in parallel if I have some help. If I do not, then parallel paths are not possible. In fact, on one-person projects, CPM scheduling is often not warranted simply because there are no parallel paths. (Naturally, a timetable is still useful, even for a one-person project.)

Figure 5.9 shows my approach to the job. I reason that while I am shopping, my teen-aged child can wash the good tableware, then set the table. Since both must be done before the meal is served, the arrow from *Set Table* terminates at the beginning of *Serve Meal*. I also assume that my spouse can prepare and serve appetizers while I am preparing the main meal, but I must have purchased the ingredients beforehand, so *Prepare & Serve Appetizers* follows shopping and precedes serving the main meal.

There is an important point here that sometimes causes a lot of problems for people trying to develop scheduling diagrams. If you absolutely know you will not have any help, then a single series of activities is all you can have. However, if it is possible to get help to do a job, then you

> **I**t is good practice to: *diagram what is logically possible to do, ignoring resource limitations.*

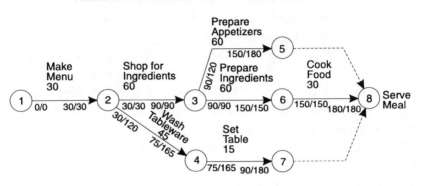

FIGURE 5.9

ARROW DIAGRAM FOR PREPARING A MEAL

should follow the practice that says to *diagram what is logically possible to do, ignoring resource limitations.* This will yield the best possible schedule. Then if you find you really can't get help, you can always revert to a single series of steps. This approach is referred to as scheduling according to *natural dependencies* (those that depend only on logic) rather than scheduling according to *resource dependencies.*

Note that I have not been concerned up to this point with activity durations. You should get the network drawn, then apply the time estimates worked out when you did your WBS. Once that is done, you can determine where the critical path is, by performing computations which will be explained in the next chapter.

At this point, you should try diagramming some small jobs that you know a lot about so that you can get comfortable with the process. Then you can move on to more complicated projects. One useful approach is to buy a model ship or airplane or a Lego™ set and develop an arrow diagram to show how it is assembled. All of these kits come with assembly instructions, but they assume a single individual will build the model. Since most contain numerous subassemblies, these can be diagrammed so that a group could assemble them in parallel. If you use a scheduling package like Microsoft Project or Superproject, which can schedule time in minutes, you can use the software to show the minimum assembly times for the model. The advantage of this approach is that it allows the scheduling of something tangible, which is easier for everyone to visualize than might be true for an abstract exercise.

COMMON PITFALLS TO AVOID

Now that you see the process, you can understand where certain pitfalls might occur. One of those was just discussed—to string a lot of tasks in series that could be done in parallel.

Another pitfall is to see an activity as totally discrete. Suppose activity D in Figure 5.10 depends on activities B and C being finished before it can be completed, but it depends on having only *half* of activity A completed. In this case, the network in the first figure gives a misleading result. The correct relationship is shown by Figure 5.11, which connects the midpoint of activity A with the input to D, using a dummy. If the critical path originally ran through activities A and D, then splitting activity A will shorten the critical path by *up to* one-half the duration of A. (We cannot tell precisely how much the path will be shortened, since B or C might become part of the critical path now.)

A problem also occurs when a *loop* is formed in the logic, as shown in Figure 5.12. These loops defy analysis and must be avoided. Most current microcomputer software performs a loop test before doing an analysis, and will exit if a loop is found. However, if the software does not tell where the loop exists, it can be very difficult to locate.

FIGURE 5.10
DIAGRAM WITH "A" PRECEDING "D"

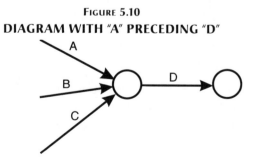

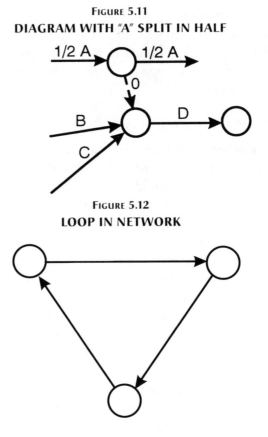

FIGURE 5.11

DIAGRAM WITH "A" SPLIT IN HALF

FIGURE 5.12

LOOP IN NETWORK

To avoid these pitfalls, it is recommended that networks be drawn on paper before entering data into the computer. In this way, you can work out all logic details and check off activities as you enter them, thus helping to ensure that nothing is omitted or connected incorrectly.

Fixed–Time Activities

Some activities require fixed time periods outside the control of management. Examples: legal minimums (30 to 90 days advance notice for public hearings), or technical minimums, such as curing time for concrete, etc.

When these become part of the critical path, it is useful to try to accomplish in parallel other activities that can be done. However, when possible, it is advisable to keep fixed-time activities off the critical path, since nothing can be done to shorten them in the event the end date must be advanced.

ACCOUNTING FOR THE WEATHER

When it is possible for weather to cause delays in completing project work, such delays must be factored into the schedule. One method is to estimate how long a project will take, then to add to that duration a fudge factor based on considering in what part of the year the project will be done.

A better method is to consider each activity individually and see what impact weather might have on that activity specifically, then add fudge factors to only those activities. By doing so, you avoid padding the entire project because of a small number of activities.

FACTOR
IN
WEATHER
DELAYS

It may also be possible to schedule activities that have large amounts of slack during those periods when weather is likely to cause delays.

OVERLAPPING WORK—LADDER NETWORKS

An earlier example showed that it may not be necessary to finish one task completely before beginning another. The technique is to overlap the work. Consider the following example. Suppose you want to dig a ditch in which some pipe will be laid. Once the pipe is laid, you will refill the trench with dirt.

Now you might be inclined to simply tie the pipe-laying task onto the end of digging, followed by filling with dirt, so you would have a sequential network.

This will clearly create the longest path to complete the project. The question is, do you need to dig the whole trench before you begin laying pipe? And do you need to lay all of the pipe before you begin covering?

The answer is no, but you must get a certain amount of trench dug before you can start laying pipe, and similarly, you must lay a certain amount of pipe before you start filling. The delay before the subsequent activity can start is called *lead* time. AOA or AON diagramming can be used to show these relationships, as shown in Figure 5.13.

The *SS or lead times* (Start-to-Start) are the times that must pass before the subsequent work can start, while the *FF or lag times* (Finish-to-Finish) are the times that it takes from the completion of a preceding task until the finish of the succeeding one.

Suppose, for example, that you want to get a one-day head start on digging the trench before you start laying pipe. Then the Start-to-Start time at that point is one day. Then suppose from the time you finish digging the trench it takes one-half day to finish laying the pipe. That means there is a lag of one-half day from the finish of digging to the finish of pipe laying. As this shows, a lead-lag network does not require that the lead and lag times be equal.

FIGURE 5.13
AOA AND AON DIAGRAMS FOR PIPELINE

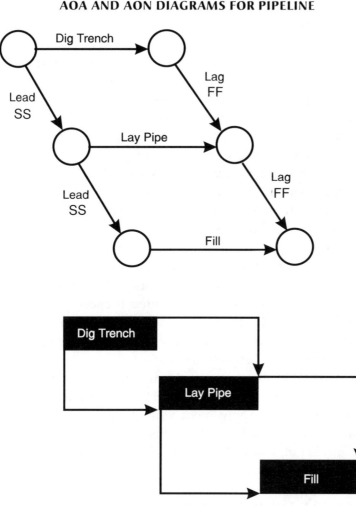

Using this approach naturally yields a path from beginning to end that is shorter than that obtained by simply connecting the three activities in series. This example illustrates one of the frequent methods used to shorten schedules when work does not have to be totally complete before a dependent task can begin. However, not all software will properly analyze ladder networks, which might be a factor to consider in deciding what software package to buy.

Another factor that may suggest the use of overlapping work in this manner is that, in many cases, both the start and finish dates for a project have been "given" before the project manager begins planning the work. The end date may be dictated by market or customer requirements, whereas the start date is constrained because one project is already in progress and must be completed before the new one can begin.

Given this fairly typical scenario, the network is developed, the critical path is computed, and the total project duration won't "fit" between the two given dates. The critical path is too long, and must be shortened.

It may be possible to shorten the critical path by putting more people on the task(s), although all work reaches a point at which adding resources does not shorten the job, and may, in fact, actually increase the time required because people get in each other's way. (Or the two may argue about how to do the job, thus wasting time.) In that case, using a ladder or lead-lag network may be the best solution.

One caution, however. It is tempting to get carried away and use ladders everywhere. I suggest that you draw a network without them, then apply them where it makes sense, but be careful to consider whether it is really *feasible* to overlap the work. If it is not, you will get a schedule that looks shorter than it can really be.

LEVEL OF DETAIL IN SCHEDULING

One question that must be considered in scheduling is just how much detail should be in the diagram. Even though a WBS may be developed down to level 6 *(level-of-effort)* for estimating purposes, you may want to develop a working schedule at level 5 *(work package level)*, rather than level 6.

There are two reasons for this. One is that most managers above you do not need or care about a lot of detail in tracking progress. They only want to know where you stand on significant portions of the work. Second, you will probably find that you cannot manage small tasks very tightly (nor do you need to). Therefore, it may be advisable to develop a schedule to level 6 only for one's personal use and to publish the working schedule at level 5.

In deciding how much detail to put into a schedule, the basic rule of thumb is that the network should be planned in no more detail than can be managed. However, there is a converse rule, which is that planning in too little detail leads to problems as well. For example, when a number of activities are lumped together and scheduled as one task, it is difficult to determine progress, and the final activity in the sequence is

> **D**on't plan in more detail than you can manage!

DON'T
PLAN
IN
MORE
DETAIL
THAN
YOU
CAN MANAGE

likely to be crunched because preceding activities were delayed until there was no time left to do the final one.

A related aspect of this has to do with activity duration. Tasks should be broken down into units of work that have relatively short durations. There is no hard-and-fast rule, but suggested durations should be in the range of four to six weeks maximum, just depending on the nature of the work. If this is not done, there is a real tendency to *back-end load* tasks by putting off work until it is too late to get it all done. Then a lot of effort is applied near the end of the task in a futile effort to finish on time. When a task has a duration longer than six weeks, it should be subdivided into "artificial" tasks, with deliverables if possible, so that progress can be reviewed and back-end loading can be kept to a minimum.

In short, there must be a balance or compromise between scheduling in too much or too little detail. As will be shown in later chapters, breaking large tasks down into manageable ones not only keeps them from being back-end loaded, but also helps with resource allocation. In addition, it is often possible to establish measurable milestones at which *tangible deliverables* will be produced, thus giving a good measure of progress on the project.

QUESTIONS FOR REVIEW

1. *What is the difference between an event and an activity?*

2. *What assumption in scheduling is the most likely to result in a schedule that cannot be achieved?*

KEY POINTS *from Chapter 5*

- Scheduling considers both the *durations* of tasks and the *sequence* in which the work must be done.

- The critical path is the longest path through a project and therefore determines the earliest end date.

- Activity-on-node notation uses the nodes to represent activities and the arrows to show the sequence in which they are performed.

- Activity-on-arrow notation uses the arrows to represent activities and the nodes to represent events.

References

1. For a detailed discussion of the history of scheduling methods, see Fleming, Bronn, and Humphries, in the reading list.
2. I am deviating here from conventional terminology. It has been common practice to call the node an event, but I find this leads to confusion, as each node really represents at least two events, the finish of one task and the beginning of following task(s). I believe the terminology that I am using will avoid that confusion.

Schedule Computations

Once a suitable network has been drawn, with durations assigned to all activities, it is necessary to perform computations to determine the longest path through the project. If start and finish dates have already been "dictated" for the project, these calculations will tell whether the required dates can be met. On the other hand, if a start date is given, the computations will tell the earliest completion date for the project.

> The *critical path* is the longest path through a project, and so determines the earliest completion for the work.

The simplest computation that can be made for a network will determine total working time on the longest path through the project and will reveal whether any latitude exists on paths parallel to the longest path. The longest path is called the critical path, since a slip on the longest path will cause a corresponding slip in the completion of the project. This computation would tell how many weeks (or days or hours, depending on time units being used) it will take to complete the project if no holidays or vacation periods exist.

Naturally, during certain parts of the year, holidays and/or vacations will intervene, so that the actual *calendar time* for the project is likely to exceed the *working time*.

It is also important to note that the conventional way to compute project working times is to ignore resources initially. In other words, activities are treated as though they have *fixed durations*, based on the assumption that certain levels of resources will be available when the work begins.

Further, these durations are estimated from historical data and are based on a person being available who has a certain skill level to do the work. As was pointed out in previous chapters, if these conditions are not met, then the actual working times will deviate from estimated times, sometimes considerably.

NETWORK RULES

In order to compute project working times, there are only two rules that are *universal* in defining how networks function. The software you use may impose additional rules, which will be presented in the user manual. The universal rules are:

> *Rule 1:*   Before a task can begin, all tasks preceding it must be completed.
>
> *Rule 2:*   Arrows denote logical precedence. Neither the length of the arrow nor its angular direction has any significance. (It is not a vector, but a scalar.)

BASIC SCHEDULING COMPUTATIONS

Although no one is likely to do network computations manually in this day of abundant scheduling software, it is important to understand how computations are made by the computer. Otherwise, it is easy to fall into the *garbage-in-garbage-out* problem.

Further, the computer output is not easily understandable unless the computation method is understood. What does "float" really mean, for example?

The following material will explain how the basic computations are performed with no concern for resource limitations. That is, these computations all are based on the assumption that the required resources will indeed be available when the time comes to do the work. This is equivalent to saying that the organization has an *unlimited* pool of people, which of course is never the case. For this reason, a schedule that assumes unlimited resources is considered to be the *ideal* or *best-case* situation, and provides a starting point for resource-constrained project scheduling. Chapter 7 deals with the allocation of resources to yield a realistic working schedule.

We will use the network developed in Chapter 5 to prepare a meal to illustrate scheduling computations. That network is repeated here in Figure 6.1, using AON notation. A solution will be presented later using AOA notation. The numbers in the duration (DU) cells are working durations in minutes. Each activity contains cells in which we can enter the *Earliest Start* and *Earliest Finish* as well as the *Latest Start* and *Latest Finish* for the activity. Other notation schemes are used in other books and with various software packages. This one just seems to me to be very simple to understand.

In order to locate the critical path and compute earliest and latest start and finish times for noncritical project activities, it is necessary to do two sets of computations. These are called *forward-pass* and *backward-pass* calculations.

Forward-Pass Computations

A forward pass is made through the network to calculate the earliest achievement times for each activity in the network. If we remember that each activity has a start and a finish, then we can talk about *Early Start* and *Early Finish* times, as mentioned above. This really amounts to having start and finish *events* for each activity, but they are not usually shown in activity-on-node

FIGURE 6.1
AON NETWORK FOR PREPARING A MEAL

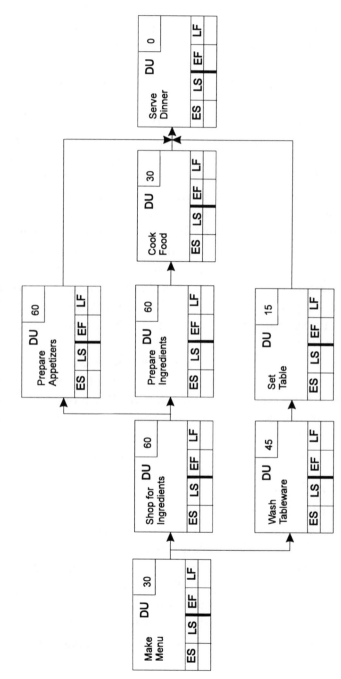

diagrams. As was stated above, the durations for the activities in Figure 6.1 are *working minutes*. The project is shown as starting at time T = 0. For schedules spanning several days or weeks, once activity start and finish times are determined, they can be converted to calendar dates, but that step will be omitted in this chapter. For our simple project, we will compute the total project time in minutes and then convert to hours.

Figure 6.2 shows the first steps in the forward-pass computation. *Make Menu* starts at time = zero. It takes 30 minutes. That means it has an *Early Finish* 30 minutes after it starts, or at T = 30. As soon as *Make Menu* is finished, two activities can start—*Shop* and *Wash Tableware*. This means that the *Early Finish* for *Make Menu* becomes the *Early Start* for these two succeeding tasks.

It takes 60 minutes to do the *Shopping*, so the *Early Finish* for that task is 90 minutes. You simply add its duration to its *Early Start* time to get its *Early Finish*. The same is done for *Wash Tableware*. Again, the *Early Finish* for each task becomes the *Early Start* for succeeding ones. We continue this process until we get to *Serve Dinner*.

At this point, *Prepare Appetizers* has an early finish of 150 minutes, *Cook Food* has an early finish of 180 minutes, and *Set Table* has 90 minutes for its early finish. Which one becomes the *Early Start* for *Serve Dinner?* Remember, Rule One presented above says that you can't start a task until all tasks preceding it have been completed. Since *Cook Food* ends the latest (has the largest early finish time), then its Early Finish becomes the Early Start for the Serving task.

Given the activity durations shown and the sequences detailed by the network, the project has a completion 180 minutes after it begins. Because we are usually trying to meet an imposed completion time for most projects, this working time can now be compared to the target to see if that target can be met, given an anticipated start date or time. If it cannot, then either the project must start earlier, the end date must slip out, or the network must be changed to compress (shorten) the critical path.

FIGURE 6.2
FORWARD PASS CALCULATIONS FOR MEAL PROJECT

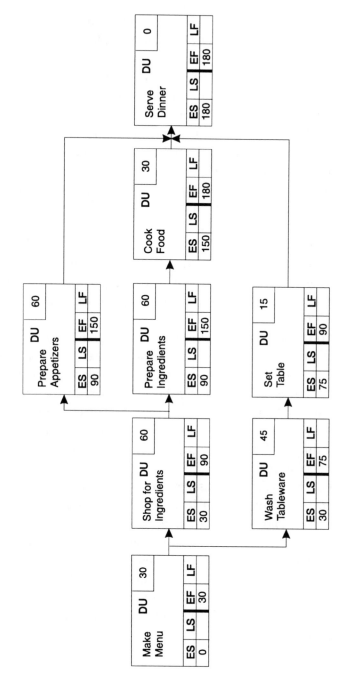

For our example, suppose we had planned to come home from work at 5:00 P.M. and have dinner prepared to serve at 7:00 P.M. Since we have found that it will take three hours to prepare the meal, this won't work. Either we will have to shorten the time of some tasks, start the process at 4:00 P.M., or revise the network in some way. Naturally, we could shave 30 minutes off the project by preparing the menu the day before. For many projects, such a solution would not be an option, so we will pretend for now that this option is not available and see what other approaches are available.

In that case, the question is, "How will the network have to change in order to finish in two hours?" The answer to this question is never obvious in a complicated network (although it is fairly obvious in this one). As a general rule, in order to see what else in the network might have to change, more information is needed. Specifically, we need to know the *latest* times by which each activity can be achieved and still meet the 180-minute completion.

You might ask, "Why not use the 120-minute completion, since that is what is required?" The answer is that a *best-case* computation is made first, so that we can see which paths have latitude and which one(s) is critical. The best case is considered to be that 180 minutes is acceptable. A shorter time is a worse case because you will have to squeeze time out of something. A longer time is also a worse case, as you are stretching the project out unnecessarily.

For that reason, we assign a 180-minute *Late Finish* to Serve Dinner, which means that it has the same early finish and late finish times, and zero duration, making it actually an *Event*. This is an example of the only kind of event actually shown in activity-on-node networks, and it is called a *Milestone*.

Now that the late finish time has been set for Serve Dinner, we do a *backward-pass computation* to determine the latest event times on all activities, which will permit achievement of the 180-minute completion.

Backward-Pass Computations

Beginning with *Serve Dinner*, and assigning a *Late Finish* time of 180 minutes to it, we subtract its duration of zero from that time to get its *Late Start* (see Figure 6.3). Naturally, that gives a *Late Start* of 180 minutes. This *Late Start* time must be the *Late Finish* for all predecessors to *Serve Dinner*, so that time is entered into the cells for each activity. Now in the case of *Prepare Appetizers*, we subtract its duration of 60 minutes from its *Late Finish* of 180 minutes, to get 120 minutes. This number becomes its *Late Start* time. For *Cook Food*, we do the same and get a *Late Start* of 150 minutes. In turn, we use 150 as the *Late Finish* for *Prepare Ingredients*, subtract its duration, and get 90 minutes for its *Late Start*.

Now notice the junction at the beginning of *Prepare Appetizers* and *Prepare Ingredients*. The *Late Start* for *Prepare Appetizers* is 120 minutes, and for *Prepare Ingredients* it is 90 minutes. Which one of these should we use for the *Late Finish* of the predecessor, *Shop*? If we allowed *Shop* to finish as late as 120 minutes, that would mean that *Prepare Ingredients* could not start until that time, and if you work forward from there to the end of the project, you will see that this will push the end time out to 210 minutes, instead of 180. We can now offer the following rules for assigning early and late times to activities that have multiple predecessors or successors.

> **Rule 1:** When two or more activities precede another, the earliest start for the successor will be the *Latest* of the late finish times for the predecessors.
>
> **Rule 2:** When two or more activities follow a predecessor, the *Latest Finish* for the predecessor will be the earliest *Late Start* for the successors.

Continuing in this way, you arrive at the late activity times shown in Figure 6.3.

Figure 6.3

BACKWARD PASS CALCULATIONS TO DETERMINE LATE TIMES

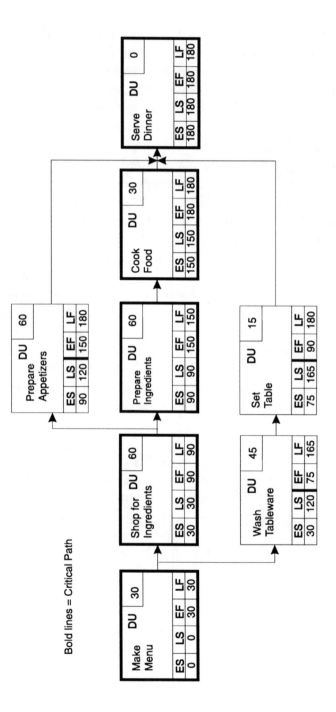

Bold lines = Critical Path

Activity Maximum Float

Now examine *Prepare Appetizers*. Note that its *Early Start* is 90 and its *Late Start* is 120. The difference of 30 minutes is called the *Activity Float*. This float represents latitude for the activity. So long as it starts no later than 120 minutes and takes no longer than its duration of 60 minutes, the project can be finished by 180 minutes.

Note the activities that run through the center of the diagram. They all have the same *Early* and *Late Start* and the same *Early* and *Late Finish* times. These activities have no float, and are called *critical*. The path

> **A**n activity is a critical activity any time it has no float.

containing those activities is, in turn, called the *critical path*. What we have done is apply *Critical Path Method* to locate that path. By making the final activity *Late Finish* the same as its *Early Finish*, we have forced one path to have no float. As you can see, it is the longest path.

The term *float* comes from the fact that *Prepare Appetizers* can start as early as 90 minutes and as late as 120 minutes, or we say it can float around for the difference of 30 minutes. Note that float is always calculated by taking the *Latest Start* minus the *Earliest Start*, or the *Latest Finish* minus the *Earliest Finish*. In equation form, you have:

$$MaxFloat = LF - EF$$

or

$$MaxFloat = LS - ES$$

where LS means *Late Start*, LF means *Late Finish*, ES means *Early Start*, and EF means *Early Finish*.

THE VALUE OF FLOAT

It is tempting to think that float is undesirable. The first suggestion people sometimes make is to finish a task that has float as early as possible and move resources onto the critical path to shorten it, so that you wind up with no float anywhere. To see why this is not a good idea, we must remember that the durations for all tasks are *estimates*, that they have 50-50 likelihoods if averages have been used, and that we often have made those estimates using poor history, so they are suspect to begin with. Given those facts, it is highly advisable to have float on all but the critical path, to compensate for unforeseen problems, estimating errors, and so on.

What about the critical path itself? That series of activities must be managed in such a way that all tasks are completed on time or the project will be delayed (unless lost time on one activity can be recovered on a later one). It is very risky to

> The best practice in managing projects is to do whatever is necessary to stay on schedule.

Do whatever **IS NECESSARY** to stay on schedule

allow a critical path task to slip, under the assumption that you will recover the time later. Murphy's Law invariably prevails when you do this. In fact, the best working rule I know is to *do whatever is necessary to stay on schedule.*

CALCULATIONS FOR AN AOA NETWORK

The calculations for AOA networks are done exactly the same as for AON networks. The only real problem is with notation. In Figure 6.4 is the same diagram for preparing a meal in AOA format. In the first edition of this book, I learned that people were confused by the notation, as I had split each node in half and placed an early time on the left side and a late time on the right. However, as was pointed out earlier, each node contains at least two events, and if several activities enter or leave, there will be several events contained. I have looked at a number of systems of notation, and no single one is unambiguous. For that reason, I have placed the early and late times on each end of all arrows. On the left end will always be the *Early Start* and *Late Start*, and on the right end will be the *Early Finish* and *Late Finish.* Each node is simply numbered for easy reference. See Figure 6.4 for this example.

FIGURE 6.4
AOA DIAGRAM FOR PREPARING A MEAL

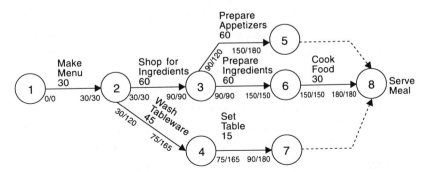

Constrained End Date Scheduling

As was mentioned above, the usual situation for most projects is that an end time (or date) has been imposed, either by contract with the customer or by management, based on business considerations. This end date may be earlier than the earliest completion date determined by the forward-pass computation, in which case the project must be started earlier or the schedule must be shortened somehow.

In many cases, as was mentioned previously, the start date for a project is also dictated by availability of resources or some other factor, so that the start date cannot be moved up. When this is true, then the critical path must be shortened. When this is done, other paths may become problems as well.

For the network just analyzed, suppose the end time were established as 120 minutes. (Or, as was mentioned previously, you want to serve dinner at 7:00 P.M., and start the project at 5:00 P.M.) What would be the overall impact on the project? To answer that question, we will impose a *Late Finish* of 120 minutes on the project and do a new backward-pass calculation. Note that there is no need to do a new forward-pass computation yet, since the forward pass only determines early times, and these will not change until an activity duration is changed or else the network is redrawn.

Figure 6.5 shows the network with the latest project completion constrained to 120 minutes. When the backward-pass computations have been completed, we find a strange thing. The float on the former critical path is now *negative!* When the float is negative, the activity or path is called *supercritical*. Note also that *Prepare Appetizers* now has negative 30 minutes of float, whereas before it had positive 30 minutes. Thus we have two supercritical paths. (*Wash Tableware* and *Set Table* still have 30 minutes of float, because originally this path had 90 minutes of float.)

It is also interesting to examine the Late times on *Make Menu* and *Shop*. These times are now negative. In the case of *Make Menu*, this is telling us that the activity needs to start 60 minutes before it is planned to start, which we already knew.

FIGURE 6.5

BACKWARD PASS WITH END TIME CONSTRAINED

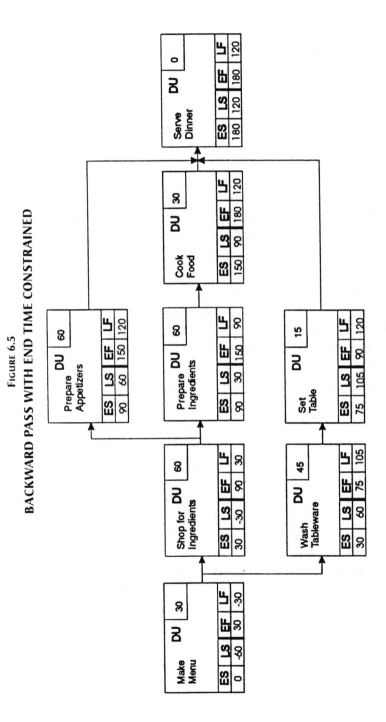

If we cannot start the project early, we will have to shorten the critical path by at least 60 minutes to meet our deadline. Let's suppose we can do this by taking 30 minutes off the time to prepare ingredients and another 15 minutes out of *Make Menu* and *Shop*. We might get time out of *Prepare Ingredients* by buying frozen vegetables rather than fresh, so they don't have to be cut up. If these adjustments are made, we now have the result shown in Figure 6.6.

We now have a situation that is not desirable as a general rule. We have two critical paths. *Prepare Appetizers* is critical, as are *Prepare Ingredients* and *Cook Food*. For this particular project, we might not be concerned about having two critical paths, but most of the time this would be very undesirable. The reason is that when you have no float, you know that if anything goes wrong with the task, so that its duration increases, then you will slip your overall project finish time by the amount of the increased duration (unless you can reduce the times taken by subsequent tasks). Having two critical paths increases risk.

For this reason, you should try to get rid of all but *one* critical path. This can only be done by changing the duration of one or more activities, by allowing the end date to be extended, or by redrawing the network to have a new configuration. Assuming that a choice must be made of which critical path to eliminate, the issue is how to decide which path would be best to get off the critical path.

There is no single answer to this problem. Float is only one kind of risk involved in a project. There are also risks from technical problems, poor estimates, weather and other uncontrollable factors, and so on. Table 6.1 is a list of some of the factors that should be considered in making a decision. The comments that follow each factor explain the rationale for deciding what to do.

FIGURE 6.6

MEAL PROJECT WITH ACTIVITY DURATIONS REDUCED

Bold lines = Critical Path

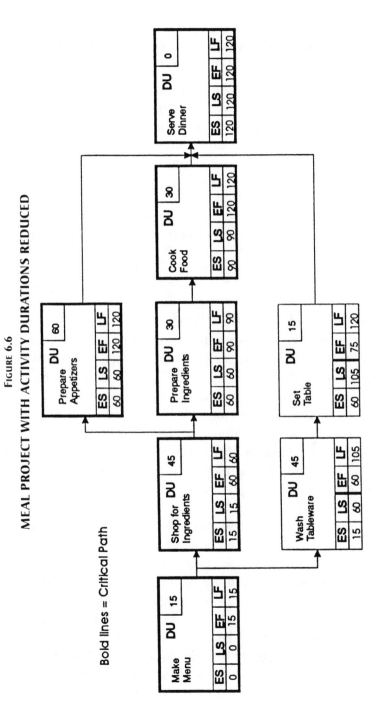

TABLE 6.1

**FACTORS TO CONSIDER IN ELIMINATING A DUAL
CRITICAL PATH**

Number of activities	Path with most activities might be most risky
Skill level of people	Path with least-skilled people could be most risky
Technical risk	Path with greatest technical risk should have float
Weather/uncontrollable	Give float to activities with uncontrollable factors
Cost	Give float to activities that cost most to do
Historical data	Least historical data—give float; historically a problem—ditto
Avail. backup plan	Give float to activities with no obvious backup
Business cycle	If business tends to get hectic at certain times, give float to activities affected
Difficulty	Float given to activities that are most difficult

REDUCING ACTIVITY DURATIONS

When it is necessary to reduce the duration of a critical path, we usually try to reduce activity durations, rather than redrawing the network. That is because we usually feel the logic is more or less sound, so changing sequences might not be an option.

Whether activity durations can be reduced depends on four factors. Can the work be done faster by increasing *efficiency* (perhaps by using a more productive person)? Can the *scope* of the work be reduced? Can extra *effort* be applied to the job to get it done faster (by increasing resources)? It is not always possible to reduce activity time by adding more resources, since a point of *diminishing returns* is reached, often because people simply get in each other's way. Can the *process* be changed?

There are, of course, two ways to increase human resources applied to a project. One is by adding bodies. The other is by working the same number of people more hours per day, which we call working *overtime*. In both cases you tend to get diminishing returns very quickly. I know of one company that measured the impact on productivity of working overtime. They measured productivity for a normal 40-hour week, then again at the end of three weeks in which people worked 50 hours per week.

EXCESSIVE
OVERTIME

DIMINISHES
PRODUCTIVITY

Productivity after working overtime was back down to the normal 40-hour-per-week level, and errors had increased.

When productivity declines without errors increasing, it is often because people are *pacing* themselves. They think like a marathon runner who knows that if she runs too fast at the beginning and uses up her energy, she will be unable to finish the race. On the other hand, when error rates increase, it is usually because people are truly fatigued.

We also find that people doing *knowledge work* suffer the same kind of problems. One study found that when people put in 12 hours of overtime on knowledge work, you probably get an increase in output from them equivalent to what you would expect in two normal working hours!

CONVERTING ARROW DIAGRAMS TO BAR CHARTS

While an arrow diagram is essential to do a proper analysis of the relationships between the activities in a project, determine activity float, and to identify the critical path, the best tool for the people actually doing the project work is the bar chart. People find it much easier to see when they are supposed to start and finish their jobs if you give them a bar chart. The schedule shown as an arrow diagram in Figure 6.4 has been portrayed as a bar chart in Figure 6.7, making use of what was learned about the schedule from the network analysis.

In this figure, the critical path activities are shown as solid bars, while those that have float are shown as hollow bars with lines trailing to indicate the amount of float that the activity has. Note that each activity is shown starting at its earliest possible time, so that float is reserved to be used only if absolutely necessary. This is the conventional method of displaying bar charts.

Note that *Wash Tableware* has 90 minutes of float and so does *Set Table*. Naturally, it is the *same float*, and initially, before the project begins, there are 90 minutes of float *available* for each activity. However, if all of the float is used up on *Wash Tableware*, there will be none left for *Set Table*, and it would therefore be critical.

This illustrates a real pitfall of bar charts. Assume that different individuals are doing two sequential activities that share a common amount of float. Since the chart does not show interrelationships of activities, it is hard for the people performing the work to tell that the float is shared. They look at the chart and think that they each have the designated float. Then, if each tries to make use of the float, the project is in trouble.

In fact, Parkinson's Law can be applied to project float. Parkinson's Law says that work always expands to fit the time allowed. When applied to float,

Parkinson's Law:
Work always expands to take the time allowed.

Lewis' Law for Float:
If you give it to them, they'll take it!

FIGURE 6.7

BAR CHART FOR PROJECT TO PREPARE A MEAL

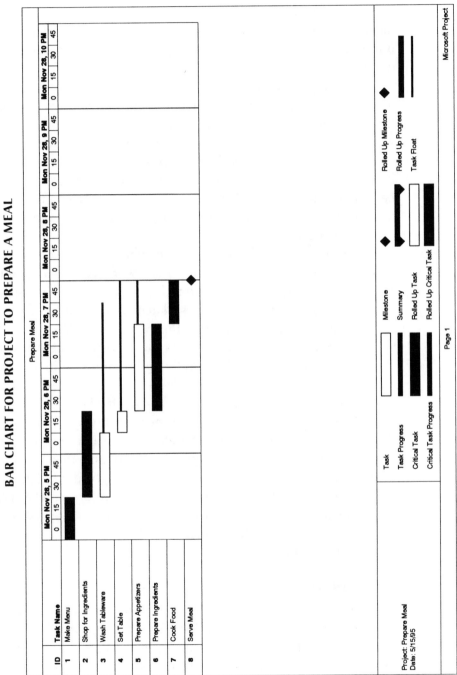

it means that *when you give them float, they take it!* For this reason, most software can be set up so that float is not printed. The implication of such a schedule is simply that the work should be done as shown.

I personally do not like that approach. I prefer to explain to team members that float is shared, and encourage them to keep float in reserve to be used only if necessary. Indeed, it is always a good idea to keep float in reserve to be used if an estimate turns out to be wrong or if an unforeseen problem causes the work to be delayed. As someone told me recently, every project should be planned as if there will be at least some percentage of the total time when the entire city will have a power blackout and nothing will get done.

McGregor formulated a management model some years ago that stated that some managers see workers as undependable, wanting only a paycheck from the job, and so on. He called this a *Theory-X* outlook, and postulated that a manager with such an outlook would tend to get the expected result.

The opposite outlook, which is more positive, he called a *Theory-Y* view. This would naturally be the more desired view, as a manager would tend to get the more positive result. It is easy to see Parkinson's Law and Lewis' Law for Float as *Theory - X* outlooks. However, I don't see them that way. In today's down-sized, right-sized, understaffed organization, people simply have to do their work in priority order and this leads to putting off things until they absolutely have to be done. Thus, if they have float, they tend to take it, but they unfortunately may take it at the beginning of an assignment, then if they have a problem with the work, there is no float left to use in getting the work done on time.

LIMITATIONS OF CRITICAL PATH METHOD

It is important to remember what was pointed out earlier—namely that the conventional critical path analysis that has been illustrated for this network assumes that unlimited resources exist in the organization, so that all activities can be done as planned. As the bar chart shows, however, a number of points exist at which activities are running in parallel. If those activities require the same resources, then there may not be enough to get the job done as shown, so that the schedule cannot be met. This subject is addressed in Chapter 7.

MULTIPLE CALENDARS

One final subject must be considered in doing basic network computations. Not all project activities can follow the same working schedule. Does everyone work Monday through Friday? Do some people only work weekends?

In some projects there may be activities that require actual working days to complete; others do not. Pouring of concrete must be done during the work week. However, that concrete may cure over a weekend. For this reason, it is important that multiple calendars be considered in scheduling.

Consider, for example, the situation in which one group works a conventional Monday-to-Friday schedule. Another group, however, works only weekends—Saturday and Sunday. This is shown in Figure 6.8.

FIGURE 6.8
MULTIPLE CALENDAR NETWORK

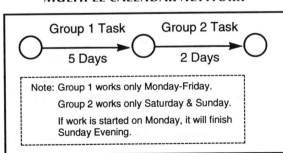

141

Now suppose the two groups are scheduled to do two sequential tasks, with group 1 working exactly one week (M-F), followed by the people in group 2, who are supposed to finish their work over the weekend. However, group 1 gets behind on their work by one day. How much is the schedule impacted? As Figure 6.9 shows, the work will slip an entire week because group 1 gets behind only one day!

This kind of problem highlights the occasional need for multiple calendars in scheduling. They are called *calendars*, since holiday and overtime dates are different for the two groups. If the software being used does not permit the use of multiple calendars, it may still be possible to "fake it" and force the schedule to reflect correct working dates, but it may be difficult to do. For this reason, selection of software should be made with this potential requirement in mind.

THE BALI BOOK SCHEDULE

In Chapter 4 we developed a WBS for the Bali book project. In Figure 6.10 is a schedule for that project in AOA format, and in Figure 6.11 is one in AON notation. This illustrates a much more complex schedule than those presented up to now. Note, however, that times are shown ignoring resource limitations that might exist.

FIGURE 6.9

WORK SLIPS ONE WEEK BECAUSE OF A ONE-DAY SLIP BY GROUP 1

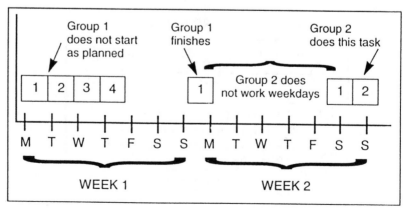

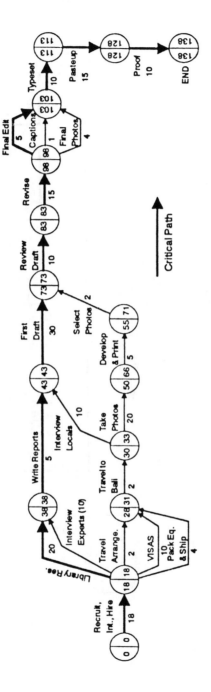

FIGURE 6.10
AOA DIAGRAM FOR BALI BOOK PROJECT

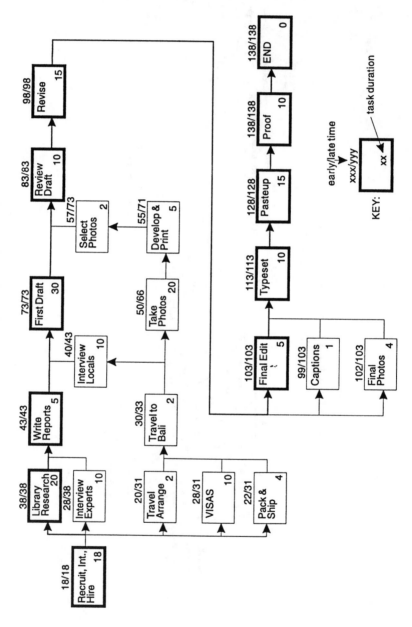

FIGURE 6.11

AON NETWORK FOR BALI BOOK PROJECT

144

QUESTIONS FOR REVIEW

1. What is the difference between a forward-pass computation and a backward-pass computation in a network?

2. To find the critical path in a network, what date is used for the final event late time?

3. Of all the ways by which an activity duration can be shortened, what two are undesirable?

4. If an activity duration is to be changed by reducing its scope, what actions should a project manager take before proceeding?

5. In a network, each activity has early finish and late finish times specified. For practical purposes, what should be the target time by which an activity should be finished?

6. In the network shown in Figure 6.12, calculate all activity early and late times and show where the critical path is.

A. Which activities are on the critical path?

B. What is the maximum float (in days) for Activity D?

C. What is the minimum float for Activity D?

FIGURE 6.12
NETWORK FOR SCHEDULING EXERCISE

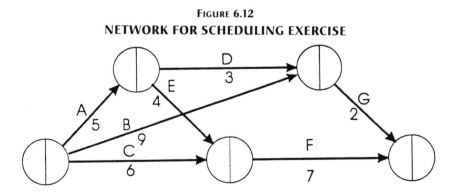

KEY POINTS *from Chapter 6*

- Scheduling is done to determine sequencing of work and to show earliest completion for a project, as well as points at which latitude exists in the work.

- The *forward-pass* computation determines earliest finish times for activities. The *backward-pass* calculation determines latest finish times.

- Basic critical path computations assume unlimited resources, and thus yield dates that may not be achievable.

- Try to get rid of all but one critical path in a network, since critical activities increase risk.

Chapter 7

SCHEDULING WITH RESOURCE CONSTRAINTS

Chapter 1 emphasized that the key to project scheduling is to solve the resource allocation problem. Every organization has a fixed number of resources. Yet project managers invariably plan projects as if their own project were the only one being done! Then when they get ready to do a particular task, they find that "Charlie" is already tied up on another job. Then the screaming starts.

"I can't get my job done on time if you don't break Charlie loose from the job he's working on," the frustrated manager bellows.

"We need Charlie on this job. The product is being shipped to upper Mongolia next Friday, and this is our big chance to penetrate that market. This job has priority over yours."

"Well give me someone else."

"Sorry. There is no one else available. You'll just have to do the best you can until we get through with the Mongolian project."

If that weren't bad enough, when Charlie is finally free to work on the lower priority project (which by now has become the top-priority job because it is running late), the manager discovers that he has Charlie scheduled to work on two activities (within the same project) at the same time, and they are both full-time jobs! He hadn't noticed that the two activities were running in parallel. Now what does he do? Have Charlie work 80-hour weeks until the jobs are complete?

This illustrates the problem with the basic PERT/ CPM procedures used to produce project schedules. They are limited because resource availabilities and requirements are not included in the scheduling process. The computation procedure assumes that resource availability is unlimited and that, given the durations assigned to activities, only precedence requirements affect start/completion times. For this reason, PERT and CPM have been criticized as a *feasible way to produce a nonfeasible result!*

Resource constrained scheduling: Why so few do it

The purpose of resource constrained scheduling is to produce a more accurate schedule by including more realism.

Capable software tools include features to add realism to the scheduling process. You can specify availability, costs, and various loadings. The software will then do the tedious arithmetic for you.

Over the last 10 years I've asked hundreds of project management software users about their use of resource-constrained scheduling, especially once they've started tracking progress. About 80% are aware it exists. About 50% have tried it. But only about 3% use these capabilities routinely—and most of these have taken vendor training. If it's so great, why do so few use it?

- It's tedious to specify, so your "model" is now more complex.
- You need small tasks and dependencies to make it work.
- It requires a high level of mastery of the tool. If you're not proficient you won't spend the time.
- It's costly (tedious) to maintain.
- It tends to give overly optimistic results!

In a word, the benefit may or may not outweigh the price.

Tom Conlon

The problem is so bad that two years ago, when I was talking with a client about doing some training for them, he said, "Don't spend too much time on scheduling."

I asked why.

"Because it doesn't work," he replied.

"I would guess that the last time you did any computerized scheduling was before 1980, using mainframe software," I said.

He agreed, and wanted to know how I knew.

I explained that the current microcomputer software is far superior to what was available on mainframes prior to 1980. I also asked him to let me go through my normal material on scheduling, as it is very important. He agreed. At the end of the class he was satisfied.

This chapter will illustrate the use of one such program, Project Workbench™, produced by Applied Business Technologies. The program was used because it represents a good trade-off among all of the characteristics that a scheduling program should have. It is doubtful that any package will have all of the characteristics that you may want, so ultimately you have to pick the one with the best overall features and use it.

The Effect of Limited Resources on Schedule Float

When network computations are made, float is calculated based on activity interrelationships and durations. When resource limitations exist, the float that appeared to be available under straightforward critical-path analysis may not exist. Float can be affected as follows when resources are limited:

- Resource constraints reduce the total amount of schedule float.

- Scheduling times are not unique; float values are not unique. When a resource is overloaded, such conflicts are solved by applying certain scheduling rules, which are called *heuristics*. The term means *rule-of-thumb*, and will be discussed later in this chapter.

- The critical path in a resource constrained schedule may not be the identical continuous series of activities that is obtained in the unlimited resources schedule. A continuous chain of zero float tasks may exist, but since task start times are constrained by resource availability and precedence relations, this chain may include different activities.

AN EXAMPLE OF RESOURCE ALLOCATION

To illustrate the resource allocation problem, a new network will be used, since the one developed in Chapter 6 is too simple. Resources will be assigned to each activity. How resources are assigned to activities depends on the nature of the work involved and the people available to do the work.

In some cases, work can be done by anyone available. Many kinds of manual labor fit into this category. For example, sweeping floors, mowing grass, and other forms of housework might be done by any available person at least 10 years of age or older. When this is true, those individuals are treated as a resource *pool*.

As another example, if a group of skilled carpenters were available, it might be possible for any of them to install a new door in a room. However, all carpenters are not necessarily equal. Some may not be able to do certain jobs, so treating them as a *pool* of resources would not work.

When workers can all do a given job, it is useful to consider how task duration varies with resource level. In Figure 7.1 is an illustration of the relationship. If 5 workers can do a task in 20 days, we say that 100 person-days of labor will be expended. This combination of labor and task duration can be portrayed as a rectangle, and the area of the rectangle represents the units *person-days*.

If it is assumed that equal-area rectangles will yield the same result so far as work is concerned, then adding labor to the task will shorten the task duration. For the example given, adding 5 workers would allow completion of the work in 10

FIGURE 7.1
EQUAL-AREA LABOR RECTANGLES

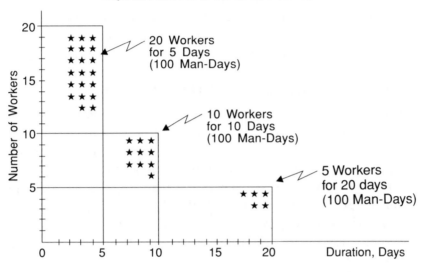

days. Putting 10 workers on the job would allow it to be completed in 5 days, or one fourth the original time.

Naturally, this can only be extended so far. For all work there must be a point at which adding workers does not shorten the job. Instead, the people will begin to get in each other's way, and the time taken to do the job will begin to increase, rather than decrease. For this reason, a project manager might choose to treat an activity duration as *fixed*, and assign only so many workers to it.

On the other hand, if the activity is such that duration can be changed by applying variable levels of resources, then there would be no exact duration for the task that would be assigned to the project. Rather, the project manager might treat the initial duration and resource level as only a starting point, and allow the actual task duration to vary in order to achieve a certain desired schedule. It might be that a prescribed end date must be met, and it is feasible to add as many resources as required to meet that deadline. Or it might be that what is desired is to finish the project in the shortest time, given a certain number of people available to do the work.

The most common scheduling method is to assume fixed-duration tasks, so that system will be illustrated first, followed by scheduling the same project using variable-duration tasks.

SCHEDULING WITH FIXED-DURATION ACTIVITIES

In most projects, the starting point would be to assume that a certain number of people will be assigned to an activity, and that it will then require so many days (or whatever time units are appropriate) to complete. In Figure 7.2 is a schedule with task durations shown. We will begin by analyzing the situation in which a pool of workers is available, all of whom can do any of the activities in the project. As was stated previously, the analysis that follows was done using Project Workbench for Windows, Release 2.0.

FIGURE 7.2
NETWORK TO ILLUSTRATE RESOURCE ALLOCATION

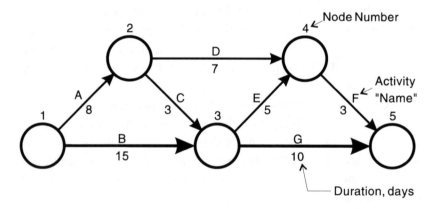

Before the computer can do a resource allocation, the number of workers available must be specified. For the project analyzed here, two categories of workers were specified, in the levels shown.

Description	Number Available	Person-Hours/Week
Senior Worker	2	80
Helper	1	40

It is helpful to understand the source of this data, as well as what the software must do to deal with it. First, consider how you decide on the resource levels needed for a project. Naturally, a number of scenarios are possible, but in many cases, you begin by considering a similar project as your starting point. You used two senior workers and a helper to do that job, so you begin with that number for the present job. Or, you go to the managers of the groups who will provide resources for your project and mutually decide about what the level should be.

That is your starting point. Once you enter this data into the computer, you will be able to tell if the level is sufficient. After all, you usually have an end date imposed, and a start date constrained by something, so, as has been mentioned in a previous chapter, you must try to fit the work between those two dates. By using scheduling software that can level resources, you can determine if the proposed schedule will work, and if it won't, you can perform some what-if analyses until you find a solution that will work. After that, you negotiate for the resources you need.

We will begin by making two Senior Workers and a Helper available. If a normal five-day work week is assumed, then there are 80 person-hours of labor available to apply to the project each week. Since one Helper is available, we have 40 person-hours of labor available each week. For simplicity, we will assume that the people are available 100% of the time. In practice, this is never true. At most, no one is available more than

80% of the time, and in most cases the figure is lower. This will be discussed in more detail later in this chapter.

Note that holidays and vacations also serve to reduce the amount of labor available during the period in which they occur, so that the schedule will reflect a total elapsed time greater than would be obtained if a constant level of labor were available. Project Workbench allows the levels of available resources to be varied upward and downward from the average level to compensate for availability of overtime or holidays. This means that vacation days can be entered for individuals when resources are tracked on an individual basis, and the schedule will be adjusted to compensate for those days.

For the analysis that follows, no vacations have been entered, but standard legal holidays are inserted into the program calendar to show the effect of having days on which no one works.

As each activity is entered into the computer, a level of resources is assigned to each task. The levels assigned are as shown in Table 7.1.

TABLE 7.1

Task	Duration	Sr. Wkr.	Helper
A	8	8	0
B	15	15	3
C	3	0	3
D	7	7	2
E	5	5	0
F	3	3	1
G	10	20	10

Notes: Durations in days; Allocations in person-days total.

Before we continue, it is instructive to see how Table 7.1 is created. As a general rule, you look at the tasks to be done and decide on a level of resources to apply. Then you ask the people who must do the work how long it will take them. So for Task A, we are going to assign a single senior worker. She says it will take her eight days to do the task by herself. She needs no help.

Task B is to be done by a senior worker. You ask him how long it will take, and he says 15 days, and he also says he needs a helper for three days during that time. Now a crucial question arises, which determines what kind of software you need. How does the senior worker plan to use the helper for 3 days on a 15-day task?

Clearly, an almost unlimited number of combinations can be used, but some of the more common ones include:

- Three days at the beginning or end of the task;

- One day each week, either at the beginning or the end of the week; and

- 20% of each day, spread linearly along the 15-day total duration. This would be equivalent to about 1.6 hours each day, and is common in laboratory settings for technicians.

The reason this question is so important is that not all software programs will handle all of the combinations. For this example, I assigned the Helper to the task for three days at the very beginning. If you use a linear spread of 20% per day, you get a very different schedule solution when the software levels resources.

Once the data has been input to the computer, a critical-path analysis can be done. The first analysis is made as described in Chapter 6, assuming that unlimited resources are available. This schedule is shown in Figure 7.3. Using January 23, 1995, as a starting date, the project will end on February 27. This corresponds to 25 working days, as was calculated for the arrow diagram previously. However, because February 20 is a holiday, it is dropped from working time, so that the actual end date is 26 days from project start (ignoring weekends).

Also note that a milestone called *Finish* has been entered into the project. This is done to force Project Workbench to show exactly when the project ends.

Figure 7.3

SCHEDULE SHOWING EARLIEST POSSIBLE FINISH

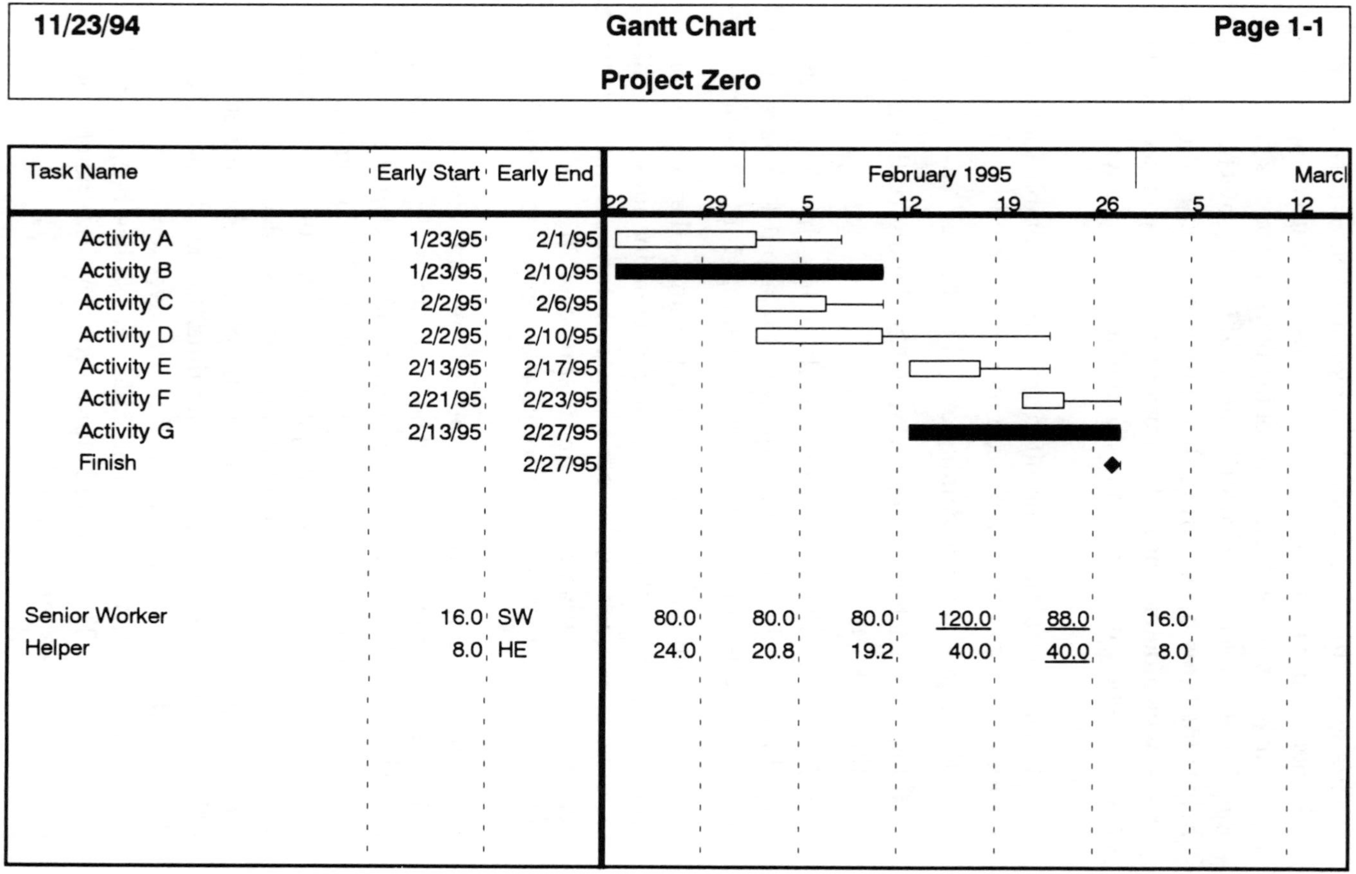
11/23/94
Gantt Chart
Page 1-1
Project Zero
Task Name
Early Start
Early End
February 1995
March
22
29
5
12
19
26
5
12
Activity A 1/23/95 2/1/95
Activity B 1/23/95 2/10/95
Activity C 2/2/95 2/6/95
Activity D 2/2/95 2/10/95
Activity E 2/13/95 2/17/95
Activity F 2/21/95 2/23/95
Activity G 2/13/95 2/27/95
Finish 2/27/95
Senior Worker 16.0 SW 80.0 80.0 80.0 120.0 88.0 16.0
Helper 8.0 HE 24.0 20.8 19.2 40.0 40.0 8.0

Note that at the bottom of the schedule the computer shows the level of each resource that will be required to do the work as scheduled. These levels are shown in person-hours required each week. Since the February 20 week is a four-day week, the levels drop that week.

On the left of the resource listing is the level of resources available in person-hours per day. When that number is multiplied by the number of working days in a week, the level of person-hours per week is obtained. For most weeks, the Senior Worker availability is 80 person-hours per week, and for the Helper it is 40. During the February 20 week, which is a four-day week, the Senior Worker level would be 64 and the helper level would be 32. So long as the level required is less than the level available, the schedule can be met as shown under ideal conditions. This is not the case, however. There are two weeks during which the required level of Senior Workers is greater than 80, meaning that they are overloaded, and in one week the Helper is overloaded.

Now we could meet the best-case schedule by increasing resource availability to meet the requirement. However, suppose we are told that this cannot be done. There is a freeze on overtime, or no additional personnel are available. What will that do to the schedule? Clearly, it will stretch out. To see the impact of this resource shortage on the schedule, a new analysis is done.

For Project Workbench, this analysis is called *Autoschedule*, with resources being considered. Figure 7.4 shows the result. The completion of the project slips to March 13. Note that the software schedules activity G to be done before it does activities D, E, and F. It gives priority to critical-path activities, delaying non-critical-path work until more resources become available. In this case, sufficient resources did not become available until activity G was completed, so the computer scheduled D, E, and F to be done then.

At first glance, the resource-leveled schedule seems strange. Why is activity D being delayed? That task is scheduled to run between February 2 and February 10. During that period,

FIGURE 7.4
SCHEDULE WITH RESOURCES LEVELED

Gantt Chart

Project Zero

11/23/94

Task Name	Early Start	Early End
Activity A	2/6/95	2/15/95
Activity B	2/6/95	2/27/95
Activity C	2/16/95	2/21/95
Activity D	2/16/95	2/27/95
Activity E	2/28/95	3/6/95
Activity F	3/7/95	3/9/95
Activity G	2/28/95	3/13/95
Finish		3/13/95
Senior Worker	16.0 SW	
Helper	8.0 HE	

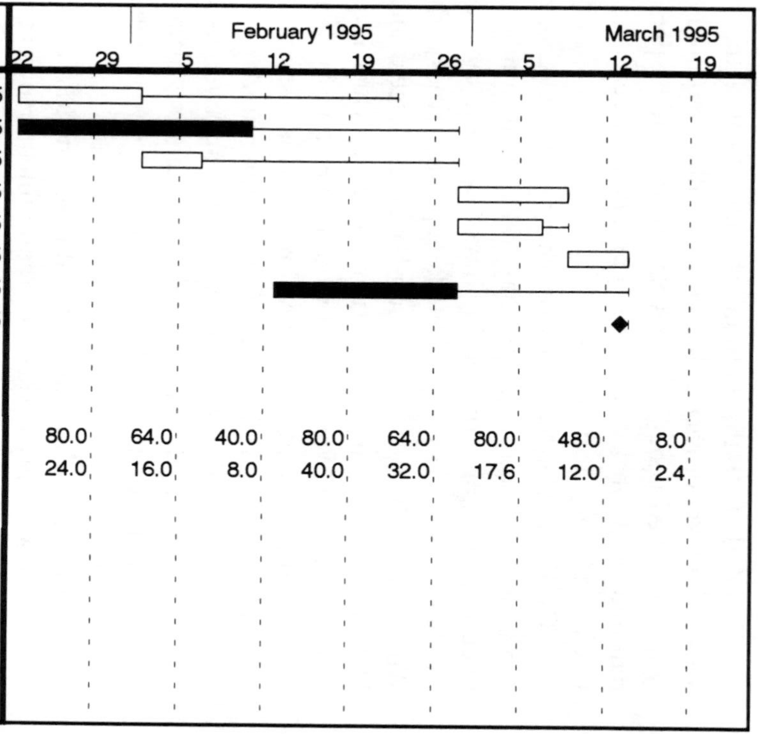

158

neither the Senior Workers nor the Helper are shown as over-loaded.

The problem is, the figures under the schedule are weekly utilization figures. If the levels are examined on a *daily* basis, which can be done in Project Workbench using a view called *QuickPlan*, then it turns out that Task D is being delayed because of the Helper. I assigned all resources to their tasks with uniform loading, and the Helper is assigned to D for two days on a seven-day task. The result is that, on February 26, the helper is needed for 10.4 hours per day (see Figure 7.5). Because only eight hours per day of availability have been specified to the software, Task D is delayed until the helper again becomes available, and this does not occur until after Task G is completed.

The delays for E and F are because we are trying to use too many Senior Workers at once. When Project Workbench looks at the tasks, it is programmed to allocate resources to the critical-path activities first and to wait until those tasks are complete before allowing resources to be assigned to other tasks. Naturally, since D, E, and F have slipped past the completion of G, we know that they are critical, even though the printout does not indicate such. In fact, Task G is shown having float, but this is timescale float only, and should not be interpreted to mean that any latitude is available for that task. The software is telling us that all tasks should be performed as shown to prevent over-loading of resources.

This illustrates what happens to many projects when sufficient resources are not available to do the work as planned. Without a good scheduling tool, the project manager often is not aware that the project is resource-limited until the work begins. Then it is too late.

To compensate, overtime may be applied to the project—in essence increasing resource availability, but this may not solve the problem, since more labor may be needed than can be gained with overtime. In the case of this network, the Senior Workers were scheduled to work 120 person-hours the week of February 12, which would be equivalent to needing another person full-

Figure 7.5

QUICKPLAN VIEW SHOWING HELPER DAILY USAGE

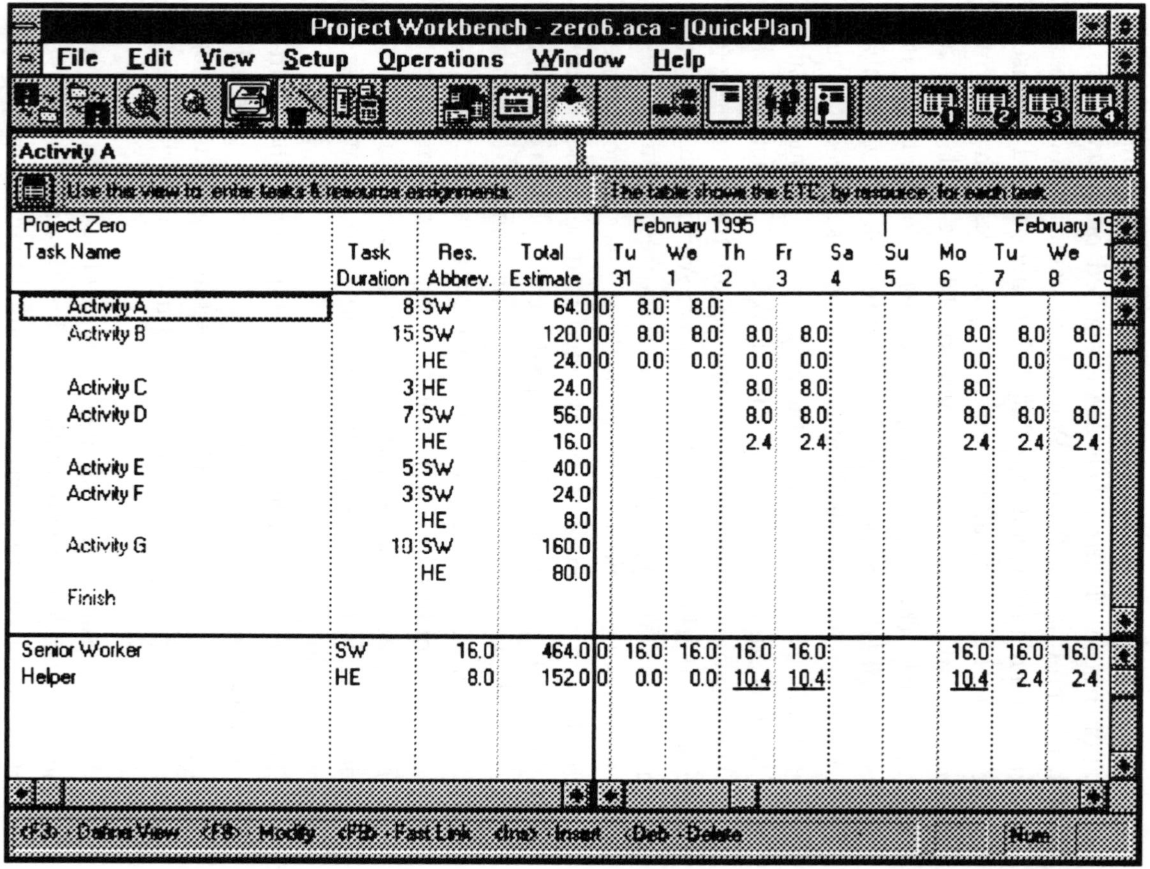

Project Workbench - zero6.aca - [QuickPlan]

File Edit View Setup Operations Window Help

Activity A

Use the view to enter tasks ( ) resource assignments   The table shows the ETE by resource for each date

Project Zero

Task Name	Task Duration	Res. Abbrev.	Total Estimate	Tu 31	We 1	Th 2	Fr 3	Sa 4	Su 5	Mo 6	Tu 7	We 8	We 9
Activity A	8	SW	64.0										
Activity B	15	SW	120.0	8.0	8.0	8.0	8.0			8.0	8.0	8.0	
		HE	24.0	0.0	0.0	0.0	0.0			0.0	0.0	0.0	
Activity C	3	HE	24.0							8.0	8.0	8.0	
Activity D	7	SW	56.0			8.0	8.0	8.0		8.0	8.0	8.0	
		HE	16.0			2.4	2.4	2.4		2.4	2.4	2.4	
Activity E	5	SW	40.0										
Activity F	3	SW	24.0										
		HE	8.0										
Activity G	10	SW	160.0										
		HE	80.0										
Finish													
Senior Worker		SW	16.0	464.0	16.0	16.0	16.0	16.0			16.0	16.0	16.0
Helper		HE	8.0	152.0	0.0	0.0	10.4	10.4			10.4	2.4	2.4

time that week. Or they could work a seven-day week, plus a small amount of overtime to get the job done.

However, studies have shown that results gained with overtime tend to be short-lived. After several weeks of working 50-hour weeks, productivity may very well be back down to what would normally be achieved in a standard 40-hour week.

There are at least two reasons for this. One is that people get tired and work output drops. Another is that they sometimes "pace" themselves. As is true in a marathon race, if a runner expends too much effort early in the race, he or she may not finish. Workers may well do the same thing, slowing down so they can endure the longer days.

These considerations alone argue against planning projects to be completed using significant levels of overtime to meet required completions. But there is an even more important reason. If overtime is being used just to meet the schedule and problems occur in the project, then there is no room left to compensate. So, as a general rule, overtime should be reserved to deal with unforeseen problems or inaccurate time estimates.

CONTOUR LOADING OF RESOURCES

It should be noted that the example shown above was done assuming uniform loading of all resources on all tasks. Project Workbench has a feature called *contour loading,* which allocates resources so that they are not instantaneously overloaded, and when the helper is contour loaded, it turns out that Task D will be done as soon as possible, thus preventing the end date from slipping quite so much. However, these solutions assume that work can actually be done as determined by the software, and that may not be the case.

Further, the amount of analysis required to arrive at optimum solutions takes so much time that it may not be worth the effort. Even for this simple schedule, several hours of analysis were required to understand exactly what the computer is doing. It is also my conviction that the schedule is an approximate model, not an exact representation of how the work should be done. It is best used as a guide, and some practical experience should guide actual practice.

Contrary to what I have heard people say, the computer is not *telling* the project manager what to do, but is simply determining solutions based on what data have been presented to it. It is still up to the manager to make a good decision about which solution is best.

SCHEDULING WITH SPECIFIC INDIVIDUALS

When resources cannot be considered *generic* or *pooled*, the resulting schedule may be different than that obtained when pooled resources are used. This is because we assume with pooled resources that all members of that pool can do each other's work. In highly skilled or professional jobs, this assumption is seldom valid. When specific individuals are assigned to tasks, the software simply schedules work so that no person is overloaded, as it did for a pooled resource in the previous example.

MULTIPROJECT SCHEDULING

The impact of resource constraints illustrated by the single project example above is magnified in scheduling multiple-project situations where several separate, independent projects are linked together through their dependence upon a pool of common resources.

Project Workbench and other software packages allow the multiproject situation to be analyzed in much the same way as was done for a single project. Such an analysis is really the only way in which an organization can practically gain control of the multiproject situation when resources are shared among all projects.

However, the data files created in these multiproject cases may become so large as to tax the capability of personal computers at the present time. I know of one company that tried to level resources across projects using a VAX, and for the huge data files that they were analyzing, no one could use the VAX until it finished its analysis.

The other option is to assign a *category* of resource to your project—such as Senior Programmer, Technician, Data Analyst, Electrician, and so on—develop your schedule, and then let functional managers assign whoever is available to do the job. In this way, you create manageable data files, and functional managers control the assignments in much the way that has been used in the past.

One problem with all of this is that we assume the world stands still from the time we create a schedule until we finish the job. Clearly this is not the case. Schedules are dynamic. Some tasks finish ahead of schedule (theoretically) and some finish late. When resources are shared across projects, this leads to interdependencies that have nothing to do with logic linkages, but with resource linkages. Thus, attempting to model such complexity soon exceeds our capability.

Related to this is an idea that I got from Marvin Patterson's book, *Accelerating Innovation.* Patterson points out that, in order to accelerate innovation, you must violate a long-held paradigm called the *lean-mean* model. When an organization is starved for resources and a small perturbation is introduced into the system, it spreads like a cancer throughout the entire body, destroying every plan in its path. The heretical conclusion is that you need slightly *excess* resource capacity to prevent such devastation, but this violates sacred precepts about how to manage properly.

Yet, Patterson's argument is easy to understand by the use of a simple analogy. Assume you are passing an 18-wheel truck on a two-lane road, and you are halfway around, with your foot on the floorboard. Around a curve ahead comes a car. It is too late to fall back and you have no power in reserve to get on around. You are in big trouble. On the other hand, if you only had the accelerator halfway down, you could press farther down and have a chance of success. The lesson is clear.

SHARPENING THE SAW

In his book, *The 7 Habits of Highly Effective People,* Stephen Covey points out that if you saw wood continuously, never stopping to

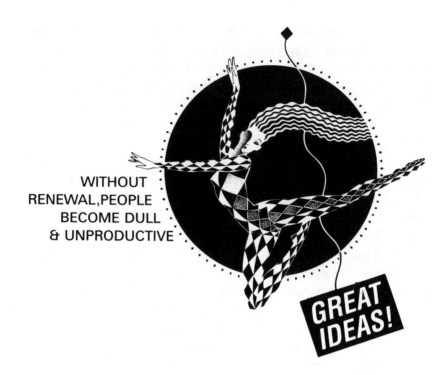

WITHOUT
RENEWAL,PEOPLE
BECOME DULL
& UNPRODUCTIVE

GREAT
IDEAS!

sharpen your saw, eventually the blade gets dull and won't cut anymore. Similarly, if people never take time to renew themselves, they become dull and unproductive. This is especially true for technical personnel.

It is said that the half-life of an engineer (including programmers, etc.) is now two to five years. The term comes from physics, relating to the decay of atomic material. If you start with a gram of uranium, after so many thousand years, you only have a half-gram left. The remainder has decayed to some other substance.

What this means for technical people is that two to five years after they graduate from a university, half of the technology they learned is now obsolete. If they are not staying current with advances in their field, they are becoming obsolete. Since these people represent the only truly renewable resource that a company has, it is clearly in the interests of the organization to renew them. Economically, you invest about $100,000 a year in most professional people. That figure represents typical loaded labor rates of around $50 per hour times about 2000 hours per year. To lose that investment makes very little economic sense.

Nevertheless, when you run under the lean-mean paradigm, people have no time to renew themselves. They are so burned out after a long day, trying to do the same amount of work that was being done before the company downsized, that they have no incentive to read current literature. Further, even if they had the inclination, consider one statistic to see how bad the problem is. In 1993 there were 90,000 articles published worldwide on cardiology. No individual could read even 10% of them! Similar statistics must apply to computer science, engineering, and so on.

Finally, we need to consider the effect of fatigue on errors. Dimancescu (1992) says the vice president of engineering at Boeing estimates fully one-third of the cost to develop a new airplane is rework. As he says, that is equivalent to having one of every three engineers on his staff to simply redo what the other two did wrong. On a multibillion-dollar program, that is a lot of money! Clearly, improving performance in terms of quality yields a big productivity boost. My belief is that two factors contribute to this statistic—inadequate planning and fatigue.

PRACTICAL SUGGESTIONS FOR RESOURCE ALLOCATION

In the example presented in this chapter, all workers have been assigned to the project as if they are available to work full-time. This is another reason why projects sometimes get into trouble. It is almost never true that a person is available to work on *anything* at a 100% rate! There are meetings to attend, nonproductive time (such as breaks, goofing off, interruptions, and so on), nonproject assignments, and a host of other reasons for the loss of availability. One company I know about had their people keep a record for two weeks of what they were doing every half-hour of the day. Prior to the study, they believed project personnel were spending about 70 to 80% of their time on projects. After the study, they found that it was closer to 25%! Under such conditions, it was no wonder projects were seldom completed on time.

History can sometimes be used as a guide to determine what percentage of an individual's time can be expected to be available on a project, and then activity durations can be established accordingly. Project Workbench does allow nonproject activities to be inserted into a project schedule, so that the impact on the project can be assessed. By doing this, a manager can decide if it is best to assign a particular job to a certain individual or whether it would be too great an impact on a project. This permits *informed decision making*, rather than having to make decisions based only on "gut reactions."

Part-time vs. full-time participation

You often don't have a choice. Specialized resources, project size and priority, policy, practices, etc. may dictate. Here's the major reason part-timers can hurt productivity. Increased communication load. Time is spent assuring understanding among more people! Especially when things change.

What's an average workday?

Time lost on non-project activities is about 40%. Sometimes called a productivity factor. Don't be afraid to specify full-time resource availability as 4 or 5 hours per day. Your task durations will be much more realistic.

Tom Conlon

One factor that may affect performance on projects more than people suspect is just how many projects a person is working on at one time. One company found that when they had their people quit working on multiple projects, focusing on one project at a time, their productivity nearly doubled!

I believe this may be more widespread than we think. It is probably the *second-order* effects of shifting around that reduce productivity the most, whereas our models for analysis generally consider only first-order effects. For example, a first-order analysis would suggest that the time it takes to do an interrupted task is identical to that taken to do the uninterrupted one. This simply is not true.

In the long run, it may make more sense to do a few top-priority projects first, then move on. I know that we usually want it all—immediately if not sooner—but that is unrealistic. Choices must be made, and prioritizing is the way to do it. As Peter Drucker has written (1974), doing the *right things* is more important than doing them right. That is, it makes little sense to be 100% efficient if you are doing the wrong thing.

> **D**igging the best hole in the world is of little use if a hole is not needed in the first place.

RESOURCE ALLOCATION METHODS

For the reader interested in how computers are programmed to perform resource allocations, a number of references are available. These include Fleming, Bronn, & Humphries; Moder, Phillips, & Davis; and specific software manuals, including the one for Project Workbench. See the reading list for titles to the books cited.

Generally speaking, all programs make use of what are called *heuristics*, or "rules of thumb," to assign resources. The problem is generally so complex that exact mathematical models are impractical to construct. Moder, et al., present a table of a number of such heuristics. Project Workbench allows the manager to select various allocation rules, which is helpful. While it is outside the scope of this work to describe these in detail, suffice it to say that control of projects can only be achieved if the resource allocation problem is solved, and abundant software exists to help.

TIME–COST TRADEOFF PROCEDURES

In Chapter 1, I showed that the cost of project work is often not linear with time. There will be a certain duration for a project that will yield a minimum cost. As the duration increases, costs rise because of inefficiency. As the duration is reduced, costs rise again, but often exponentially, due to diminishing efficiencies, premium labor costs, and so on.

However, there are times when reducing time is crucial. One computer manufacturer found that if they were one month late to market with a new computer, they may lose one-third of their total product sales. That is enough to completely wipe out their profits. As Tom Peters has asserted so strongly in his book, *Liberation Management*, speed is life. We all must get fast or go broke.

To illustrate how time-cost tradeoffs are done, consider the schedule in Figure 7.6. Only four tasks are involved. Two workers are available at the rate of eight hours per day, and their loaded labor rate is $400 per day ($50 per hour). I have referred to them as Worker 1 and Worker 2, so that we can see exactly where in the project they are applied. The project will cost $11,200 and will take 15 days to complete. The early start is November 7, 1995, and the early finish is November 25. (Note that I am treating the Thanksgiving holiday as a standard working day.)

Now suppose we want to finish the project before Thanksgiving starts. Can we add resources and shorten task durations? It all depends. Some tasks are not labor-intensive in a *body* sense. That is, you cannot put two people on them and do them faster. However, you can let the one person assigned work more hours per day and get the calendar duration down.

The simplest case is the one in which tasks are labor-intensive, so that extra people can be added *or* you can work overtime to get them done faster. Assuming that in our example, we note that Tasks B and C are only eight days total duration, while Task A is 10 days. This means that the worker assigned to B and C is idle for two days. If this person were allowed to work on Task A immediately after finishing C, could we shorten A, and if so, by how much?

FIGURE 7.6

SCHEDULE *CRASH* IN ITS INITIAL FORM

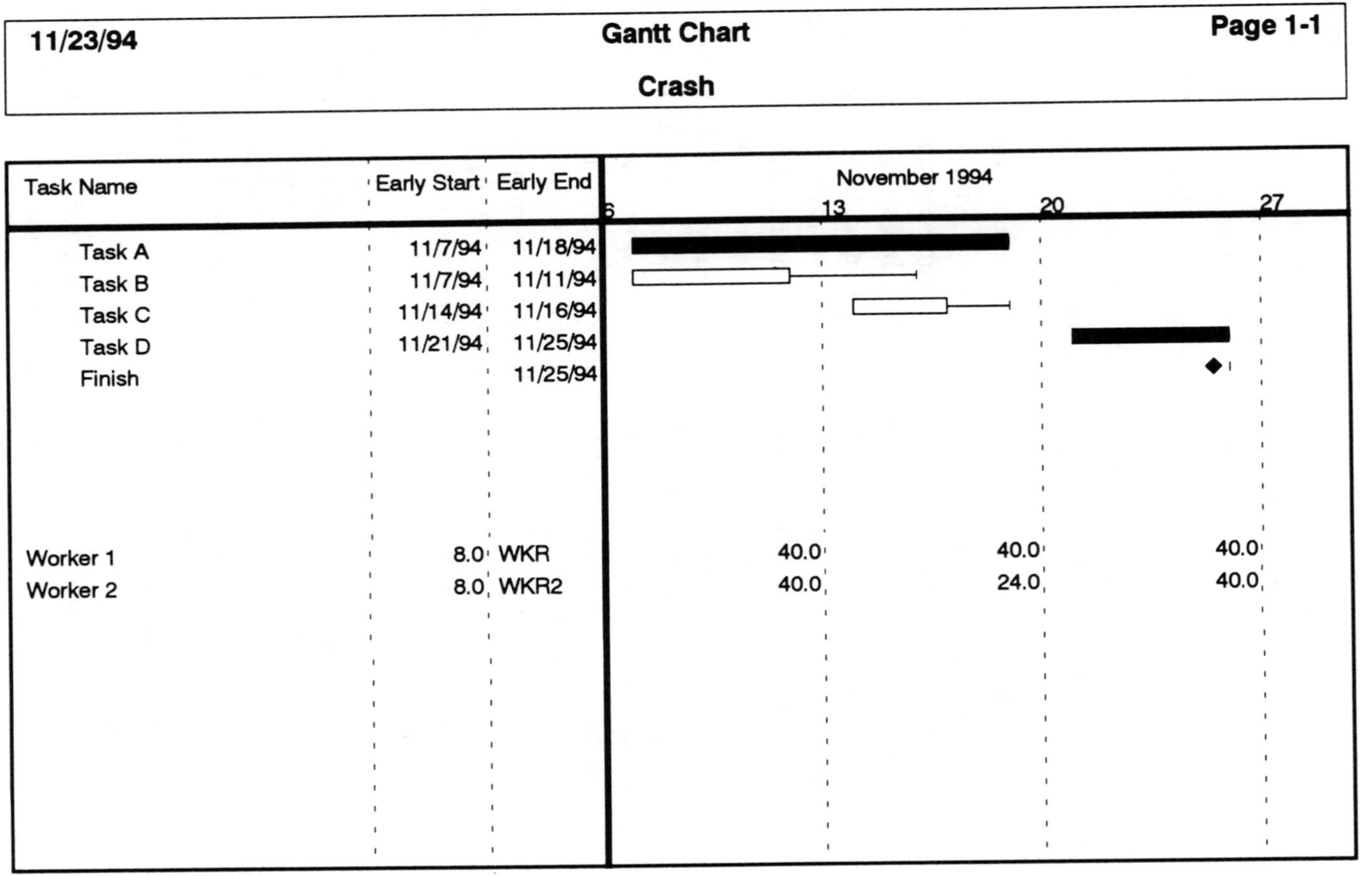

| 11/23/94 | Gantt Chart | Page 1-1 |
| | Crash | |

Task Name	Early Start	Early End	November 1994
Task A	11/7/94	11/18/94	
Task B	11/7/94	11/11/94	
Task C	11/14/94	11/16/94	
Task D	11/21/94	11/25/94	
Finish		11/25/94	
Worker 1	8.0	WKR	40.0 40.0 40.0
Worker 2	8.0	WKR2	40.0 24.0 40.0

169

We are saying that two people will be working on A during that time. If one person is going to take two days to complete A and we assign two workers, we can pretend that it will only take one day to complete. This yields the schedule shown in Figure 7.7. Note that it has only shortened A by one day, so we have gained a day on the schedule.

What about the cost? The cost has remained constant at $11,200, because we are simply using a worker who was idle, and we have made a linear tradeoff. However, we have not shortened the project to 10 days. To do that might require overtime.

In order to have Project Workbench deal with overtime, we have to add new *resources,* called overtime resources. I have added Worker 1 OT and Worker 2 OT, each with four hours per day availability, and labor rates of $75 per hour. In other words, I am going to assume that my workers can each work twelve hours per day, but I will pay them time and one-half for the four hours overtime each day.

Now let us begin with Task D. It already has both workers assigned to it and takes five days to do. If we have both of them work overtime, how much faster can they do the work? We are increasing the labor applied from 16 person-hours a day to 24. A linear tradeoff would suggest that duration would be reduced by 33.3%, to a total of 3.33 days. However, we know that a linear tradeoff is optimistic. I would assume that the duration would only drop to four days. Using that figure, we arrive at the schedule in Figure 7.8.

We have now pulled the schedule down to 13 days, rather than 15, and we have increased costs from $11,200 to $12,800, or by $1,600 total. In other words, reducing the schedule by two days has cost $1,600, or a total of $100 per hour on the average. (These numbers are calculated by Project Workbench in the CSSR report, which is not printed here. This is one example of how the software can help with what would normally be tedious calculations.)

Clearly, further reductions in time are possible by applying overtime to the remaining tasks. But this simple example shows

Figure 7.7

PROJECT *CRASH* SHORTENED BY ONE DAY

Figure 7.7
PROJECT *CRASH* SHORTENED BY ONE DAY

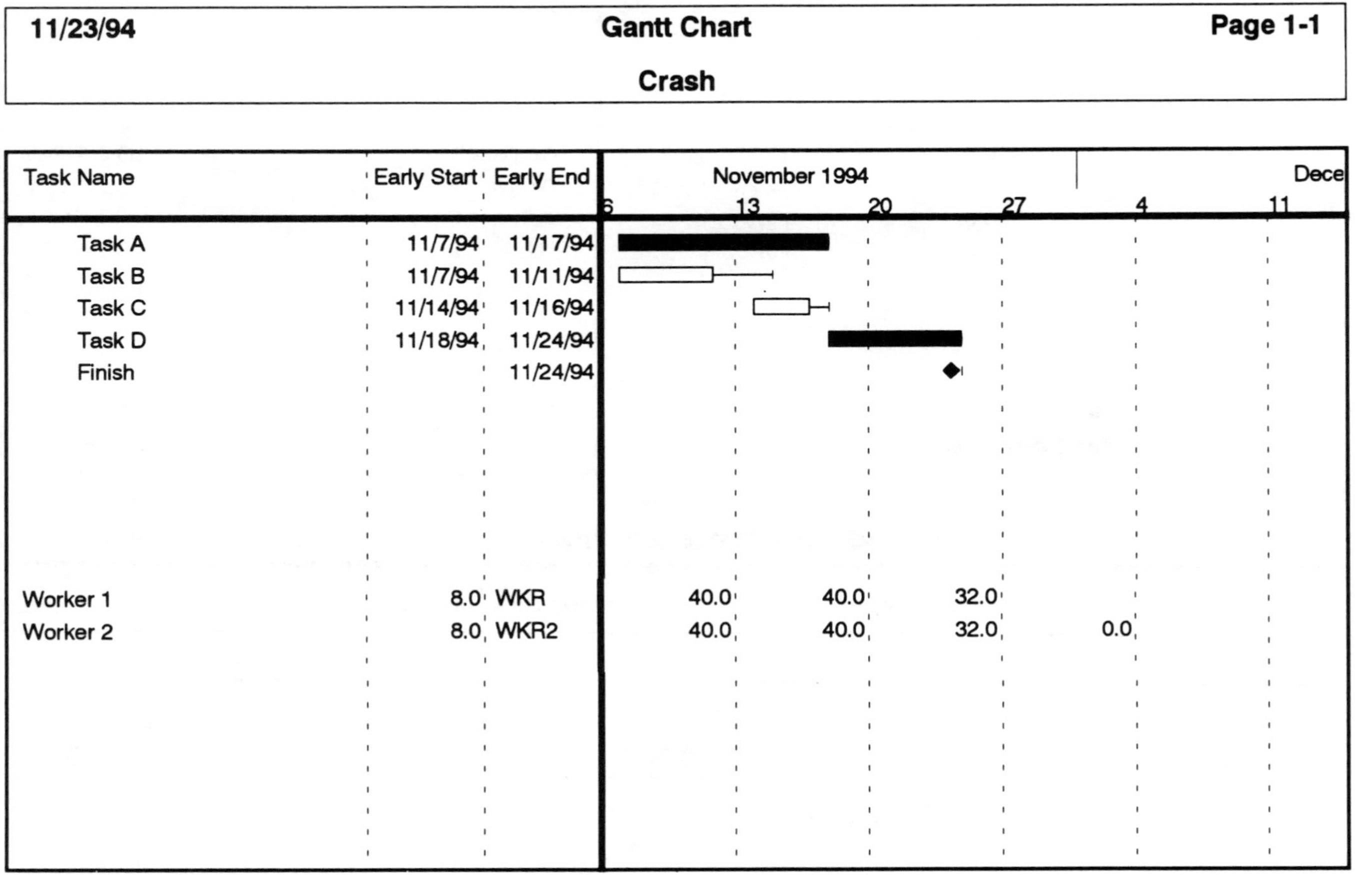

FIGURE 7.8

SCHEDULE WITH OVERTIME APPLIED TO TASK D

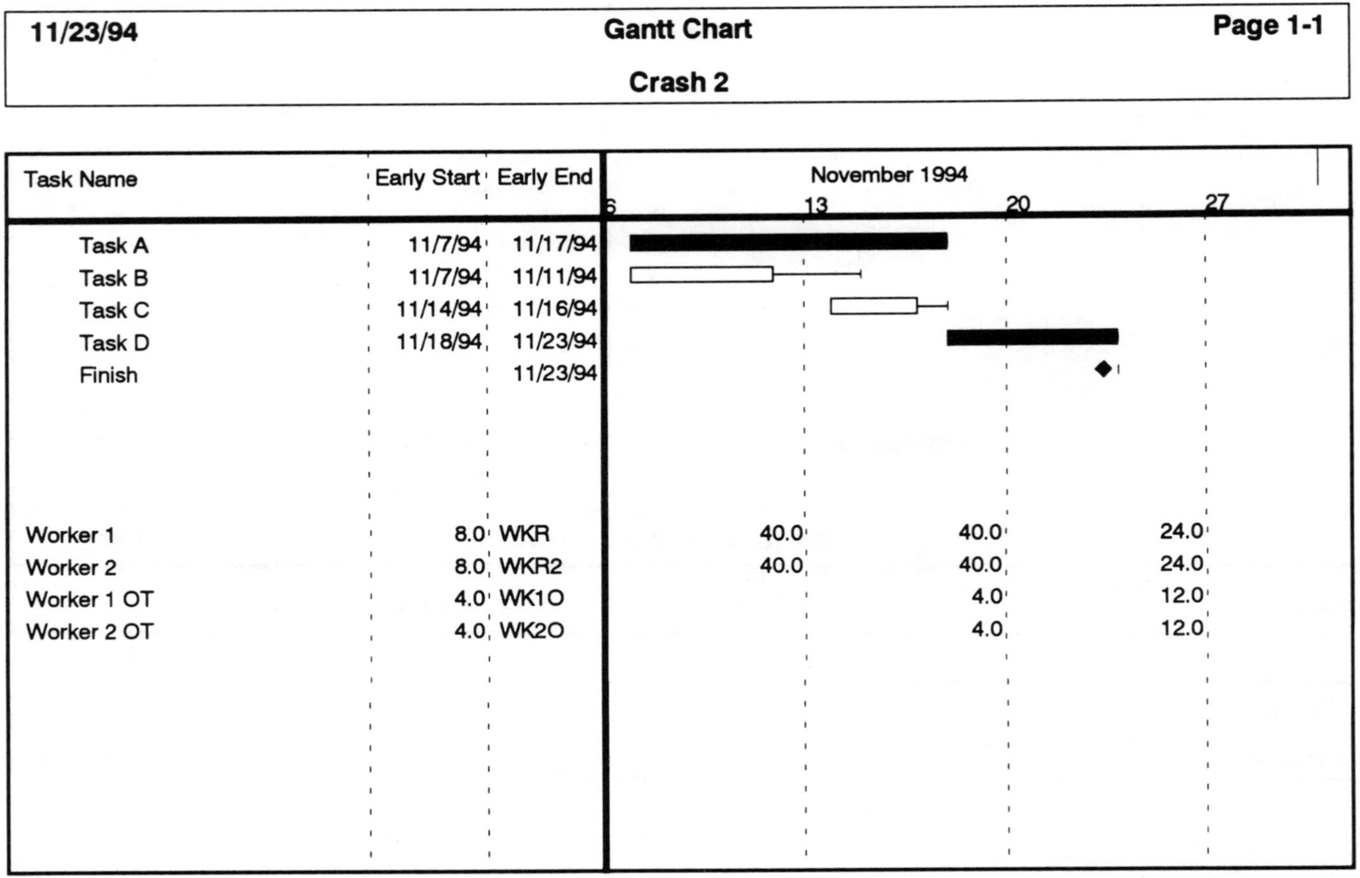

how time-cost tradeoffs are made, and illustrates how costs start to rise sharply as time is reduced. I submit that it is not possible to do this analysis manually. As the length of one task is reduced, parallel tasks may become critical. If, for example, we reduce the duration of Task A by another day, then B and C will become critical. As I pointed out in Chapter 6, this increases project risk. In fact, many attempts at time-cost tradeoffs produce schedules that look feasible but simply can't be met. The assumptions of efficiency reductions may be very inaccurate. Nevertheless, there are times when it is necessary to do them, and this illustrates the approach.

QUESTIONS FOR REVIEW

1. *What is the difference between a fixed-duration and a variable-duration activity?*

2. *If one person can complete a task in 10 hours, how long would it probably take for two people? For four people?*

3. *On what kind of task would adding people probably not significantly shorten the working time?*

4. *Why should you begin by having a person allocate no more than 80% of his or her time to a project?*

KEY POINTS *from Chapter 7*

- When resource limitations are considered, a schedule may not have the float that was determined by standard CPM analysis.
- Resources can be allocated in a "pooled" fashion when the workers can all do the same work; otherwise, they must be allocated by name.

- The software can show how vacations and holidays will extend working times, so that their impact can be assessed.

- Scheduling can be improved in some cases by allowing activities to be *variable-duration*.

- "What-if" scenarios can be tried quickly with the computer, so that an informed decision can be made about how a project should be scheduled.

THE PERT STATISTICAL APPROACH

Imhotep left the pharaoh's palace and hurried back to his office. He was visibly shaken, walking like a zombie, hardly noticing friends as he passed them on the street. In fact, if he had been capable of hearing, he would have heard several exclaim to their companions, "What's wrong with Imhotep? He looks like he just saw a ghost."

But Imhotep did not hear them. He was so shaken by

The reader who has no knowledge of statistics should consult a basic text before reading this chapter, since it is outside the scope of this work to explain the statistics involved. A suitable work is the book by Walpole, cited in the reading list.

pharaoh Zoser's new assignment that he was deaf to all outside noises. The thought kept racing through his mind, "Nothing even faintly approaching this monument in size and splendor has ever been created by man."[1]

There had been no preparatory phase, no small pyramids on which to develop experience. In fact, Imhotep thought, only a generation ago Egypt had been a semitribal state. Now it was a highly organized society. But this? This was madness. And if he failed . . . Who knew the bounds of the pharaoh's wrath? And with no experience on which to base his plans, how was he to say with any degree of certainty how long the pyramid would take to construct? He hurried into his office, took out a sheet of papyrus, and began to make sketches. By the gods, he had to do this right!

* * *

Nothing much has changed in the nearly 5,000 years since Imhotep faced the biggest challenge of his career. Project managers are still required to plan and estimate jobs for which they have little or no experience to use for comparison. And some of them do encounter the wrath of the "pharaoh" in their own organization if the job is not completed on time and within budget.

We don't know, of course, if Imhotep gave the pharaoh a target completion date (or if one was imposed on him). We do know that the job was of enormous complexity. By the time it was finished, the step pyramid rose to a height of about 60 meters (197 feet) had a base dimensioned 125 by 110 meters (410 by 361 feet), and contained around 850,000 tons of stone. As Mendelssohn says:

> *[What is] surprising is the realization that the immense technological advance required for pyramid building was not due to a technical revolution. The methods of using stone as a building material and the metal and stone tools employed had been well-known in the Second Dynasty. What was new in Zoser's time was the degree to which all these activities were suddenly escalated. Pyramid-building was a milestone in the history of man because it was his first true application of large-scale technology . . . The keys to the problem were manpower and organization.*[2]

As we have seen in previous chapters, estimating is made easier by using the Work Breakdown Structure to subdivide the project into smaller units. However, you still arrive at individual tasks whose durations and costs must be estimated.

When those tasks or activities are similar to others that have been performed a large number of times, CPM scheduling is generally applied, using estimates of activity durations that are based on historical data. Again, these estimates are assumed to be the mean or average time that it has taken to perform the activity in the past.

However, when a project contains a majority of activities for which no experience exists—that is, no historical data is available—then the estimating difficulty becomes significant. Numerous slang terms exist to describe the kind of estimating that is done under this condition, and all of them have to do with the word "guess." When no experience is available to use as a guide, the only thing that can be done is make the best possible guess, based on *whatever* relevant experience one has.

It seems clear, however, that the more unique an activity is, the less certain the estimate of its duration, and therefore, the more *risky* the project will be in terms of control. And since a lot of projects (such as research and development) fall into this category, the question naturally arises whether there might not be some method that could be employed to reduce estimating risk.

It was in response to this problem that PERT was developed around 1958 as a joint effort between the Navy and the Booz, Allen & Hamilton consulting firm, and originally applied to the Polaris submarine project.

EMPIRICAL FREQUENCY DISTRIBUTIONS

To understand PERT estimating, consider an activity that has been performed in the past many times under essentially the same conditions. You might find that duration ranged from seven to 17 days. Now suppose that you count the number of times the activity required seven days to perform, eight days to

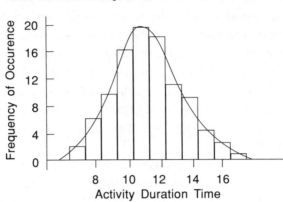

FIGURE 8.1
EMPIRICAL FREQUENCY DISTRIBUTION

perform, etc., and you display the resulting information in the form of an empirical frequency distribution, or histogram, as shown in Figure 8.1.

As we know from statistics, if an infinite number of observations are made, the width of the intervals in this figure approaches zero, and the distribution will merge into some smooth curve. This type of curve is the theoretical probability density of the random variable. The total area under such a curve is made to be exactly one, so that the area under the curve between any two values of **t** is directly the probability that the random variable **r** will fall in this interval. When this is done, the curve is called a *normal distribution curve.* It is also often called a bell-shaped curve.

Once the normal distribution curve exists for an activity, it is then a simple matter to extract the average-expected-activity duration from the curve and to use that time as the estimate for how long the work will take.

However, under those conditions when no such distribution exists, we could still say that the problem is to arrive at our *best approximation of what the average expected duration would be* if we *could* perform the work over and over to develop the normal distribution curve. It is the answer to this question that forms the heart of the PERT system.

PERT System of Three Time Estimates

Even though a project may consist of activities for which little or no experience exists, most planners will have some relevant experience, so in most cases it is possible to make an educated "guess" of the *most likely* time the work will take. In addition, estimates can be made of how long the work would take if things go better than expected and, conversely, if things go worse than expected. These are called the *optimistic* and *pessimistic* conditions, respectively.

They are not defined as best- and worst-case, however. See Table 8.1 for the exact meanings of the terms *optimistic* and *pessimistic*.

TABLE 8.1
TERMS USED IN PERT ESTIMATING

Definitions:

a = **optimistic performance time:** the time that would be improved only one time in twenty if the activity could be completed repeatedly under the same essential conditions.

m = **most likely time:** the modal value of the distribution, or the value that is most likely to occur more often than any other value.

b = **pessimistic performance time:** the time that would be exceeded only one time in twenty if the activity could be performed repeatedly under the same essential conditions.

These three estimates can be thought of as representing aspects of the normal distribution curve, which could be developed if the work were performed a sufficient number of times. Another way to think of them is to say they represent *information* or data about the work in question. Taken together, perhaps a computation of the distribution *mean* can be made.

This is the essence of the PERT system, although what has been presented is an admittedly simplified presentation. In fact, the original development of PERT did not assume a normal distribution. It is, however, easier to understand the concepts if normal distributions are used. The interested reader should consult

Moder, Phillips, and Davis (see reading list) for a more thorough treatment of the statistics involved. For our purposes, all that matters is the application of the method.

PERT COMPUTATIONS

In order to combine the three estimates to calculate the expected mean duration for the activity, a formula was derived, based on principles from statistics. The estimate of average expected time to perform an activity is given by the following expression:

$$t_e = \frac{a + 4m + b}{6}$$

where

t_e = expected time
a = optimistic time estimate
m = most likely time
b = pessimistic time

These values of t_e are used as the durations of activities in a PERT network. Given those estimated durations, the network calculations are identical to those for CPM. A forward-pass computation yields earliest times for events and a backward-pass provides latest times.

ESTIMATING PROBABILITY OF SCHEDULED COMPLETION

When you have done PERT estimates, you can now compute a *confidence interval* for each activity and for the critical path, once it has been located. To do this, the standard deviation of each activity distribution must be known. With PERT software, such a computation would be automatically made by the software. However, if CPM software is used to do scheduling, the calculations can be made externally, perhaps using a spreadsheet (which is very simple to construct, incidentally).

A suitable estimator of activity standard deviation is given by:

$$s = \frac{b - a}{6}$$

where **s** is the standard deviation of the expected time, t_e.

Once the critical path has been determined for the network, the standard deviation for the total critical path can be calculated by taking the square root of the sum of the variances of the activities on the critical path. Thus, in the case of only three activities on the critical path, the standard deviation would be given by:

$$s_{cp} = \sqrt{s_1{}^2 + s_2{}^2 + s_3{}^2}$$

From statistics, we know that there is a 68% probability of completing the project within plus-or-minus one standard deviation of the mean, 95% within two standard deviations, and 99.74% within three standard deviations. The normal curve is shown in Figure 8.2 for reference:

FIGURE 8.2
A NORMAL DISTRIBUTION CURVE

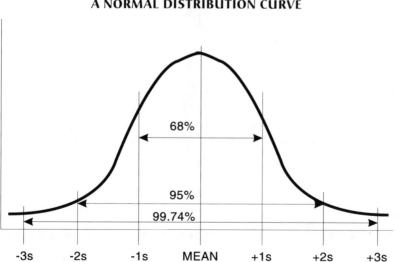

AN EXAMPLE

To illustrate how PERT works, we will consider a single activity, for which estimates are made by two different planners. The estimates given by each person are shown in Table 8.2, together with the calculated values for t_e and s.

Note that the standard deviation for the estimates made by person one is only 0.5 day, meaning that the spread on the normal distribution curve is quite small. For person two, the standard deviation is 1.8 days. For convenience, we will call this 2.0 days even. The normal distribution curve, using these two different sets of numbers, would look as shown in Figure 8.3.

TABLE 8.2
ESTIMATES MADE BY TWO INDIVIDUALS

Estimator	Optimistic	Most Likely	Pessimistic	PERT Time	Std. Dev.
1	9	10	12	10.2	0.5
2	9	10	20	11.5	≈ 2

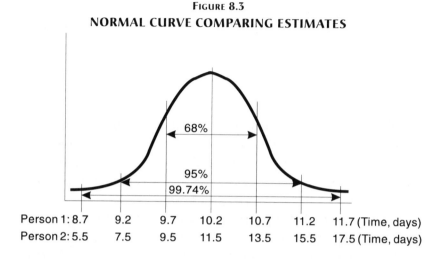

FIGURE 8.3
NORMAL CURVE COMPARING ESTIMATES

Person 1: 8.7	9.2	9.7	10.2	10.7	11.2	11.7 (Time, days)
Person 2: 5.5	7.5	9.5	11.5	13.5	15.5	17.5 (Time, days)

The impact on the activity estimate is that the *confidence interval* for person two is four times wider than that for person one for a *given probability* of completion of the task.

> **To illustrate, there is a 68% probability that the activity will be completed in the range of 9.7 to 11.7 days if the estimates made by person one were used, whereas the 68% confidence interval is 9.5 to 13.5 days if the estimates made by person two were used.**

What is meant by these statistics is simply that person one has greater confidence or less *uncertainty* about his estimates than person two. Does that mean he is more correct? No. It is simply a reflection of the different experiences of the two individuals.

Perhaps because person two has had less experience with this particular activity than person one, he is not sure how long it will take. Therefore, the PERT system would tell him to use an activity duration of 11.5 days as his best estimate of mean duration, whereas person one would only use 10.2 days. This can be thought of as automatically providing some "padding" for the person who has the least confidence in his estimates, although I am using the word "pad" here in a different sense than it is normally used.

Using PERT

The fact that PERT requires that three time estimates be made for each project activity, and that these be plugged into formulas to calculate a time estimate and standard deviation, means additional work compared to CPM. For this reason, many planners consider PERT to be not worth the effort.

Not only that, but people question the validity of the entire process. They argue that, if all three estimates are guesses, why should the weighted composite of three guesses be any better than just using the most likely estimate in the first place? Indeed, there is merit to this argument. As I see it, one principal advantage of PERT is that it makes everyone realize that durations used to specify the completion of work are not exact, but carry with them *probabilities.*

As was discussed in Chapter 4, it may be better to use DELPHI to arrive at an estimate, or perhaps have several individuals estimate an activity duration independently of one another and simply average them. In any case, the interested reader is referred to the work by Moder, Phillips, and Davis, and to the *Project Management Handbook,* by Cleland and King, for a more in-depth treatment of PERT and probabilistic methods in project scheduling (see the reading list).

QUESTIONS FOR REVIEW

1. *Referring to the normal distribution curve on page 181 (fig. 8.2), if an activity has an expected duration of 15 days and a standard deviation of 1 day, what is the probability that it will be completed within the range of 14 to 16 days?*

2. *If the critical path in a project has a duration of 20 days and consists of three activities having the following characteristics, what is the probability that the project will be completed by 21.36 days after it starts?*

TASK	DURATION	STD. DEV.
A	6	.7
B	9	1.1
C	5	.4

KEY POINTS *from Chapter 8*

- PERT is used when very little experience exists on which to base estimates of activity durations.

- Three estimates must be made for each activity: most likely, optimistic, and pessimistic.

- These estimates are combined in a formula to yield an estimate of the average expected duration for an activity.

- Standard deviation can then be computed for each activity and a confidence interval can be used to specify the probability that the activity will be completed in a certain range of times.

- A confidence interval can also be specified for the critical path, once it is located in the network.

- A major advantage of PERT may be that it compels everyone to realize that estimates are not exact, but carry probabilities of completion.

References

1. I have paraphrased a passage from the book by Mendelssohn, *The Riddle of the Pyramids*, page 35. See the reading list for complete citation.
2. Mendelssohn, page 35.

Chapter 9

CONCEPTS OF PROJECT CONTROL AND EVALUATION

In his book, *The Abilene Paradox*, Jerry Harvey relates the story of Captain Kohei Asoh, a Japan Air Lines pilot, who, on November 22, 1968, landed his DC-8 jet, with 96 passengers and 11 crew members on board, $2^1/_2$ miles out in San

> **P**redicting the future is easy. It's trying to figure out what's going on now that's hard.
>
> *Fritz R. S. Dressler*

Francisco Bay, but in nearly perfect alignment with the runway on which he was supposed to land. According to Harvey, Captain Asoh landed the jet so smoothly that many of the passengers were unaware that they were in the water until someone pointed out a sailboat floating nearby. No one was injured, not even bruised, and they were all extricated from the plane and ferried safely to land in inflatable life rafts.

The inevitable hearing was convened by the National Transportation Safety Board (NTSB) shortly afterward, and everyone expected Captain Asoh to be hung up by his toes in downtown San Francisco, totally disgraced.

Captain Asoh was the first witness called to testify, and as he took the stand, all eyes and ears were attuned to the battering he was certain to endure. The investigator opened the hearing with the obvious question, "Captain Asoh, in your own words, can you tell us how you managed to land that DC-8 Stretch Jet $2^1/_2$ miles out in San Francisco Bay in perfect compass line with the runway?"

Captain Asoh never hesitated. His reply was straightforward and honest. "As you Americans say, Asoh screwed up!"

With that, the inquiry was essentially over. All that remained was to tidy up details. What more is there to do when the accused admits his guilt?

Harvey calls this the *Asoh defense*, and suggests that it should be invoked more often. Certainly, when things go out of control, when Murphy's Law works its wrath on managers, the Asoh defense may make more sense than trying to cover one's behind.

It certainly worked for me. At one point in my career, when I was a young, inexperienced project manager, I sent a set of drawings to our machine shop to have some prototype parts made. The machinist screwed them up, and they wouldn't work. When I asked him why he had botched a relatively simple machining job, his reply was essentially the Asoh defense.

"Because I'm dumb," he said.

With that, there was nothing more to be said, except, "Well, do them over and make them right this time."

CONCEPT OF CONTROL

One of the primary responsibilities of a project manager is to ensure that things are done as they are supposed to be done—in other words, that control of a project is maintained. As was true for Captain Asoh, landing the plane in San Francisco Bay is unacceptable, and bringing a project in late and over budget is similarly taboo.

In short, a project manager is expected to meet the *good, fast, cheap* objectives discussed in Chapter 1. If this is to happen, proper project control is necessary. Therefore, the design of a project control system is very important. However, before the system can be designed, it is essential to understand the basic concepts of control, by answering the questions in Figure 9.1.

To repeat the definition offered in Chapter 1:

> **Control is achieved by comparing where one is with where one is supposed to be, then taking corrective action to resolve any discrepancies that exist.**

Although the word *control* often refers to power, authority, command, or domination, the definition offered above is more like what is involved in aircraft or marine navigation. The pilot is guiding a vessel by comparing his course to the planned route in order to arrive at a predefined destination.

The central idea in this meaning of control is that *information* is used to maintain satisfactory progress toward a desired goal; in other words, this is an *information systems* definition of control. Information systems

> The right information cannot be extracted from the wrong data.
>
> *Russell L. Ackoff*

are designed around concepts of *feedback systems,* and this is the model that should be applied to project control systems. A simple feedback system is shown in Figure 9.2 to illustrate the point.

This way of looking at control in terms of information processes, rather than in energy terms, is helpful because it leads to insight into how a manager must deal with people. When control is thought of in terms of energy or power, it inevitably leads to authoritarian management, in which the manager tries to achieve control by closely monitoring workers and giving orders for them to follow. Such a control method is ineffective for at least two reasons.

FIGURE 9.1
CONCEPT OF CONTROL

FIGURE 9.2
FIRST-ORDER FEEDBACK SYSTEM

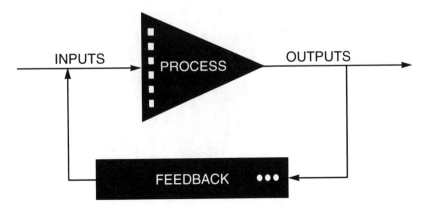

For one thing, the manager is burdened with having to closely monitor workers, which does not give him or her much time to do anything else. Thus, planning and other management activities tend to suffer. Further, such a method of control is not very effective if a number of workers must be monitored, since the manager cannot easily practice surveillance on all of them at once.

The second reason why authoritarian management does not work well is simply that today's worker does not readily accept it. People today expect more autonomy, and do not willingly let managers treat them like pawns. However, when they do accept authoritarian management, they absolve themselves of responsibility for the outcome of their efforts. As long as they do what they have been told to do, if the outcome is unacceptable, they can respond to the manager with, "Well, I did what you told me and it didn't work. What do you want me to do now?"

AUTHORITARIAN MANAGEMENT

DOES NOT WORK

For these reasons, a manager must ultimately establish a situation in which workers achieve self-control, so that *work* is *controlled—not workers.* The objective must be to get the work done, not make workers perform in lock-step fashion. Attempts to constrain and regiment workers generally lead to resentment and an atmosphere that stifles creativity, which is just the opposite of what is needed. Control should be viewed as a tool that the worker can use to work more effectively and efficiently.

Consider, for a moment, the word *organization.* It has the same root as the word *organism.* The human body is an example of a complex organism. If any organ of the body does not function correctly, the entire organism suffers. In the same way, if any member of a project team does not function correctly, it will have an adverse effect on the entire project. Therefore, we can say that:

> **A manager is only in control if every member of his team is in control of his own work.**

The best way to see this is to consider the words *macro* and *micro* control. The project manager is interested in achieving macro control of the project. That is, at the top level of the Work Breakdown Structure, the project is supposed to be in control. Following the WBS model, we can think of the Work Package or Level-of-Effort as points where micro control is exercised. Clearly, if micro control is not achieved, no macro control will exist, since top-level control depends on what is happening at the lowest levels of the project. And so, the individual must be in control of his or her own work so that micro control will exist.

The term most often used to designate what the manager must achieve is *empowerment.* Employees must be empowered to do their jobs with the minimum supervision that is consistent with the individual's capability. Enabling individual members of a project team to achieve self-control is absolutely essential if real project control is to be accomplished.

It is clear to me that the word *empowerment* is not understood by a lot of people. Nor is participation or employee involvement. One chief executive is reported to have said, "I'm not letting the monkeys run the company." This demonstrates contempt for the workforce for one thing, and a total lack of understanding of empowerment for another. Empowerment does not mean that managers *abdicate* their leadership roles or practice totally nondirective leadership. It does not mean that the employees can just do whatever they want to do. It does not mean that there are no boundaries. It simply means that *within* those boundaries employees are free to carry out their assignments using their own judgement, skills, and methods; that they can make unilateral decisions affecting how they do their work; and that they accept responsibility for the outcomes of their effort.

In order to show how this can be achieved, a *Standard Operating Procedure For Empowering People* is presented in Table 9.1. Each point will be explained below.

TABLE 9.1

HOW TO EMPOWER PEOPLE

Standard Operating Procedure For Empowering People

The employee needs:

1. A clear definition of what he or she is supposed to be doing, with the purpose stated.

2. A personal plan on how to do the required work.

3. Skills and resources that are adequate to do the work.

4. Feedback on progress that goes directly to the person from the work itself.

5. A clear definition of his or her authority to take corrective action when there is a deviation from plan. And that authority cannot be zero!

1. The first step is to be sure that each team member is clear on what his or her objective is. Ideally, the person would participate in the development of those objectives, so that clarity is automatically achieved. Note also the need to state the *purpose* or reason for doing the job. This is very important.

   To illustrate, I have used an exercise in some of my classes in which I tell groups, "You have fifteen minutes. During that time, you can do anything you want to do, so long as you do it together and report to the rest of us what you've done." They give me some strange looks. I repeat the assignment and go sit down.

   The typical conversation in the groups sounds something like this:

   "Anybody have any ideas?" asks one member. The others stare blankly or screw up their faces in serious contemplation.

   "Whatever we're going to do, we'd better get with it," says a member, staring intently at her watch. We've only got 14 minutes left."

   The emerging leader presses them. "Okay, give me some ideas."

   "How about if we go outside and see how many cars there are in the parking lot from each state?"

   The others look a bit distraught, but no one has anything better to offer. "Only 13 minutes left," chimes the time-keeper.

   In desperation, they divide the parking lot into zones, run outside, count cars, come back and consolidate their lists, then give a report. "There are 10 from Indiana, 1 from North Carolina, 8 from Illinois, and 2 from Michigan."

   All groups do something similar. Then we process the exercise. I ask how they felt about the vagueness of the objective. They agree it was vague, but they weren't too

**What do you do
when you get fuzzy objectives?**

concerned, as they expect such stupidity from seminar instructors, and besides, there weren't any serious penalties for failure.

I ask those who are officers from corporations if they ever get fuzzy directives from corporate headquarters. "Is there any other kind?" they ask.

"What do you do when you get fuzzy directives?" I ask.

"We try to figure out what should be done, and we do it."

Personally, I find this frightening. These are some of America's finest. Rather than ask for clarification, they try to second-guess headquarters and do what they think should be done. I know the reason. They have been conditioned to not ask questions, as they don't want their bosses to think they're stupid. I submit to you that guessing often leads to absolute proof of their stupidity, when they do the wrong thing and it must be done over.

But this has been ingrained in us because many teachers tell students not to ask stupid questions. It seems obvious that you would be better off to invoke the Asoh defense, admit to your stupidity, and ask for clarification, than to risk wasting valuable time and resources doing the wrong thing. Simply say, "I may be dense, but I don't understand what you want me to do. How about going over it again." Or you can say, "Let me see if I'm with you." Then you summarize.

I once heard that Einstein told someone, "Please go slowly. I do not comprehend quickly." If Einstein, the genius, could ask for clarification, and could admit to needing time to think, surely the rest of us poor mortals can do the same.

Next, I ask the groups, "Why did you feel that you had to do anything at all? I told you that you could do *anything* you wanted to do. Why didn't that include doing nothing? Just hang out together. Vegetate."

"No, we couldn't do that," they protest.

"Why not?"

"We didn't want to waste time," they reply defensively.

As if counting cars is a good use of time, you understand.

Most people chuckle when they hear this story. I did too, until one day I realized how profound is the implication of what they are saying. They don't want to waste time. They want to do something that has at least some semblance of meaning. And they are unanimous, regardless of level in the organization.

This is exactly what the gurus have been saying for years. People thrive on doing *meaningful, worthwhile* things.

They don't thrive on having jobs simplified to the point that they are mindless, robotic tasks, yet that is what we have done. We have deprived our workers of the opportunity to feel a sense of accomplishment through such practice.

Clearly, this says that the purpose of a project should be explained. People should be told why it is important and what their contribution is. This is a vital step in developing commitment and motivation to the project team.

2. Each team member must also have a personal plan that will determine how his or her objective is going to be achieved. Again, it is most helpful when each member has participated in planning the project at his or her level of involvement. Why do they each need a personal plan? Because if you have no plan, you have no control. It is true at the project level, and it is true at the individual level. Further, remember that if you don't have control at the micro level, you won't have it at the macro level. A personal plan may not be very involved—perhaps nothing more than a daily planner with tasks prioritized and times allotted. But it must exist!

3. The project manager must be sure team members have all the resources needed to do the job. These include tools, equipment, and supplies or material. In addition, the individual must have the necessary skills to do the job or must be given training. It may be necessary to include in the project budget the expense of providing team members training in specialized areas for which no training budget is normally provided by the overall organization.

4. Feedback must go *directly* to the person doing the job *from the work itself*—not back through some circuitous route, such as the Management Information System (MIS). If you have ever had the experience of driving while someone navigated for you, and about three seconds after you passed a turn they told you about it, you know how frus-

trating such an experience is. It all boils down to *not being in control!* You didn't have the map, and the road signs meant nothing to you, so you couldn't exercise control.

In an analogous way, one of the problems with some management information systems is that, by the time information flows through the system to tell about a deviation from plan, it is too late to make a smooth correction. You have already "missed the turn," and must now backtrack. This is not to say that MIS is not useful. It is, for overall checks-and-balances, but not for micro-level control.

5. Finally, the individual must have a clear definition of his or her authority to take actions to correct for deviations from plan, and that authority *cannot be zero!* If the individual must ask someone else what to do every time there is a deviation, the person has no control, the manager does.

Naturally, there will be limits, as stated above. Further, the limits will vary with the experience, maturity, and proven performance of the individual contributor. Whatever those limits, the normal approach is to say that so long as the person is within a certain percent tolerance around the target (such as plus-or-minus 10%) she is to correct for those small deviations herself. On the other hand, if she finds the deviation exceeds the 10% limit, she must consult with her manager and they will jointly decide what to do about the problem.

WHY CONTROL SYSTEMS SOMETIMES FAIL

While the procedure presented above is sound, it will not function in a climate of fear, distrust, or antagonism. When people know that they will be punished for making mistakes, they will first play it safe. They are unlikely to invoke the Asoh defense.

This ultimately means that they won't do much of anything innovative, which means *risky*, since innovative things often don't work. Further, if they play it safe and still have problems, they will then try to hide those problems until the problem becomes so big it can no longer be hidden.

Unfortunately, learning to trust someone requires that we first be willing to take a risk. If you have ever had a teen-aged child who learned to drive and it came time for him to go off for his first solo drive, you know that the only thing you can do at that point is sit down and pray that he comes home safely. You cannot drive around with him until he is 40 years old. You have to take a risk and let him go. The same is true with your employees. If you never take the risk, you will never find out if they can be trusted.

Much has been written on the need to establish an organizational climate that fosters openness, honesty, and innovation, and it is outside the scope of this book to address the subject. Tom Peters has a great deal to say in his book *Thriving On Chaos* about how to promote good working relationships, and his points are relevant to project teams as well. It must be remembered that project management is not just a set of tools, it is a

discipline, and the "bottom line" is that success is only possible if people are managed properly.

As Peters says, there is no limit to what a properly *trained,* properly *informed,* and *empowered* employee can contribute to a company. Note the conditions: trained, informed, and empowered. You cannot contribute effectively without proper skills. You can't make good decisions unless you have information (especially about the "big picture"), and you can't make a significant contribution without being empowered.

Unfortunately, some employees can't easily make the transition from being disempowered to empowered. It takes some time.

As a fellow told me once, "I've been working here 20 years. During that time, they wanted me to hang my brain on the gate outside. Now they want me to carry the whole load."

For 20 years he had been treated as a pair of hands. Then the company decided they wanted him to think as well. It was a struggle. Some make it, and some don't. But we have to try with everyone.

COMPONENTS OF A PROJECT CONTROL SYSTEM

The feedback system shown previously is a very simple one that systems people call a *first order* system. It is not very elegant, and has some serious limitations as a model on how to achieve control in project management.

For those readers unfamiliar with feedback systems, a good analogy for the first-order system is the thermostat in one's home. In the winter, the system provides heat and the desired room temperature is preset by adjusting the thermostat to the proper level.

It should be clear that every system is designed to work properly only under certain conditions. For example, the home heating system might be designed to maintain the room at 70 degrees Fahrenheit so long as the outside temperature does not go below minus 30 degrees. When the outside temperature drops below that level, the heater will run continuously, but the room temperature will begin to drop below the preset level of 70 degrees.

To maintain the desired room temperature, the system would have to increase its heating capacity, but it cannot do this. Thus, it keeps running, without being able to adequately heat the house.

In a similar manner, a project may run into unexpected obstacles, which fall outside the boundaries for which the project control system was designed. Everyone is following the plan to the letter, but they are not getting the desired result. What is needed is to change the approach. However, a first-order control system does not have that capability. Something more flexible is needed. The third-order system shown in Figure 9.3 is the answer.

FIGURE 9.3
A THIRD-ORDER SYSTEM

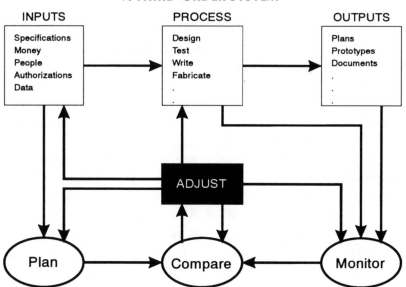

The system in Figure 9.3 has the same basic elements as the first-order system of Figure 9.2. There are Inputs, Processes, Outputs, and Feedback. However, the third-order system feeds information about the system outputs to a *comparator*, which weighs them against the original plan. If there is a discrepancy, that information is passed to an *adjust* element, which must decide if the discrepancy is caused by something being wrong with the processes, the inputs, or the plan itself.

Once that determination is made, the adjust element calls for a change in the plan, inputs, or the process itself. Note also that the adjust element has an arrow going back to the monitor. If a deviation is detected, the monitoring rate is increased until the deviation is corrected, then monitoring is decreased to its original level.

The real-world analogy is that if you were monitoring progress on a project weekly and a problem occurred, you might begin to monitor daily. If the problem becomes serious enough, your monitoring rate might increase to several times each day. Once the problem has been solved, you would revert to your weekly monitoring.

Comparing performance against plan can be difficult when the work cannot be quantified. How do you know what percentage of a design is complete, for example? Or if you are doing a mechanical drawing of a part, is the drawing 75% complete when 75% of the area of the paper is covered? Probably not. Measuring progress in *knowledge work*, to use Peter Drucker's term, is very difficult.

This often leads to strange results. Suppose a member of the project team has agreed to design a new golf club, and has promised to finish it in ten weeks. At the end of week one, she reports that the design work is 10% complete. At the end of week two, the work is 20% complete. In week three she hits a small snag and gets a little behind, but by week four she has caught up again. Figure 9.4 shows a plot of her progress.

Everything goes pretty well until week eight, when she hits another snag. At the end of that week, she has made no progress

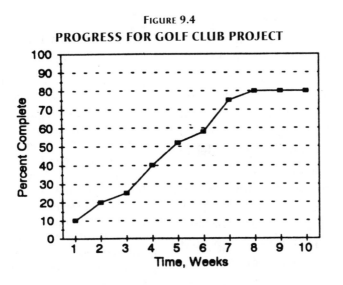

FIGURE 9.4
PROGRESS FOR GOLF CLUB PROJECT

at all. The same is true the following week, and the following, and the following.

What happened? For one thing, the 80/20 rule got her. In the case of knowledge work, it says that 80% of the work will

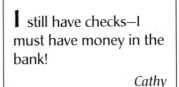

I still have checks—I must have money in the bank!

Cathy

be consumed by 20% of the problems encountered, and they will always happen near the end of the job.

The real issue, though, is how she measured progress in the first place. Chances are, at the end of the first week, she reasoned somewhat like Cathy in the comics and said to herself, "I'm at the end of the first week on a 10-week job. I must be 10% complete." And she would be in good company, because that is exactly what a lot of people do when *estimating* progress on knowledge work.

Note the word *estimate!* Assessing progress when work is not easily quantifiable is estimating, and subject to all the difficulties discussed in Chapter 4. This shows the limits of our ability to achieve control in management.

It is for this reason that two practices are advisable. First, work should be broken into small "chunks" that permit progress to be monitored fairly frequently, perhaps in intervals no greater than two weeks. Second, tangible deliverables should be used as signposts to show progress. In design, a drawing is tangible evidence of progress. For software development, printed code or a performing system are evidence that work is complete. Having it "in one's head" is impossible to verify.

PROGRESS REPORTS

The earned value report, which will be introduced in Chapter 10, is one way of reporting progress. In addition, written reports may be desirable, especially to explain the earned value report. Care should be taken to keep paperwork in projects to a minimum, so the report form shown in Figure 9.5 should be filled out only if necessary. If everything is proceeding smoothly in a project, the written progress report can consist of one line: "Everything is okay."

> **W**hy so many things are 90% complete.
>
> People resist recognizing that real work is bigger. Only near the end are rough issues that have been put on the back burner actually addressed. The project seems to get bigger about as fast as work is being completed. Two reasons: underestimation, progress not measured accurately. We discover "undiscovered tasks" as we better understand the project, its users, and impacts better. Some details just aren't visible early on. We may also get trapped by the notion, "Can't go back more than once. Look worse to reestimate again later."
>
> *Tom Conlon*

CHANGES TO THE PLAN

In Chapter 2, I said that significant changes to the plan should be made and signed off by stakeholders affected by those changes. This may not involve the entire group of stakeholders who signed the plan originally.

FIGURE 9.5
PROJECT PROGRESS REPORT FORM

Project Progress Report
Project:
Prepared by: Date:
For the period from   to:
Accomplishments for this report period are:
We are on schedule ☐, ahead ☐, behind ☐

List any changes to project objectives:	List any changes that have occurred to our business climate:

What unanticipated problems do we now face?	

What needs to be changed?	List anyone whose approval is needed for those changes:

List any additional *anticipated* problems:	Action steps that I plan to take:

Comments:	

What constitutes a significant change must be agreed-upon in advance. For example, a significant change to the budget might be considered to be plus or minus 10%. Thus, if during project execution it is determined that total project costs are likely to be 10% greater than forecast originally, then new funding would have to be approved by the financial officer, marketing director, and engineering director (as an example).

Not only should this procedure be followed if the project is forecasted to be overspent, it should also be done if an *underspend* is predicted. I know, this is foolhardy! No one ever gives money back, since they will have their budget cut next time if they do. That is the result of gameplaying in organizations, however, and does not constitute proper management practice. Money that is not needed in a project should be freed up as soon as possible, so that it can be used elsewhere in the organization. Failure to do so results in what the economists call *opportunity cost* to the organization. The money could have been used in a beneficial way, but the opportunity was lost because funds were already allocated to a project.

One change that is particularly troublesome is revision of project scope. Scope defines how much work is going to be done—that is, the *boundaries* of the project. Scope has a way of creeping up during the life of a project. Usually it happens because the client discovers that you can do something he didn't know you could do, or finds that the competition has a feature not originally asked for, and asks if you can do the additional work.

The trap here is that, in order to be cooperative, you may agree to the added work without asking for additional time, resources, or funding. It might, in fact, be possible to absorb a minor change in scope, because the impact to *good, fast, cheap* is not great. However, when several minor changes are added together, they may collectively result in a significant change, and both you and the client may wind up in trouble.

The client may not want to pay the final bill—but when the client is the marketing department, the bill has already been paid by the company by the time the project is complete, so at that point it is too late to do anything about it.

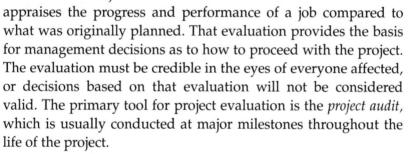

Watch out for scope creep!

Further, the project manager often is blamed for coming in over budget. Memories at the end of a project may suffer convenient amnesia! No one seems to remember that the scope of the project grew. All they know is that the project manager did not meet original targets.

PROJECT EVALUATION

As the dictionary definition says, to evaluate a project is an attempt to determine if the overall status of the work is acceptable, in terms of intended value to the client once the job is finished. Project evaluation

e•val•u•ate: to determine or judge the value or worth of

The Random House Dictionary

appraises the progress and performance of a job compared to what was originally planned. That evaluation provides the basis for management decisions as to how to proceed with the project. The evaluation must be credible in the eyes of everyone affected, or decisions based on that evaluation will not be considered valid. The primary tool for project evaluation is the *project audit,* which is usually conducted at major milestones throughout the life of the project.

PURPOSES OF PROJECT EVALUATION

Earlier we saw that the last phase of a project involves a post-mortem analysis, which is conducted so that the management of projects can be improved. However, such an audit should not be conducted only at the end of the project.

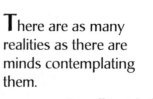

There are as many realities as there are minds contemplating them.

Russell L. Ackoff

Rather, audits should be conducted at major milestones in the project, so that learning can take place as the job progresses. As Peter Senge has shown in his book, *The Fifth Discipline*, the organization that knows how to *learn* has a real competitive advantage. This must be true of project learning as well as general learning.

Further, if a project is getting into serious trouble, the audit should reveal such difficulty so that a decision can be made to continue or terminate the work. Consider, as an example, a company that develops new products. Figure 9.6 shows cash flow in such a project as a function of time.[1]

Reading the time line from left to right, we have the following events. There is some time labeled T_o at which the *opportunity* to sell a product occurs. If you had the product at that time, you could start selling it immediately. Unfortunately, you may not have a product that meets the needs of customers at that time. Further, you don't even know that the need exists.

The next point, T_p is the time at which the need for the product is *perceived* by the company. They are now aware that a market exists for the product. However, they still do not have it. In addition, they cannot begin to develop it immediately. No funding is available, or no personnel to work on the project. So another time delay occurs until point T_b, where *development* work begins.

FIGURE 9.6
CASH FLOW IN A DEVELOPMENT PROJECT

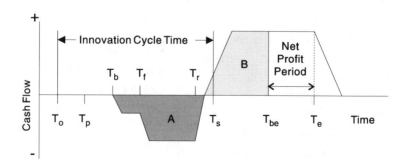

At this point, cash flow for this product starts going negative. The company is spending money to develop the product, but there is nothing to sell. Note that there may be an initial phase where some investigation or feasibility work is performed, so negative cash flow does not reach its maximum level for a short period. If the initial study is positive, then full-scale development begins and cash flow reaches its maximum negative value.

The next point, T_r is when the product is *released* to production. Then comes point T_s, the point at which first *sales* are made. At this point, cash flow becomes positive and remains positive until T_e is reached. This is the point where the product effectively reaches *extinction*. A few more units may be sold, but the product is obsolete in the market.

Between T_s and T_e is another point, labeled T_{be}. This is the *break-even* point, where the money spent to develop the product is recovered. This point is the one where the area under the positive-cash-flow curve equals the area under the negative cash-flow curve. The area to the right of the break-even point is the *profit* the company will make on the product before it becomes extinct.

Now consider the extinction point, T_e. This point is not fixed in time. If a competitor brings out a new product that is superior to the old one in some way, then the current product becomes extinct. This means that the extinction point can move leftward, and could conceivably happen before break-even is reached. Should that happen, the company not only will make no profits, it will lose money on the product.

In volatile markets like the computer business, this happens frequently. Some markets are more stable, so T_e does not move around very much. I know of one company that experienced a shift forward in T_e before they could release a new product. They decided to cancel the development project because they realized that they would ultimately lose money on the job. It cost them over $100 million to close down the project, but they considered that move the only one that made sense.

Note that every organization wants to minimize the delays between T_o and T_p and between T_p and T_d. They also want to keep the development time short if there is a possibility that extinction can move leftward.

What this emphasizes is the need to use audits together with environmental scanning to decide if projects should be continued. In general, project managers do not make such decisions, but I believe we must understand how they are made and perhaps even make recommendations occasionally that projects should be canceled.

Marvin Patterson, who was vice president of product development at Hewlett-Packard, in his book *Accelerating Innovation*, writes that if a company is not canceling *any* product-development projects, they are probably in error. On the other hand, if they cancel too many, then there is something wrong with the project selection process. That is, jobs are being done that should never have been started.

How many should be canceled? How many is too many? That is hard to answer in any quantitative way. Only careful analysis of overall project returns can provide the answer.

In summary, following are some of the general reasons for conducting periodic project audits:

- Improve project performance together with the management of the project.

- Ensure that quality of project work does not take a back seat to schedule and cost concerns.

- Reveal developing problems early, so that action can be taken to deal with them.

- Identify areas where other projects (current or future) should be managed differently.

- Keep client(s) informed of project status. This can also help ensure that the completed project will meet the needs of the client.

- Reaffirm the organization's commitment to the project for the benefit of project team members.

- Learn what is being done well and what needs improvement so that the information can be used before the project ends, as well as later.

CONDUCTING THE PROJECT AUDIT

Ideally, a project audit should be conducted by an independent examiner, who can remain objective in the assessment of information. However, the audit must be conducted in a spirit of learning, rather than in a climate of blame and punishment. If people are afraid that they will be "strung up" for problems, then they will hide those problems if at all possible.

Even so, this is hard to achieve. In many organizations the climate has been punitive for so long that people are reluctant to reveal any less-than-perfect aspects of project performance. Chris Argyris (1990) has described the processes by which organizations continue ineffective practices. All of them are intended to help individuals "save face" or avoid embarrassment. In the end, they also prevent organizational learning.

To reiterate what was said above, it seems clear that auditors must be chosen carefully. An auditor with a *blame-and-punishment* mentality is certain to create more problems than solutions.

THE AUDIT REPORT

There may be varying degrees of audits conducted, from totally comprehensive, to partial, to less formal, cursory examinations. A formal, comprehensive audit should be followed by a report. The report should contain as a minimum the following:

1. *Current project status.* This is best shown using earned-value analysis, as presented in the following chapter. However, when earned-value analysis is not used, status should still be reported with as great a degree of accuracy as possible.

2. *Future status.* This is a forecast of what is expected to happen in the project. Are significant deviations expected in

schedule, cost, performance, or scope? If so, the nature of such changes should be specified.

3. ***Status of critical tasks.*** The status of critical tasks, particularly those on the critical path, should be reported. Tasks that have high levels of technical risk should be given special attention, as should those being performed by outside vendors or subcontractors, over which the project manager may have limited control.

4. ***Risk assessment.*** Have any risks been identified that highlight potential for monetary loss, project failure, or other liabilities?

5. ***Information relevant to other projects.*** What has been learned from this audit that can or should be applied to other projects, whether presently in progress or about to start?

6. ***Limitations of the audit.*** What factors might limit the validity of the audit? Are any assumptions suspect? Is any data missing or suspect of contamination? Was anyone uncooperative in providing information for the audit?

As a general comment, the simpler and more straightforward a project audit report, the better. The information should be organized so that planned versus actual results can be easily compared. Significant deviations should be highlighted and explained. In Figure 9.7 is a form used for very simple project audits. For more comprehensive ones, the form will not be enough; an audit report should be created, capturing the same information.

FIGURE 9.7
A PROJECT AUDIT FORM

Project Audit or Post-Mortem Analysis

Project:

Prepared by: Date:

For the period from   to:

Evaluate the following objectives:
Performance was on target ☐, below target ☐, above target ☐
Budget was on target ☐, overspent ☐, underspent ☐
Schedule was on target ☐, behind ☐, ahead ☐

Overall, was the project a success? Yes ☐   No ☐

If not, what factors contributed to a negative evaluation?

What was done really well?

What could have been done better?

What recommendations would you make for future project application?

What would you do differently if you could do it over?

What have you learned that can be applied to future projects?

QUESTIONS FOR REVIEW

1. How is control exercised in project management?

---

2. Why is empowerment a useful concept to apply in projects?

---

3. Why does an individual need a personal working plan?

---

4. What is one factor that might keep a project audit or post mortem from being very effective?

---

5. At what points in a project should audits be conducted?

KEY POINTS *from Chapter 9*

- Control should be thought of in terms of information, rather than power.
- Work is controlled, not workers.
- People should be empowered by applying the standard operating procedure provided in the chapter.
- People will not admit problems if they are punished for having them, and innovation will be reduced.
- A third-order feedback system is the best model for use in project control.

Reference

1. This figure is adapted from one by Marvin Patterson in his book *Accelerating Innovation* (Van Nostrand, 1993), p. 4.

Chapter 10

PROJECT CONTROL USING EARNED–VALUE ANALYSIS

MEASURING PROGRESS

Even though there are limits in assessing exactly how much work has been done on a project, there can be no control unless some

> **var • i • ance:**
> any deviation from plan

measurement is done. The most widely used method of measuring project progress is through *variance* or *earned-value* analysis.

Variance analysis allows the project manager to determine "trouble spots" in the project and to take corrective action. As was mentioned previously, there are three areas of the project that the project manager is expected to control. These are the *good, fast, cheap* objectives. Because of the difficulty of quantifying the performance objective (good), variance analysis is usually not applied to measure quality, but is only used to track the cost and schedule targets. In that case, the project manager will have to monitor the quality targets, using whatever standards can be developed, and take necessary steps to ensure that they are met.

To see how this works, let us consider a small bar chart schedule as shown in Figure 10.1. There are only three tasks involved. During the first week, we spend $800 on Task A, as it is the only one active at that time. Note that the $800 expenditure is the product of 40 hours of labor applied during the week, at a loaded labor rate of $20 per hour. The term *loaded labor rate* means the direct salary paid to the person plus the overhead (fringe benefits, electricity, building rental, etc.) involved in doing work.

In the second week, we have both Task A and Task B active. The labor cost for Task B is $3,000. It is derived from the product of 100 hours of labor (which would be several people working) times a loaded labor rate of $30 per hour. The reason I have varied the labor rates is because in many organizations labor rates are different for each department or craft involved in a project. Thus, this is the most general case.

FIGURE 10.1
SCHEDULE TO ILLUSTRATE CUMULATIVE SPENDING

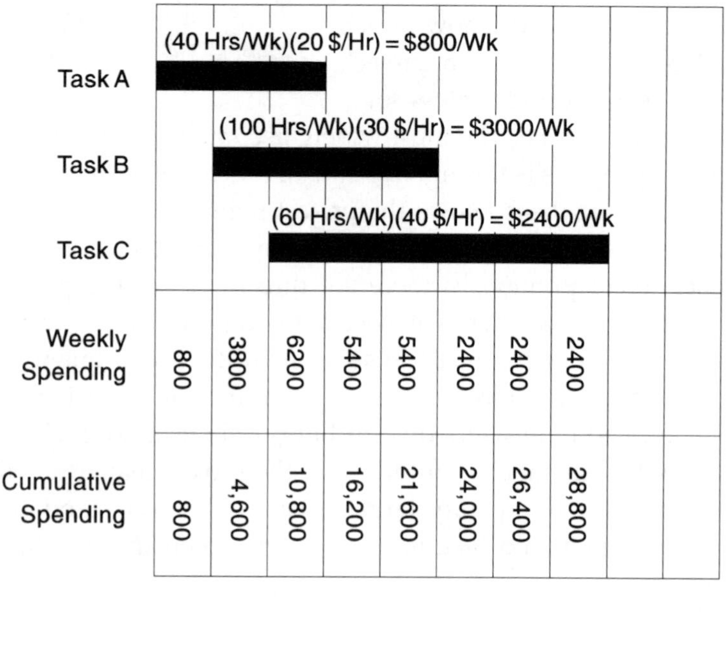

Task A	(40 Hrs/Wk)(20 $/Hr) = $800/Wk									
Task B		(100 Hrs/Wk)(30 $/Hr) = $3000/Wk								
Task C			(60 Hrs/Wk)(40 $/Hr) = $2400/Wk							
Weekly Spending	800	3800	6200	5400	5400	2400	2400	2400		
Cumulative Spending	800	4,600	10,800	16,200	21,600	24,000	26,400	28,800		

In the third week, all three tasks are active, so the total expenditure during that week is $6,200. The weekly expenditures of labor dollars are shown under the bar chart. The line under the weekly figures shows the *cumulative* expenditure for labor. If these figures are plotted, we arrive at a cumulative spending curve, as shown in Figure 10.2. Now, since this curve is derived directly from the schedule, it represents the *planned expenditure of effort* on the project. It is, therefore, a *baseline plan* for the project, expressed in labor dollars. Further, since control consists of comparing progress to plan, and this curve represents the plan, we can track progress against it and determine where corrective action must be taken to correct for any deviations from the plan.

This curve is called a Budgeted Cost of Work Scheduled (BCWS) curve. It forms the heart of the method for tracking projects called *earned-value analysis.*

Note that we do not include any expenses for materials or capital equipment in these figures. We are going to track work or

FIGURE 10.2

CUMULATIVE SPENDING FOR SAMPLE BAR CHART

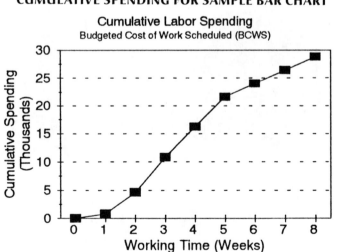

217

effort only with this graph. However, we certainly want to keep up with materials and capital expenditures; we simply do so in a different part of our accounting reports.

BCWS curves can often be plotted automatically by transferring spending data from a scheduling program (which calculates labor expenses on a daily or weekly basis by multiplying

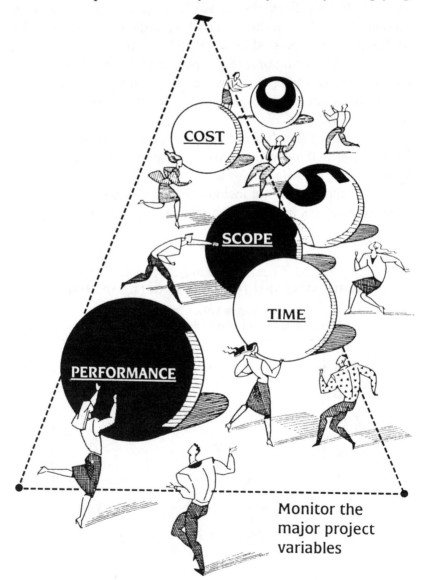

Monitor the major project variables

labor rates times manpower expended) to a graphics program using a DIF file or some other file-transfer format.

As we have said, we want to monitor all four of the major project variables, *performance, cost, time,* and *scope.* If we track progress against this curve, we can monitor all but performance, as was mentioned above. If the labor expenditures go up or down, we will see a deviation from the planned expenditure. Likewise, if the scheduled work is not on target, a point can be plotted and compared to the target, and a deviation can be detected. Finally, if the scope of work to be done changes, the BCWS curve will shift up or down, and progress will then be tracked against the new curve. As has been stated previously, a significant change in scope should be approved before being implemented.

As for the schedule and cost objectives, the following terms define what is to be monitored:

- *Cost Variance:* Compares only deviations from budget and provides no comparisons of work scheduled and work accomplished.

- *Schedule Variance:* Compares planned versus actual work completed. This variance can be translated into the dollar value of the work, so that all variances can be specified in monetary terms.[1]

In order to make cost and schedule variance measurements, three variables are used. The first, BCWP, has been introduced above. All three variables are defined in the following paragraphs, together with examples of how they are calculated.

- *BCWS* (Budgeted Cost of Work Scheduled): The budgeted cost of work scheduled to be done in a given time period, or the level of effort budgeted to be performed in that period. This is the *target* or *plan* that one is supposed to follow. The calculation method for this variable was illustrated above, so it will not be repeated here. Do note that the budgeted cost of work scheduled for a given time period is generally the sum of two or more products. For the example schedule in Figure 10.1, during week three, it is the sum of expenditures on tasks A, B, and C, or $6,200.

- **BCWP** (Budgeted Cost of Work Performed): The budgeted cost of work actually performed in a given period. BCWP is also called **earned value.** It is a measure of how much work has been accomplished.

It is easiest to understand if you first assume you are making something tangible, like widgets. Assume you were supposed to make 1,000 widgets, each of which has a value to the company of $50. This is the *value* of widgets, not their cost.

Now assume that during the time being tracked you made only 800 widgets. They are all good, so they still have a value to the organization of $50 each, or a total of $40,000. But you have made only 80% of the number of widgets that the schedule called for. We can then conclude that you are behind schedule, since you have made fewer widgets in the time period than you were supposed to make.

Similarly, for any kind of work, we can compute BCWP by simply looking at what was supposed to be done (BCWS) and looking at the percentage of work actually completed. For example, if Task A in Figure 10.1 has been worked on for one week, and the person only completed 80% of the work that first week, we can calculate BCWP as:

$$BCWP = 0.80 \times BCWS = 0.80 \times \$800 = \$640$$

- **ACWP** (Actual Cost of Work Performed): The amount of money actually spent in completing work in a given period. This is the amount of money paid to workers (wages only—no material costs are included in any of these figures) to do the work that was completed during the time period in question.

To continue with the above example, assume that the work completed was done at a labor rate of $22 per hour, and that the person doing Task A actually worked 40 hours. The ACWP, then, is:

$$ACWP = \$22 \times 40 = \$880$$

Now, from these figures, we can calculate deviations from planned performance, using the following formulas:

$$Cost\ Variance = BCWP - ACWP$$

$$Schedule\ Variance = BCWP - BCWS\ (dollar\ value)$$

Plugging numbers into these formulas, we have the following results:

$$Cost\ Variance = \$640 - \$880 = -\$240$$

A negative cost variance means that the project is spending more than it should—thus, a negative variance is *unfavorable*.

$$Schedule\ Variance = \$640 - \$800 = -\$160$$

Again, a negative schedule variance means that the project is behind schedule, and so is also *unfavorable*.

Looking at these two figures together tells us that the project has gotten behind schedule in the amount of $160 worth of work, and that labor cost is over by $240. Thus, the project is both behind schedule and overspent at the same time.

This analysis can tell us the status of a project for all possible combinations. To show how this is done, we will analyze project status by comparing ACWP and BCWP against BCWS in graphic form. Consider the curves in Figure 10.3. On a given date, the project is supposed to have involved $50,000 (50K) in labor (BCWS). The actual cost of the work performed (ACWP) is 60K. These figures are usually obtained from Accounting, and are derived from all of the time cards that have reported labor applied to the project. Finally, the budgeted cost of work performed (BCWP) is 40K. Under these conditions, the project would be behind schedule and underspent.

To understand this, the project has spent 60K to accomplish only 40K worth of work. That means an overspend of $20,000. The plan called for 50K worth of work to be done, but they have only completed 40K worth, so they are behind schedule as well.

One point is important to note before we proceed. It is not enough to understand what a variance means. You must next find out what *caused* it, and then you must decide what to do to

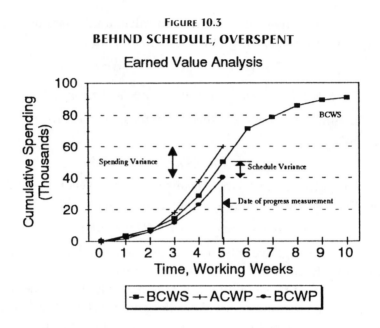

FIGURE 10.3
BEHIND SCHEDULE, OVERSPENT

correct for it. You must also determine if the figures are correct. Is the actual scope of work completed represented by the BCWP number? If not, then the project is not really where it is supposed to be. How about the quality of the work done? Sometimes, when deadlines are tight, people meet the schedule by sacrificing quality. Only when you are sure that both scope and quality are where they are supposed to be can you proceed with the analysis.

Assuming that the scope and quality are correct, when a project is overspent and behind schedule at the same time, it is usually because a snag has been hit. People are putting in the hours, but making no progress solving the problem. Or the work has turned out to be much more difficult than expected. That means that original estimates are optimistic.

What do you do? Can you salvage the project? Can you help the people doing the work? Can you get back on schedule and budget, or is the slip permanent? If the costs continue to increase and progress continues to slip, should we consider canceling the project? These are just some of the questions that must be answered. I will talk more about canceling projects later on, when I introduce another measure, the critical ratio. For now, let us continue with other scenarios.

Figure 10.4 illustrates another combination of variances. The BCWP and ACWP curves both fall at the same point, 60K. This means that the project is ahead of schedule, but spending correctly for the amount of work done. To see this, the project has spent 60K and has accomplished 60K worth of work. However, the plan called for 50K worth of work, so the status is ahead of schedule.

Is there any potential problem with being in this position? At first glance, there is none. However, if you consider how a project can be in this position, you find that more resources must have been applied than were planned, but at the planned labor rate (since there is no spending variance). Then the question is, where did the project manager get the extra people? In most environments, resources are shared, so it may be that this project

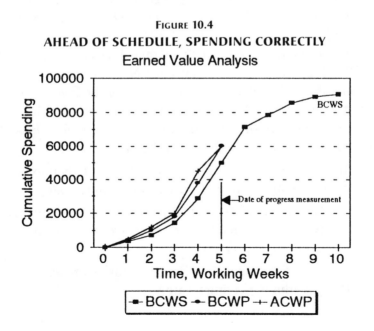

FIGURE 10.4
AHEAD OF SCHEDULE, SPENDING CORRECTLY

is ahead of schedule at someone else's expense. However, in construction work, it may be that you had planned for some weather delays, but the weather has been good, so you have gotten ahead of schedule. Labor costs, though, have been what you planned.

Another consideration is cash flow. While the project is ahead of schedule, can it be funded at the rate being spent? If not, then the work would have to be decelerated. For a construction project, you might be getting progress payments based on work completed. To you, this variance looks good. You did the work in advance, and want to be paid for it. Your customer, however, may not be able to advance the money at the rate you are earning it, so they won't be happy with your "good fortune."

The next set of curves illustrates another status. In Figure 10.5 the BCWP and ACWP curves are both at 40K. This means the project is behind schedule and underspent. This project is probably starved for resources (possibly the victim of another project manager being ahead). Labor is costing what it is supposed to cost, but not enough work is being done to stay on schedule. The problem for this project manager is that she will probably go over budget in trying to catch up, since premium labor will most likely be required.

Finally, Figure 10.6 looks like Figure 10.3, except the ACWP and BCWP curves have been reversed. Now the project is ahead of schedule and underspent. The accomplished work has an earned value of 60K, but the actual cost of that labor has been only 40K. There are three possibilities that can explain how this project manager achieved the result shown.

1. Actual labor rates were considerably lower than expected, and the people were more efficient than anticipated.

2. The project team had a "lucky break." They had expected to have to work really hard to solve a problem, but it turned out to be very easy.

3. The project manager "sandbagged" his estimates. He padded everything, playing it safe.

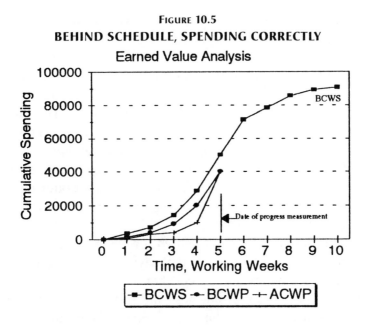

FIGURE 10.5
BEHIND SCHEDULE, SPENDING CORRECTLY

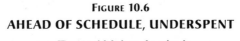

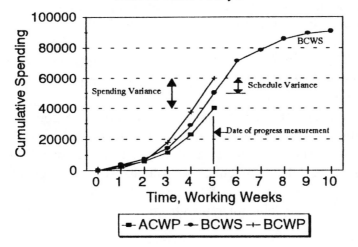

FIGURE 10.6
AHEAD OF SCHEDULE, UNDERSPENT

If you believe situation one, you will believe anything. It is very unlikely that both variances would happen at the same time.

Situation two happens occasionally. When all the planets are aligned—about once in a zillion years, you say. You bet!

Situation three is the most likely explanation. The project manager was playing it safe. And he would tell you that there is no problem. After all, the project will come in slightly ahead of schedule and underspent, which means he will give money back to the company. No problem. The controller no doubt has the budgeted funds in an interest-bearing account, so the company is earning interest on the money.

Right. But banks are not known for being overly generous with interest, and there is a rule that says that if you can't make a greater return on an investment than the interest a bank will pay, you should go out of business and just put your money in the bank. You don't need the aggravation of being in business, and you aren't very good at it anyway.

As a matter of fact, the economists would say that there is a real *opportunity cost* involved in this project. The company has lost an opportunity to get a good return on its investment because the money was budgeted for this project, and therefore could not be used anywhere else. This is another problem with padding.

The question is, naturally, what is reasonable. We certainly cannot expect to have zero variances in a project. And this is true.

However, there is no easy answer to the question. As was mentioned in Chapter 4, well-defined construction projects can be held to very small tolerances—as small as plus or minus 3%. Research and development projects are likely to run higher tolerances, perhaps in the range of 15 to 25%. Each organization has to develop acceptable tolerances based on experience.

REFINING THE ANALYSIS

The only problem with the analysis presented here is that it is an *aggregate* figure, and would not permit determination of what area of the project a problem exists in, and may even hide a problem completely. For that reason, the variance analysis needs to be conducted on a task-by-task basis.

This is usually done at the Work Package level, but it can be at any level of the Work Breakdown Structure at which one wishes to track project progress. By summing the individual Work Package figures, the aggregate figure can be used to gauge the overall "health" of the project, while a line-by-line accounting can be used to spot specific problem areas.

The importance of this was brought home to me by a client who reported that they had been using aggregate analysis to gauge project status for some time, and they discovered that a $100,000 overspend in one area of a project was being counterbalanced by a $100,000 underspend in another area. It looked as if the project

> **D**etailed activities—when they're useful.
>
> Detailed activities are very helpful in estimating. (I've never seen a project shrink in size as it is defined in more detail!) However, detailed activities are less useful in tracking progress because they're often not what we really end up doing to develop a work product or accomplish an objective. Detailed activities describe what we think we're going to do when we plan the work. But we usually don't have to perform those exact steps to achieve the result we promised. So when we come to tracking progress, we often find that in producing a required work product we performed only some of the activities we defined, and performed many others we never defined. Not only is it hard to record the status and effort on detailed activities, they don't really give an accurate measure of progress. Advice: Do define detailed activities to estimate realistically. But record actual effort spent at a level higher where the WBS is more stable. And try to measure progress in terms of physical results, e.g., drawings produced, modules tested, change requests evaluated, etc.
>
> *Tom Conlon*

was in good shape, but such huge variances indicate a lack of control, and should be addressed.

Variance thresholds can be established that define the level at which reports must be sent to various levels of management within an organization.

By combining cost and schedule variances, an integrated cost/schedule reporting system can be developed. In Figure 10.7 is a form that illustrates the use of this concept to track a project. The form has been filled in with some data to illustrate the various combinations of the numbers and their meanings.

The Critical Ratio

Part of the C/SCSC system involves calculation of two ratios that indicate how well the project is doing. One of these is called a *Cost Performance Index* (CPI) and the other is called a *Schedule Performance Index* (SPI). The CPI is the ratio of BCWP and ACWP (BCWP/ACWP). The SPI is the ratio of BCWP and BCWS (BCWP/BCWS). Meredith & Mantel (1985) describe a control-charting method that can be used to analyze progress in projects.

For readers unfamiliar with control chart methods, the idea is that, if you make a widget and measure some attribute of it, that attribute should have some average value and some standard deviation. The standard deviation will be a function of the capability of the process to hold certain tolerances. For example, if you were making steel rod that has an average diameter of 0.25 inch, and the standard deviation is 0.01 inch, you would expect that 68% of the rods made would have a diameter that is in the range of 0.25 ± 0.01 inch. Likewise, 95% of the rods would have a diameter that falls in the range of 0.25 ± 0.02 inch, and 99.74% of all rods would have a diameter in the range of 0.25 ± 0.03 inch.

Now suppose you took a sample from the production line and measured the diameter, and you found a rod with a diameter of 0.29 inch. This is outside the three sigma limits for the distribution, so there is a chance the process might be out of control, and you should check it right away.

Figure 10.7

EARNED VALUE REPORT FORM

Earned Value Report

Project No.: Date: 23-Nov-94 FILE: PROJRPT2

Description: Page______of _____

Prepared by: Signed:

	Cumulative-to-date			Variance		At Completion				
WBS #	BCWS	BCWP	ACWP	Sched.	Cost	Budgeted	Latest Est.	Variance	Critical Ratio	Action Required
				0	0			0	NA	NA
				0	0			0	NA	NA
				0	0			0	NA	NA
				0	0			0	NA	NA
				0	0			0	NA	NA
				0	0			0	NA	NA
				0	0			0	NA	NA
				0	0			0	NA	NA
				0	0			0	NA	NA
				0	0			0	NA	NA
				0	0			0	NA	NA
				0	0			0	NA	NA
				0	0			0	NA	NA
				0	0			0	NA	NA
TOTALS	0	0	0	0	0	0	0	0	NA	NA

NOTE: Negative variance is unfavorable. If Critical Ratio <0.6, INFORM MANAGEMENT!

( ) = NEGATIVE VALUES

There are other rules for interpreting charts. For example, if you measured samples of rods and found that eight samples in a row fell above or below the nominal 0.25 inch diameter, there is a chance that the process is drifting. You would check immediately and see what is happening, before you make too much unacceptable product.

Meredith and Mantel applied this idea to monitoring projects. They calculate a *critical ratio*, which is the product of the CPI and SPI, using the following formula:

$$CriticalRatio = (SPI) * (CPI)$$

or

$$CriticalRatio = \frac{BCWP}{BCWS} * \frac{BCWP}{ACWP}$$

As is true for control charts used to monitor manufacturing processes, rules can be devised for responding to the critical ratio. Meredith and Mantel (1985) suggest limits and actions as shown in the diagram in Figure 10.8. These limits are only suggestions, and the project manager will have to devise limits that are appropriate for his/her own programs.

Using a spreadsheet allows the process of interpretation to be automated. The progress report in Figure 10.7. is set up with an "IF" formula in the final column. This formula looks at the critical ratio calculated in the previous column and subjects it to tests. Based on those tests, the formula returns the words "OK," "CHECK," "RED FLAG," or "NA," meaning no critical ratio has yet been calculated in the cell being tested. The tests are simple. In words:

Print "OK" if the critical ratio (CR) is between the values 0.9 and 1.2.

Print "CHECK" if the CR is between 0.8 to 0.9 or 1.2 to 1.3.

Print "RED FLAG" if the CR is above 1.3 or below 0.8.

In addition, if the ratio falls below 0.6, company management should be informed, as progress is so much worse than expected that the project may be a candidate for cancellation.

FIGURE 10.8
A CRITICAL RATIO CONTROL CHART
Critical Ratio Control Limits

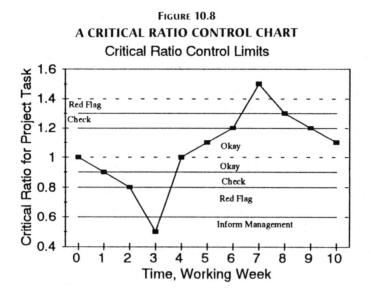

This is because to have a critical ratio so low means that the project is usually behind schedule and overspent.

Following is the IF-formula for a Lotus or QuatroPro spreadsheet with the critical ratio in cell K10 and the IF-formula in cell L10. The formula is one contiguous flow; it is broken only because it would have to be printed in unreadable type to make it fit on one line.

@IF(K10>1.3#OR#K10<0.8,"RED FLAG",@IF(K10>1.2#AND#

K10<1.3#OR#K10>0.8#AND#K10<0.9,"CHECK","OK"))

THE NEED FOR ALL THREE MEASURES
Occasionally project managers fall into the trap of trying to track their projects using only BCWS and ACWP. As long as they see no difference between what they had planned to spend and what has actually been spent, they think the project is running smoothly. However, we saw from the above examples that this may not be true, and the manager would not spot a problem until it had perhaps gotten serious.

In fact, a controller from one organization told me that he constantly sees this happen in his company. For a long time the project goes along being underspent or right on target. Then the project manager realizes that the work is not getting done as required, and a big effort is applied to catch up. The usual result is that spending overshoots the planned target. This is illustrated by the curves in Figure 10.9.

VARIANCE ANALYSIS USING HOURS ONLY

In some organizations, project managers are not held accountable for costs, but only for the hours actually worked on the project and for the work actually accomplished. The argument used to justify this way of working is that project managers usually have no control over labor rates. This is because an individual may be assigned to the project by his functional manager simply because he was the only person available who could do the job, but his rate is 25% higher than what the project manager expected to pay when original estimating was done.

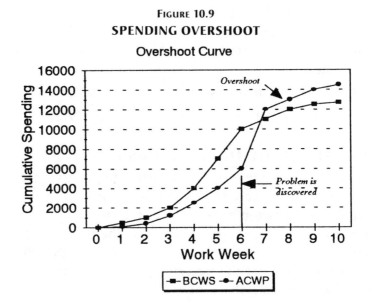

FIGURE 10.9
SPENDING OVERSHOOT

The other cause of problems is that the accounting department may change burden allocation rates (for valid reasons), which causes total labor costs to go above original estimates. This naturally creates a cost variance in the project, but one over which the project manager had no control, and so the argument is that he should not be held accountable.

In this case, the same analysis can be conducted by stripping the dollars off the figures. This results in the following:

BCWS becomes Total Planned (or Scheduled) Hours

BCWP becomes Earned Hours (Scheduled hours x percentage of work accomplished)

ACWP becomes Actual Hours Worked

Using the new numbers, it is possible to compute the following variances:

Schedule Variance = BCWP - BCWS = Earned Hours - Planned Hours

Labor Variance = BCWP - ACWP = Earned Hours - Actual Hours Worked

There is one inaccuracy introduced by this modification. ACWP is actually the composite of two variances—a labor rate variance and a labor hours variance. When money is stripped off, you lose the capability to see that costs are varying because of labor rate changes. In some environments, that may be acceptable.

TRUE PROJECT COST VERSUS APPARENT COST

The shape of a cumulative spending curve for a project is a function of how labor is applied. The typical curve has a soft "S-curvature," which occurs because the initial phase of work is preparatory in nature and only a few people can get started at once. Then the work accelerates and finally tapers off near the end of the project as "loose ends" are wrapped up. However, other shapes are possible. Figure 10.10 shows three possibilities.

Curve A is the typical curve. Curve B is obtained when resources are allocated linearly to the project—that is, resources

FIGURE 10.10
THREE POSSIBLE SPENDING CURVES

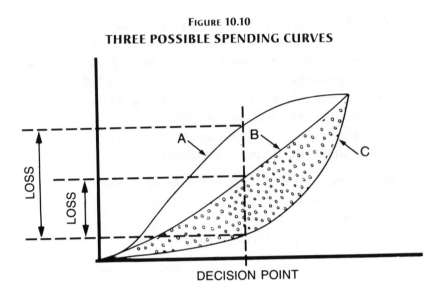

DECISION POINT

are level-loaded. Curve C shows what happens when the project is back-end loaded. There is a long period in which the work progresses slowly, then accelerates. Note that all three curves result in the exact same total project cost at the end.

However, they all have advantages and disadvantages. Curve A would be useful when the organization gets progress payments for work completed. Curve B would be an advantage when cash flow is a problem.

Curve C would be helpful if some preliminary work must be done to decide whether to scrub the project or continue. Assuming that the decision could be made in all three scenarios, if the project were canceled, the differences between points where the curves intersect a vertical line would represent the different losses that would occur. Naturally, the losses would be smallest with Curve C.

The next point that is important is to consider the area between any two curves. For example, the area between Curves B and C has been shaded. The units on that area are dollars multiplied by time, or the *time-value-of-money*. We have a special name for that product. It is called *interest!* Therefore, the area between any two curves represents the difference in the cost of capital for each project.

In the case where progress payments are being received, that interest advantage would be obtained with Curve A. The money comes in fast and the company can invest it.

When money is being borrowed, however, the interest advantage would be obtained with Curve C. The money is held as long as possible, then spent rapidly.

The problem with Curve C, however, is that back-end loading a project increases risk of being late. Chances are always good that problems will occur near the end of a project, and if it is already loaded heavily to meet a deadline, there may be no chance of adding resources to deal with last-minute problems.

The point of all this is that by allocating resources to a project correctly, the project manager can actually affect the *true cost* of the work, even though the *apparent cost* would be the same for several different plans.

AN EXAMPLE USING PROJECT WORKBENCH™

To illustrate project tracking with software, we will use the schedule developed previously to show resource allocation. For your convenience, the schedule is repeated in Figure 10.11.

Assume that we want to show status at the end of the first week. The week ends on June 21, so we can set the report date accordingly.

Only two tasks are scheduled to have any work done on them during this period. For Task A, Tom Trump was scheduled to do five days of work on an eight-day-duration activity. Let's say that Tom has gotten behind. Instead of having all five days of work completed, he has only 40% of the total done. That means he has done a little more than what should have been done in three-days. He estimates that it will take almost all of the remaining five days to complete the job. However, he has actually put in a total of four days' effort on the job, meaning that his labor costs should be about half of the total originally planned for the job.

For Task B, Charlie Clark was supposed to do three days of work up-front, simultaneously with five days of work for Sue Simms being required. We will say that they have done exactly what was planned and are right on target. The total duration for Task B was originally planned to be 15 days. We will say that what was planned in the first five days has been accomplished. Does that mean that the work is 33% complete?

For this task the answer is no. The work is not linear. More work per day is done in the first three days than in the remaining 12 days. This is where earned-value analysis provides a good measuring method. From the original plan, we find that the loaded labor rate for Charlie Clark is $160 per day and for Sue Simms it is $240. This means that the BCWS for the first five days of the activity is:

$$\$160 \times 3 = \$480 \text{ for Charlie Clark}$$

$$\$240 \times 5 = \$1200 \text{ for Sue Simms}$$

$$TOTAL: = \$1680 = BCWP$$

The total expenditure for the activity would be 10 more days of work by Sue Simms, added to the total for the first five days, or:

$$BAC = \$1680 + 10\ (240) = \$4080$$

That is, the total planned cost for activity B is $4080. If everything is right on target at the end of the first five days, then the amount of work completed is the ratio of the two figures, or:

$$\% \text{ Complete} = BCWP/BAC =$$

$$1680/4080 = 41\%$$

The question is, how do you show this on a schedule diagram? For a 15-day task, if you show 41% complete, it would look like six days of work are finished, which is not the case in a timescale sense. There are still 10 days of work remaining for Sue to do. This illustrates the difficulty of showing progress on bar charts. Only earned-value analysis provides a viable way of presenting status. In the case of Project Workbench, if you

Figure 10.11
PROJECT ZERO BEFORE WORK HAS STARTED

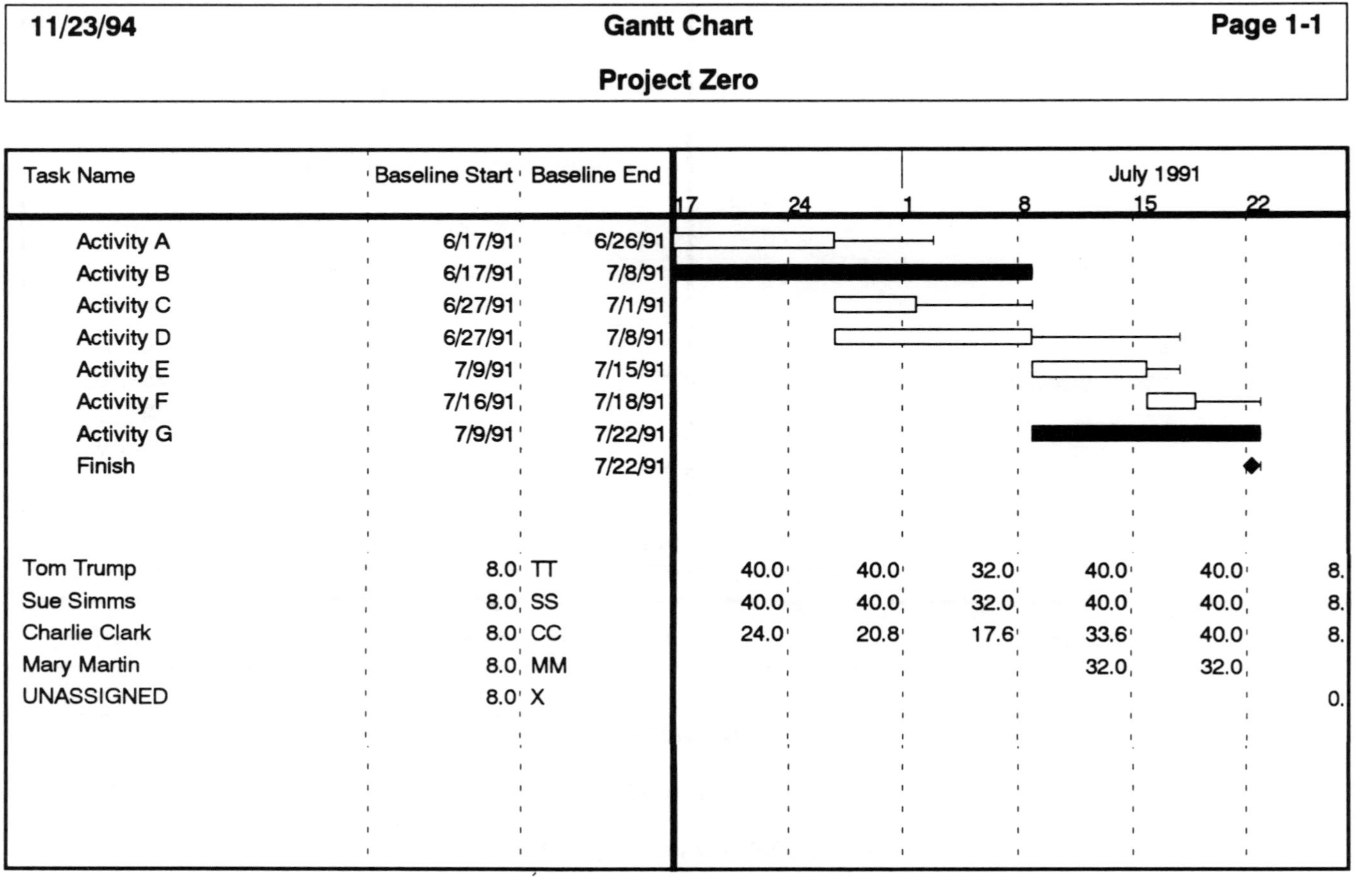

11/23/94	Gantt Chart	Page 1-1
	Project Zero	

July 1991

Task Name	Baseline Start	Baseline End	17	24	1	8	15	22	
Activity A	6/17/91	6/26/91							
Activity B	6/17/91	7/8/91							
Activity C	6/27/91	7/1/91							
Activity D	6/27/91	7/8/91							
Activity E	7/9/91	7/15/91							
Activity F	7/16/91	7/18/91							
Activity G	7/9/91	7/22/91							
Finish		7/22/91							
Tom Trump	8.0	TT	40.0	40.0	40.0	32.0	40.0	40.0	8.
Sue Simms	8.0	SS	40.0	40.0	40.0	32.0	40.0	40.0	8.
Charlie Clark	8.0	CC	24.0	20.8	17.6	33.6	40.0		8.
Mary Martin	8.0	MM					32.0	32.0	
UNASSIGNED	8.0	X							0.

237

FIGURE 10.12
SCHEDULE SHOWING PROGRESS

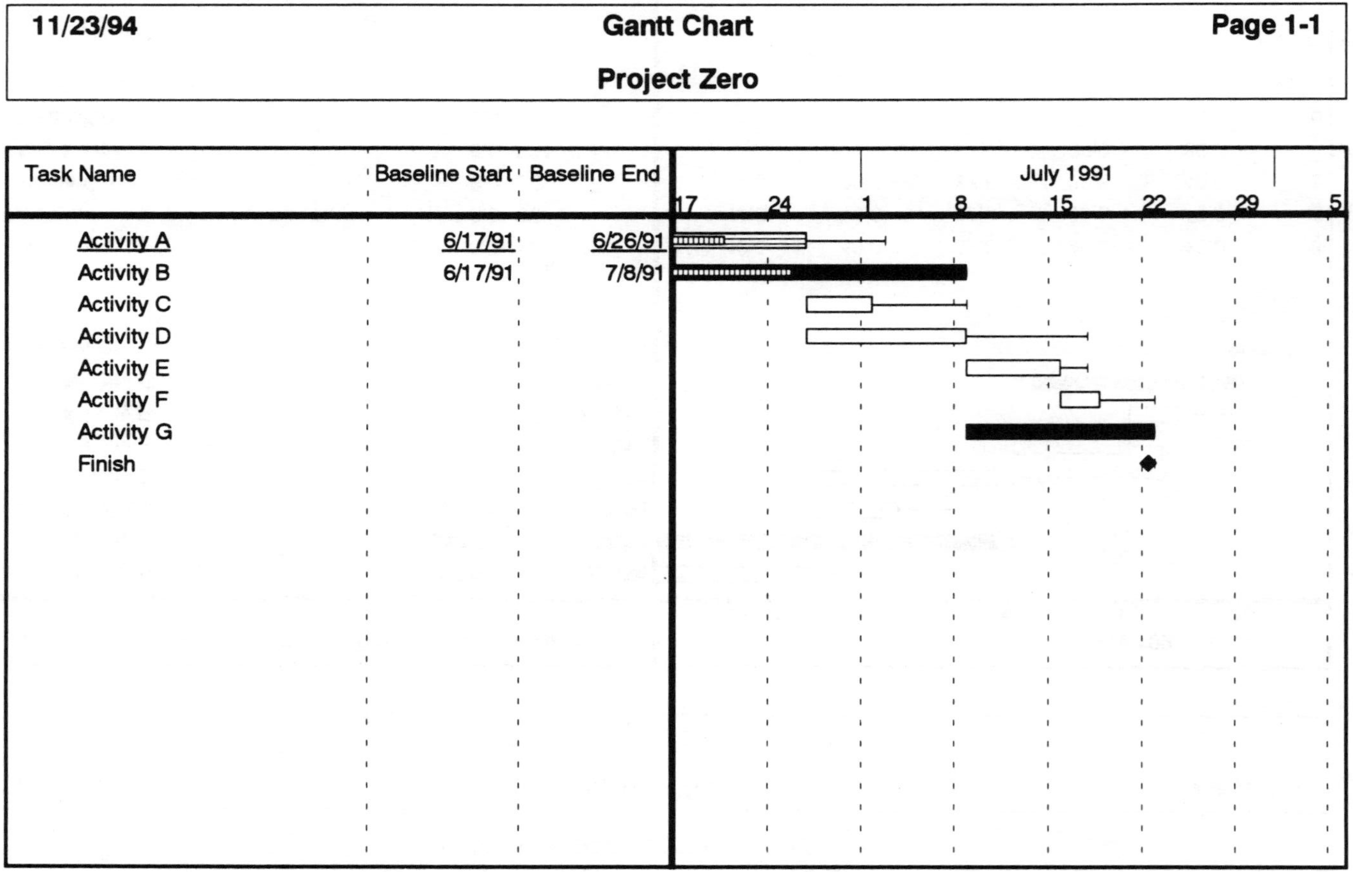
11/23/94
Gantt Chart
Page 1-1
Project Zero
Task Name
Baseline Start
Baseline End
July 1991
17
24
1
8
15
22
29
5
Activity A
6/17/91
6/26/91
Activity B
6/17/91
7/8/91
Activity C
Activity D
Activity E
Activity F
Activity G
Finish

choose to display percent complete, you have the schedule shown in Figure 10.12, which indicates that 41% of activity B is finished, and this is a bit misleading. The only way in which progress reporting on a bar graph can be shown unambiguously would be to separate the tasks being performed by each person so that you can report on them individually, and even this method is not perfect, since most work is a bit nonlinear.

However, an earned-value analysis is very clear in showing status. An earned-value report printed from Workbench is shown in Figure 10.13. The report shows that activity A is behind schedule and overspent already, and the EAC shows that the task is expected to cost $2,160, compared to the original $1,920 figure, or an overspend of $240, which is the extra day of work that Tom expects to put into the activity in order to complete it. Sue is not forecasting an at-completion variance, so the total project variance is $16,720 minus $16,480, or $240.

QUESTIONS FOR REVIEW

1. *What is the meaning of the term earned value (BCWP)?*

2. *If BCWP is a larger number than BCWS, is work ahead or behind schedule?*

3. *Why is it not acceptable to use only a comparison of ACWP and BCWS to track progress?*

4. *Why is it necessary to report progress at a low level of detail, rather than simply as a summary?*

5. *Of what value is a critical ratio?*

6. *How is work progress measured between milestones?*

Figure 10.15
EARNED VALUE REPORT FOR WORKBENCH

11/23/94	Cost Schedule Status Report (CSSR)							Page 1
				Project Zero				
Task Name	BCWS	BCWP	ACWP	SV	CV	BAC	EAC	VAC
Activity A	1,200.00	768.00	960.00	-432.00	-192.00	1,920.00	2,160.00	-240.00
Activity B	1,680.00	1,672.80	1,680.00	-7.20	-7.20	4,080.00	4,080.00	0.00
Activity C	0.00	0.00	0.00	0.00	0.00	0.00	480.00	-480.00
Activity D	0.00	0.00	0.00	0.00	0.00	0.00	2,000.00	-2,000.00
Activity E	0.00	0.00	0.00	0.00	0.00	0.00	1,000.00	-1,000.00
Activity F	0.00	0.00	0.00	0.00	0.00	0.00	600.00	-600.00
Activity G	0.00	0.00	0.00	0.00	0.00	0.00	6,400.00	-6,400.00
Finish								
Totals	2,880.00	2,440.80	2,640.00	-439.20	-199.20	6,000.00	16,720.00	-10,720.00

KEY POINTS *from Chapter 10*

- By analyzing deviations from plan (variances) a project manager can spot developing problems in time to take corrective action before they become serious.

- Earned-value analysis translates both schedule and budget measures into dollar values and tracks them against the original planned expenditure of effort, again translated into its dollar value.

- If a project is tracked only as an *aggregate,* it is possible to miss problems. Each activity in the project schedule should be tracked using earned-value analysis.

- The Critical Ratio is the product of the Schedule Performance Index and the Cost Performance Index.

Reference

1. In some organizations, project managers do not deal with costs, but rather with *labor hours.* Once standard variance analysis has been presented in terms of cost, a method of dealing with working hours will be presented.

Chapter 11

DEVELOPING THE PROJECT ORGANIZATION

An organization is a group of people who must **coordinate** their activities in order to meet their objectives. (Note the similarity to the definition for a team.) Coordination requires good communication and a clear understanding of the relationships and interdependencies among people. There is no **single best** organization structure; rather, the formation used must be one that optimizes performance by balancing human (or social), reward, and technical requirements (see Figure 11.1.)

Every organization consists of three central components, as shown in Figure 11.1. These components are related to each other in such a way that if one changes, it affects the other two.

A good example of this was the introduction of personal computers into organizations in the early 1980s. The impact has been enormous. Not only have people changed the way in which they interact, but the reward system in many organizations has changed as well. People who would not or could not become computer literate have, in some cases, found themselves "stuck" in dead-end jobs. They cannot advance or get as high raises as their peers who have gained computer skills.

FIGURE 11.1
COMPONENTS OF AN ORGANIZATION

The personal computer has also made it possible for people to do work at home that formerly would have required them to be at the office to do. They can even work while in hotels, planes, and so on, making their productivity greater than before.

But there are negatives as well. The computer has changed our concept of time. When I first started teaching seminars on how to use personal computers in project management, we were using the original VisiCalc™ spreadsheet, mostly on Apple II computers. Initially, people voiced a lot of "Wow!" and "Look at that!" comments as they watched the speed with which the computer could recalculate the row and column totals in a spreadsheet. Within three years, they were saying, "Darn, this thing is really slow!"

Jeremy Rifkin discusses this in more detail in his book, *Time Wars.*[1] Because of this change in our concept of time, we tend to want everything *yesterday,* and this is certainly pertinent to our concept of how long it should take to complete various activities in a project.

The point of this discussion is that the three components of an organization must be managed as well as the project itself. And since these three components will be affected by the form of organization chosen, then making the best choice is important.

Organization structure is dictated by communication needs together with such factors as technology and its rate of change, task complexity, resource availability, the nature of products and services being provided, competition, and decision-making requirements.

The *formal* organization is the one defined by the organization chart, which is established and sanctioned by company management. The *informal* organization, however, consists of the everyday relationships and communication patterns that exist among people, and may differ considerably from the formal structure. It may, in fact, be more important in determining where the company goes than the actual formal structure. The *project* organization is the one shown by a Linear Responsibility Chart.

The formal structure must provide each individual with a clear understanding of the authority, responsibility, and accountability given to him so that his work can be accomplished.

- *Authority* is the power granted to individuals so that they can make decisions that others are expected to follow. Authority is usually conferred by one's position.

- *Responsibility* is the obligation that individuals have to perform their assignments effectively.

- *Accountability* means that the individual is totally answerable for the satisfactory completion of a specific assignment.

In Chapter 9, a standard operating procedure was presented for empowering people, and it was pointed out that no

FIGURE 11.2
AUTHORITY-RESPONSIBILITY-ACCOUNTABILITY FIGURE

person can exercise control unless he or she has some authority to take corrective action when there is a deviation from a predetermined target. In addition, I said that people do not accept responsibility for the result of their actions if they are managed in an authoritarian way. So long as they do what they are told, if the outcome is not the one desired, they are not responsible. Rather, the person whose orders they were following is responsible.[2]

A consequence or corollary of this is that they also will not take any *initiative*. They finish one thing and wait to be told what to do next.

The lesson to be learned from all this is that we cannot delegate responsibility without also delegating authority commensurate with it, but organizations try to do so all the time.

TRADITIONAL ORGANIZATION

The traditional organization structure is a hierarchical form with a single manager at the top, to whom middle managers report. This line of reporting relationships continues downward to the lowest level of the organization. This form continues to be the predominant structure used in most organizations. In Figure 11.3 is an example of the traditional form.

There are some definite advantages to organizing a project in hierarchical form. Because the members of the group report to the project leader or one of her staff, loyalty is to the project, rather than to some other part of the company. Communication channels are well defined, and there is good control over personnel, since each employee has a single boss. This means that a manager has flexible use of personnel.

On the other hand, if the project group is fairly small, and there are several disciplines involved, problems are created by the hierarchical structure. For example, I am an electrical engineer. If I were to set up a project in hierarchical form, and if there were one programmer in the group, I would have a problem, since my knowledge of programming is very limited.

I would be unable to evaluate the quality of the programmer's work, and I would have no idea if his estimates of activity durations were reasonable or not. In addition, if I only had about enough work to keep the person busy for 85% of the time, I would have to pay for his full-time salary but only get an 85% return on my investment.

Consider also what happens when the programmer has difficulty with a technical problem. There may be no one else in the group to help him. If he were back in a group of programmers, he would be able to call on them to help.

It was for these and other reasons that other forms of project organization were tried in the 1950s and 1960s, culminating in a form that has become almost synonymous with project management. This is the *matrix* form, shown in Figure 11.4.

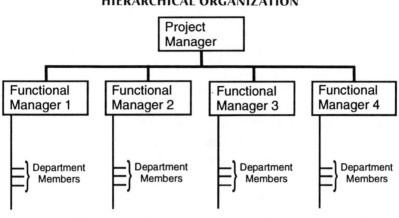

FIGURE 11.3
HIERARCHICAL ORGANIZATION

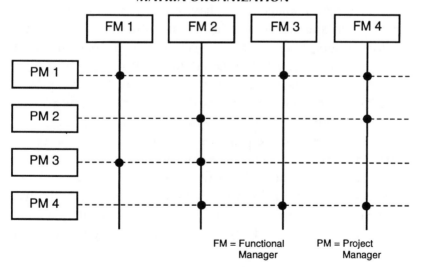

FIGURE 11.4
MATRIX ORGANIZATION

FM = Functional Manager   PM = Project Manager

MATRIX ORGANIZATION

The matrix form is intended to take advantage of pure functional structure in achieving the needs of a multidisciplinary project. It is ideally suited for companies, such as construction, that are "project driven."

A primary reason for using the matrix form is given by the answer to several questions. "Why should it be necessary to physically remove a technical person from her functional group? Why not leave her in her group and let her supervisor, who is herself a technical specialist in that discipline, worry about the quality of this person's work, her day-to-day work assignments, and so on." Indeed, why not?

So matrix leaves a company organized along functional lines (programmers, chemists, electrical engineers, carpenters, plumbers, accountants, and so on, in their own functional departments), and as projects are set up, people are drawn from those departments on an as-needed basis. The functional departments are shown in Figure 11.4 as having solid lines running vertically, a simplified illustration of the *vertical lines of authority* that exist in a hierarchical structure.

The project managers then have dashed lines of "authority" running horizontally across the hierarchical organization, and the dots at intersections indicate that a person (or persons) from the department above is assigned to work on the project as required. The dashed line is used to indicate that the project manager has limited (really *no*) authority over the person in the functional group.

This means that the project manager cannot give orders to people and "enforce" them by using his authority over the person, because he has none. Instead, he must get work done using *influence*, and a rule of thumb is that a project manager who has a matrix organization had better have very good interpersonal skills, together with good negotiating skills. He is going to need them!

In the end analysis, of course, we have already pointed out that authoritarian management does not work well in today's society, so both the project manager and the functional manager need good interpersonal skills.

MAKING MATRIX WORK

It is generally agreed that matrix organization is the only way to "fly" in managing projects, but such a form is extremely difficult to manage. Because people from each functional department are shared among a number of projects, there are always conflicts in which the same individual is needed on two or more projects at once. There are conflicts caused by disagreements about how work should be done. And there are problems caused by the fact that individuals assigned to a project really have their primary loyalty to their functional department, and not to the project.

In my experience, several important issues must be attended to if a project manager is going to be successful in a matrix organization. First, the relationship between the project manager and functional managers is absolutely vital to cultivate. I don't mean that a project manager must go out and drink beer with a functional manager every afternoon, or even socialize with him at all, for that matter.

What I mean is that a project manager must be on good terms with functional managers, should understand what makes them "tick," should understand their values and their ways of thinking, and should work to establish a relationship of respect with them.

To put it bluntly, if a functional manager "hates your guts," and you need that manager to go a little beyond the "call of duty" for you, then you are in trouble.

Second, since resources are shared across all of the projects in an organization, if a project manager sees that her work is going to slip, which means that people from a functional department won't be needed when originally planned, then she should advise the functional manager *immediately!* It is a difficult-enough job to juggle resources across a number of projects without being caught unawares on Monday morning by a project manager who announces that she doesn't have any work for those people as she had planned.

Third, project managers should have input to the performance appraisals that are written by functional managers on their people. This is one way to gain some commitment and loyalty to the project on the part of functional department members.

Finally, a project manager must be able to remove from her project any person who cannot or will not perform satisfactorily. Since they were hired by functional managers, a project manager cannot fire people from the organization, but she must be able to "fire" them from the project. Otherwise, how can she be held accountable for the overall project work?

I know that this is idealistic in some respects. I have lived with it first-hand. When a functional manager is told that a per-

A P.M. must be able to remove people who cannot (or will not) perform satisfactorily!

son is not performing and that you want someone else, he may say, "He's all I have to give you. Take him or leave him."

When that happens, the only recourse is to make the best of it or appeal to a higher authority in the organization and let them intervene. In any event, dealing with a problem employee in a matrix organization is a real problem, and one for which there are no easy solutions.

CROSS–FUNCTION MANAGEMENT

Even though matrix organization seems to make sense from a purely logical point of view, the form is still considered extremely difficult to manage. The fact that project managers cannot control allocation of resources is one particular reason why matrix projects so often fail.

In recent years there has been a developing trend to manage projects using a technique called *cross-function* management. Dimancescu (1992) argues that cross-function management is necessary to making today's organizations more competitive. He says:

> The new paradigm of cross-function management recognizes that *process*, or *how we get things done* must be treated as a strategic corporate priority. It argues that competition is won by treating all parts of the firm as a single unified whole. (p. 8)

> The objective of a cross function is to focus on critical process issues that cut across the whole enterprise. These . . . include . . . *quality, cost control, delivery, . . . purchasing, personnel training, research, and information management.* (p. 15)

Figure 11.5 shows one aspect of how cross-function management is supposed to work in managing projects. Note that the organization still employs vertical "chimneys," or functions, but the project coordinates efforts across those chimneys to achieve optimum results.

I believe the application of cross-function management in projects is the future of project management as it will be practiced. However, as Dimancescu points out in his book, we do not yet have good approaches to managing across functions.

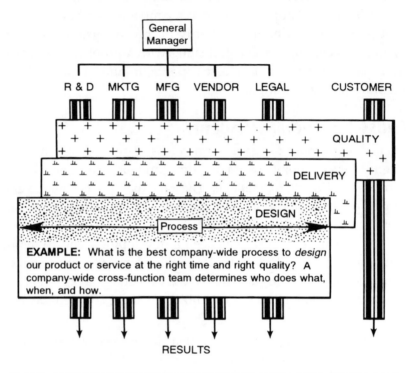

FIGURE 11.5
CROSS-FUNCTION PROCESS TEAMS

Cross-function process teams. Based on Dimancescu (1992)

QUESTIONS FOR REVIEW

1. *What is one of the major problems with the matrix organization?*

2. *What is the distinction between cross-function management and cross-functional management?*

3. *What is one of the most important things a project manager can attend to in either matrix or cross-function management?*

KEY POINTS *from Chapter 11*

- An organization is established to coordinate the work of a number of people.

- The organization consists of human, technical, and reward systems. A change to one of these will affect the other two.

- Hierarchical structure has serious disadvantages for running multidisciplinary projects.

- Matrix is almost synonymous with project management because of its advantage in dealing with many disciplines.

- Success in matrix requires very good interpersonal skills on the part of all managers.

References

1. See reading list for citation.
2. This is sometimes called the "Eichmann defense." Adolf Eichmann contended that he was only following orders and that he was in no way responsible for the fate of the Jews in his concentration camps.

Chapter 12

STAFFING A PROJECT

The way in which a project is staffed depends on the type of organization structure being used. In a hierarchical project organization, team members may be hired into the company for specific assignment to the project itself. They may also be recruited from functional groups that already exist in the company. Either way, they are "hired" to work only on a single project. In the matrix organization, the functional manager usually determines which specific personnel will be assigned to a project on a strictly as-needed basis. Those individuals still "belong" to their functional manager, not to the project manager.

Determination of how many people in each skill category are required for a project may be solely the project manager's job in the hierarchical-project setup (also called "pure-project" form), while it would be negotiated in the matrix.

THE STAFFING PROCESS

Naturally, the first step is to determine what must be done. The WBS is the tool used to show exactly what tasks will be involved in the project. Once it has been developed, it is possible to decide what kind and how many people from each skill category must be used on each task.

In some organizations, project managers might be able to decide what organizational form will be used, whether matrix or hierarchical. Usually, however, that decision has been made by top management and is established as a standard. If a choice can be made, it should be done at this point.

If matrix is used, functional managers will assign individuals to the project. Often project managers have preferences for certain individuals, either because they are known to do good work or the project manager has worked with a person before and likes working with him. It may be possible to request that person and get him, but in a shared-resource environment, that may be possible only in the event that the person is the *only* one who can perform a certain task. Otherwise, functional managers generally are pretty free to assign personnel on an availability basis.

If the project manager has any say about who is assigned to the project, he may need to interview and select people. If so, there are some guidelines for conducting interviews following this section of the chapter.

If possible, when matrix is the organization form, have people assigned to the project before final planning is complete, so that they can participate in preparing those plans. In this way, they will feel greater commitment to the plan than if it is just handed to them as a *fait accompli.*

In any event, work hard to get the person selected started off on the right foot. If the person is very inexperienced, he or she will need a lot of "hand-holding" at first. Regardless of experience level, all members of the team need to have a very clear understanding of the project objectives and the approach being taken to get there. The success or failure of a project may well depend on how the project is "kicked off."

SELECTION INTERVIEWING GUIDELINES

Too many managers do all of the talking during a selection interview. You can't learn anything about the other person if you're talking. Ask open-ended questions as much as possible—those that require that the person elaborate, rather than just giving you "yes-no" answers. Following are some examples of what you might ask:

- What are the greatest strengths you think you would bring to this job?

- What accomplishments during your career do you feel best about (work or nonwork)?

- What new skills have you developed recently?

- What did you do to increase your responsibilities or improve your job in your last position?

- What level of supervision makes you most comfortable?

- Will you be able to meet the particular requirements of this position (e.g., travel, overtime, weekend work, heavy deadline pressure)?

- Besides economic rewards, what do you look for in your work life?

- What could I tell you about this position or the organization to help you determine if this is the right job for you?

You can also ask how the prospective employee would handle various situations. For example, "If the general manager came directly to you and gave you a work assignment, how would you handle the situation?"

Tell potential hires both the *good* and *bad* (or negative) aspects of the job. Studies have shown that when employees are told only good things about a job, they feel surprised and perhaps a bit

> **Don't use esoteric interviewing methods unless you have been thoroughly trained in them.**

cheated when they begin to discover the negatives. The ultimate result is depressed motivation, and in many cases, turnover. If you oversell the position, chances are you can't deliver and the new employee will feel cheated.

QUESTIONS FOR REVIEW

1. *What is the first step in the staffing process?*

2. *Which of the tools is used as a first step in staffing?*

3. *What is the difference between staffing a project organized in pure project form versus one in matrix form?*

4. *What is one main guideline that should be followed in interviewing candidates?*

KEY POINTS *from Chapter 12*

- The starting point for staffing a project is the Work Breakdown Structure.
- Once tasks have been identified, decide what skill-level person will be required.
- Ask open-ended questions in an interview, so that the applicant does most of the talking.
- Don't use esoteric interviewing techniques unless you have been thoroughly trained in them.

Chapter 13

THE ROLE OF THE PROJECT MANAGER

The previous chapters of this book have presented the *tools* of project management. These tools are a necessary but not sufficient condition for success as a project manager. To these must be added skills in

> **A** one-track mind can-not effectively manage a two-track railroad.
>
> *Russell Ackoff*

dealing with people. After all, except for very small, one-person projects, the job of the project manager is to *get work done by other people.*

During the week prior to revising this chapter, I taught a three-day class in project management for a group of 24 engineers. These young men had all graduated from engineering schools within the past two years and joined my client company. They were finishing a year-long training program of which the project management class is just one part.

In our sessions during that week, the discussion about the project manager's role became very animated at times—to use an understatement. Much of what was said comes out in most of

my classes on project management attended by more-experi-
enced people. This class, however, made me realize just how difficult the project manager's role is for a new manager, and
showed me how inexperienced individuals view that role initially. I decided to use that class as the basis for this chapter, and
am indebted to my participants for their questions, challenges,
and understandable skepticism, all of which forced me to think
through the issues in detail.

In discussing the control of projects, I presented the standard definition of control, which has been given in this book:
Control is comparing where you are to where you are supposed
to be, then taking action to correct for any deviation.

"We can't take corrective action," they told me. "We don't
have any authority over the people who work on our projects."

Of course, this is why I have written in Chapter 9 that a
manager only has control if his or her people are in control of
themselves, and that those people must be empowered, using
my Standard Operating Procedure, so that they are able to exercise self-control.

"The people can't even do that," they argued. "If they need
to buy something or work overtime, our policies and procedures
require that such actions be approved by someone else, so they
can't act unilaterally."

What they said is true. However, it misses an important
point. Just because an action must be approved by someone else
does not mean that it cannot be taken. Nor does it absolve the
individual of the responsibility for getting that approval.

What impressed me about this expression on their part is
that they, like so many individuals in organizations, feel *powerless* to act at all. There is a certain paralysis that sets in when a
problem exists. It can be explained in part by the widespread use
of authoritarian management for so many years, in addition to
authoritarian parenting and teaching.

People have been told what to do by their parents, teachers,
and supervisors for so long that they have come to view the
world as a place in which they have no power to affect their own

lives. Thus, instead of being active, they become reactive, and view the organization (and the world) as tying their hands so that they cannot exercise control, even when they are managers.

Now that the problem has been recognized, enlightened managers are trying to correct it. We are trying to adopt more participative styles, and we are trying to empower people. Self-managed work teams represent one such attempt to give the worker more control over his or her work and eliminate authoritarian practices.

Unfortunately, the initial reaction to such a move is distrust. "They're up to something," the worker says. "They're just trying to get more work out of us without paying us any more."

There are also mixed messages: "We want you to manage this project," they are told. "It's your baby, and you are responsible for seeing that it comes in on time and on budget." Then they are told, "But don't do anything drastic without checking with me first, and if you want to buy something, we have to get my signature, my boss's signature, the plant manager's signature . . . and if it's for more than $5,000, it will have to be signed by the president."

EMPOWERED TEAM MEMBERS ARE MORE LIKELY TO TAKE INITIATIVE THAN POWERLESS INDIVIDUALS

However, my response was this: While it is true that you do not have direct authority to control many aspects of your project work, you must take steps to break roadblocks by appealing to those individuals who do have the authority to act.

Furthermore, it seems to demonstrate that the "power" of authority is misunderstood. People think that if they only had authority, they could move mountains. They argue that the organization will not give them any authority, and therefore, they cannot move even a tiny ant hill.

What they don't realize is that, even if they had authority, it would not guarantee that people would automatically do what must be done. As I have already said, authoritarian management leads to difficulty. So even if they had authority over people, it would not guarantee compliance, nor would it be the best way to work. Interpersonal skills must be used to get things done. That means *influence.*

In support of this, one of the participants told me that he works hard at building relationships with people in the plant. He gets to know them. He finds out how they think, what they like to do in their free time, and so on. Then when he needs to get something done, he requests it as one friend to another, and he usually gets cooperation.

Yet his boss views his small talk with those people as a waste of time, which is true of a lot of managers. "We're here to work," they say, "not to socialize." Still, this young man is able to get things done that his boss cannot accomplish.

As for the matter of the organization not giving a manager any authority, I learned early in my career that you have as much authority and responsibility as you are willing to take. The manager who *exercises* authority—that is, makes decisions, behaves proactively, and who takes responsibility for his actions, is the one who eventually rises to the higher levels of the organization. The manager who "cries in his beer" that he can't get anything done stays where he is.

There is a saying that conveys this idea nicely: "It is always easier to ask forgiveness than to get permission." That is the essence of the proactive manager's attitude.

Some simple examples will illustrate the point. In most organizations, requisitions for purchased parts, equipment, and tools must be signed by an approving individual. I asked them if those individuals ever "sit on" their requisitions.

"It happens all the time," they all chimed in.

"What do you do about it?" I asked.

"Just wait until they sign it," several of them said.

"Then you aren't managing the project," I told them. "You're just being reactive. You have to let that person know that the requisition must be signed by a certain date, or the following consequences will result: The project will be late; it will cost the company so many dollars; the customer will cancel the order; there is a penalty clause in the contract; or whatever the result will be.

You have to keep pestering him until either that requisition is signed or he throws you out of his office and tells you not to bother him any more. Then, if he does that, you revise your schedule to show the impact of the delayed items, and publish it. That is your responsibility."

"And polish up your resume," someone chirped.

We all had a good laugh. Then we admitted that there are definitely some risks. Nothing comes without a cost—or at least a potential cost.

Another issue that was discussed is the difficulty of managing a project when someone in another department does not act as required by the project plan. The project manager has no authority to tell that person what to do. However, if the success of the project depends on that person's performance, and the manager is unable to influence him to get moving, then the only recourse is to enlist the help of someone in the organization who can gain that individual's compliance, even if it is through the use of authority. To simply sit around and say, "My project was late because they didn't do their work as planned" is an unacceptable response if the project manager took no action to deal with the problem.

Then someone in the session asked, "What am I supposed to do when someone does not do their part on time?"

"In the first place," I told them, "if other people are supposed to deliver something to you by a certain time, it is your responsibility to be checking with them ahead of time to see how they are doing. There should be no last-minute surprises. You should know in advance that they are going to be late, and should be taking steps to prevent such schedule slips by working with those people to do whatever is necessary. If they need more help, you have to "lobby" with other managers to get that help. If it is a technical problem, you may have to pitch in and help them solve it. Again, at the expense of sounding like a stuck record, it is the proactive approach that is necessary."

DEALING WITH RESISTANCE

One of the more common complaints from managers is that other departments are sometimes difficult to deal with. They won't cooperate. They build boundaries around themselves and refuse to cross them.

Invariably, when I ask the person who complains about resistant people, "What's in it for them to do what you want done?" they have no answer. They have usually not taken the time to find out what is important to the other person, and all they care about is getting their job done.

The macho manager would say, of course, "What's in it for them is keeping their jobs. That's why they should cooperate." That response, however, is based on contempt for people at the worst, or a failure to understand basic psychology at the least. People do what they do because they get something out of it. So to fail to help others get what they need in the process of doing what you need done is to be very unrealistic in your expectations. The "savvy manager" knows this and tries to be sure the person will get a fair exchange in the interaction.

Sometimes the refusal to cooperate is caused by the people in the department feeling threatened. To illustrate, one project

Sometimes the REFUSAL to cooperate is caused by someone feeling threatened!

manager told me that his company had a problem with high scrap rates, which were costing the company several hundred thousand dollars a year. He was given the assignment to determine the primary cause of the high scrap.

He designed an experiment in which half of the raw material was held aside and the other half was run through Process 1, which was very carefully controlled. Then the material was sent through the subsequent processes and the scrap level was measured.

A few weeks later, the remaining material from that lot was run through process 1, which was again carefully controlled; then it was put through the remaining steps. The scrap rate was considerably higher than before. This proved that the material was not the cause of the problem, nor was Process 1. The cause was in the subsequent steps.

When he pointed this out, he got a very defensive response. Naturally, the people who performed those steps were being told that they were doing something to cause high scrap rates, and they did not want to admit it, because people do not like to be "blamed" for errors.

Here again, this is an outcome of our traditional way of dealing with people. Instead of blaming and punishing people for problems, which does not solve the problem, we must enlist their support in solving those problems. Otherwise, people hide problems or resist changing their ways, since to do so would be to admit that what they were doing was wrong.

What I suggested to this manager was to adopt a new approach the next time. "People don't argue with their own data," I told him. "If you can run the same experiment next time, with them totally involved in the design, implementation, and *interpretation of the data*, and then ask them how to solve the problem, you won't be as likely to get much resistance." It will be their data and their interpretation. People don't argue with their own data.

THE NEED FOR FLEXIBILITY

All of the foregoing should reinforce the need for a project manager to have good people skills, and because she must deal with so many different people, all of whom have different personalities and dispositions, she must have a great deal of flexibility in her approach. The same is true when solving nonpeople problems. A person must be flexible in her methods.

Most managers think they are fairly flexible. They believe they are able to change their approach to solving a problem if the first method fails to work. On the contrary, I have seen a number of managers get trapped into simply using "more of the same" in dealing with a problem that does not yield to the first "attack." The problem with this is explained by the Law of Requisite Variety:

> **In any system of men or machines, the element in the system with the greatest flexibility in its behavior will control the system.**
> *Ross Ashby*

Consider the system diagram in Figure 13.1. The system involves a process that converts inputs into outputs and uses feedback to keep the process functioning as required. This system model can be applied at the interpersonal level, in which the process involves the interaction of the project manager (element A) with the rest of the project system (element B). Of course, the manager wants to ensure that the element represented by B does what is required. That is, he wants to be in control of the outputs from the system.

The law of requisite variety says that the element inside the system (A or B) that has the greatest flexibility (variety) will control the behavior of the system. So if the manager is to control, he must have greater flexibility than the remainder of the elements that make up the project system.

A corollary of the law can be stated as follows:

> **If you always do what you've always done, you'll always get what you've always gotten.**

FIGURE 13.1
FIRST-ORDER FEEDBACK SYSTEM

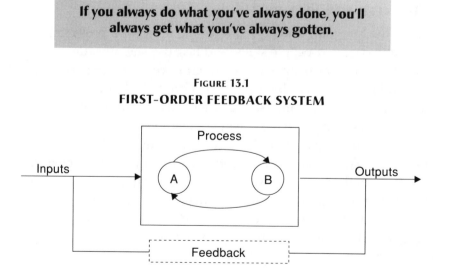

This is almost the opposite of the old adage "If at first you don't succeed, try, try again." We might say instead:

> **"If you try repeatedly and don't succeed—try something different!"**

Developing flexibility is a lifelong task. Only when we have a big "bag of tools" at our disposal can we hope to be able to deal with all of the situations we are sure to encounter.

Unfortunately, rather than develop flexibility in themselves, too many managers attempt to reduce the variability in the system. They do this by imposing rules on the people in the organization. These are usually called *policies* and *procedures*.

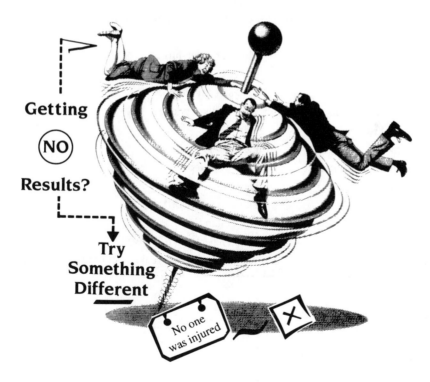

In order to maintain control, they try to limit the behavior of the people who report to them. The net result is the one that we have discussed. People begin to feel powerless (which is exactly the intent of the policy, when you get right down to it). For this reason, Tom Peters[1] has argued forcefully for the need to get rid of the myriad of policies which only serve to strangle the organization, and give employees more autonomy. I agree with him wholeheartedly.

ATTRIBUTES REQUIRED OF PROJECT MANAGERS

As a summary of what is required of a project manager, I have asked people in my classes to list what they think it takes to make a good manager. In Table 13.1 is a list which contains some of the more significant characteristics listed by those participants.

TABLE 13.1
ATTRIBUTES OF PROJECT MANAGERS

Good listener	Mutual ownership
Supportive	Buffer to rest of organization
Organized	Visible leadership
Clears roadblocks	Technical knowledge
Mutual respect	Fair
Team builder	Flexible
Knows own limitations	Open-minded
Sense of humor	Delegates
Gives feedback	Honest/trustworthy
Good decision maker	Understanding
Follows up	Challenges team to do well
Shares experience	Knows strengths/weaknesses of team members

KEY POINTS *from Chapter 13*

- A project manager must be proactive.
- You have as much authority and responsibility as you take.
- Authoritarian management causes people to feel powerless.
- People don't argue with their own data.
- A project manager must have flexibility.

Reference

1. See his book, *Thriving On Chaos,* for more on this.

Chapter 14

LEADERSHIP IN
PROJECT MANAGEMENT

In Chapter 9 it was pointed out that authoritarian practices are ineffective in managing projects. On top of that, the project manager seldom has authority over many of the people assigned to the project anyway, so he cannot practice authoritarian management, and if he tries under those conditions, he is likely to incite a rebellion. If he is to succeed, he must have the ability to deal effectively with people. This certainly involves leadership, in addition to other interpersonal skills.

WHAT IS LEADERSHIP?

The term "leader" is used very loosely in organizations. Dozens of books have been written on how to practice leadership. The topic has been widely researched and numerous definitions exist, many of them not very satisfactory. It seems obvious (though it is often overlooked) that no one is a leader unless he or she has followers.

In addition, not all managers are leaders, even though they are supposed to be exercising leadership as a normal part of their jobs. Perhaps it is this fact that causes some observers to say that we have a crisis in leadership in our country today.

To *manage* means to handle. To *lead*, by contrast, means to take someone to a destination. We manage things, but we lead people. In my opinion, Vance Packard summed up what we mean by leadership with the definition shown in Table 14.1.

TABLE 14.1
VANCE PACKARD'S DEFINITION OF LEADERSHIP

Leadership appears to be the art of getting others to want to do something that you are convinced should be done.

Vance Packard
The Pyramid Climbers

How you get people to *want* to do something constitutes the practice of leadership, and is the focus of this chapter.

To determine how leaders influence their followers, Kouzes and Posner conducted an extensive study of leaders and documented their findings in a book entitled *The Leadership Challenge*.[1] They write that leaders appear to adopt a three-phase strategy in getting people to follow them, which they call VIP—vision-involvement-persistence. Leaders have dreams or *visions* of what could be. They also recognize that they cannot get there alone, so they work to create *involvement* of others. Finally, they are *persistent* in working toward their goal.

THE PRACTICE OF LEADERSHIP

Kouzes and Posner say that vision, involvement, and persistence are expressed through five fundamental practices that enabled the leaders they studied to get extraordinary things done. When they were at their personal best, those leaders practiced the steps shown in Figure 14.2.[2]

FIGURE 14.1
VISION, INVOLVEMENT, PERSISTENCE

Challenging the Process

Kouzes and Posner[3] say that every case they studied in which a person performed at their personal best involved some kind of challenge. It might have been a business turnaround, some innovative new product, or whatever, but there was always a change in the status quo. Rather than be satisfied to let things continue the way they had always been done, these leaders pushed for a new way.

INSPIRING A SHARED VISION

James McGregor Burns, in his study of political leaders,[4] pointed out that people only follow someone who they believe can take them to a destination that they want to reach. Another way of saying this is that they must see something of value

FIGURE 14.2
KOUZES AND POSNER'S STEPS

5. Encouraged the heart
4. Modeled the way
3. Enabled others to act
2. Inspired a shared vision
1. Challenged the process

in following the other person—they must have some of their needs met.

A sense of purpose, mission, or vision creates in people a great motivation, and leaders are able to create such a shared vision. As Kouzes and Posner say, "A person with no followers is no leader, and people will not become followers until they accept a vision as their own. You cannot command commitment, you can only inspire it."[5]

Gail Sheehy supports the importance of a sense of purpose, when, in her book *Passages*, she reports that she surveyed some 60,000 Americans and found that those who were most happy, contented, and productive had some overriding sense of *purpose* in their lives—something bigger than themselves—that drove them. Leaders are able to bring such a sense of purpose alive for their followers.

ENABLING OTHERS TO ACT

A number of years ago David McClelland studied the motivations of corporate executives and found that the need for power is a dominant driving force among those individuals.[6] However, McClelland found that the power motive can be expressed in two ways—the *personal power* motive and the *social power* motive.

He argues that the most effective leaders are those who appeal to what he called the social power motive, which is expressed as the drive to do things together. In today's vernacular, we would say that such leaders *empower* their followers. Rather than tie their hands through domination and restriction, effective leaders make people feel stronger.

Reinforcing McClelland's position, Kouzes and Posner say that there is a one-word test to determine whether someone is on the way to success as a leader. That word is *we*. Leaders can't do it alone.

Some try, however. McClelland found that ineffective leaders are inclined to use the personal power motive, which is characterized by the word "I." These leaders tend to be authoritarian, self-centered, and insensitive to the wants and needs of their followers.

By listening to leaders talk, McClelland found that you can tell which power motive they generally adopt. You hear the word "we" with those leaders who have social power as a driving force, whereas the word "I" predominates for the others.

The Chinese sage Lao Tse knew about this aspect of leadership and described it several thousand years ago, as the quote in Table 14.2 shows.[7]

TABLE 14.2
THE WAY OF SUBTLE INFLUENCE

Superior leaders are those whose existence
 is merely known;
The next best are loved and honored;
The next are respected;
And the next are ridiculed.

Those who lack belief
Will not in turn be believed.
But when the command comes from afar
And the work is done, the goal achieved,
The people say, "We did it naturally."

Modeling the Way

Effective leaders lead by example. They are role models for their followers. They practice what they preach, and they also live their values. Employees are very quick to point out the discrepancies between a manager's stated values and his behavior. When a manager's behavior is not consistent with his stated beliefs, people ultimately will lose respect for him.

Encouraging the Heart

Difficult objectives can cause people to become frustrated, exhausted, and disenchanted. Leaders must encourage them in order to keep them from giving up. The leader has to show them that they can win. In addition, leaders must give themselves encouragement.

THE SELF-FULFILLING PROPHECY

The self-fulfilling prophecy is one of the most important principles from psychology, at least for leaders. The principle is that you tend to get what you expect from others. Thus, if you expect poor performance from a person, you will tend to get it, and conversely.

Support for the Self-Fulfilling Prophecy

A well-known account of the experiments that indicated that the self-fulfilling prophecy might be valid was published by Rosenthal and Jacobson.[8] Children were given aptitude tests, and were then paired up according to test scores, race, and sex. Thus, two black boys having equal scores would be paired, and so on. Their teacher was not told the actual test scores. Instead, for each pair of children, the teacher was told that one child was average, while the other was a "late bloomer." The average child would do all right in school, but the late bloomer could be expected to do really well that year. So the teacher was told.

Later that school year, academic performance of the children was checked, and the late bloomers were found to be doing better, on the average, than their counterparts. The only logical explanation for this is that the teacher somehow brought about the expected performance based on the bias presented by the experimenter. But how was this done?

Subsequent studies showed that teachers were more supportive of the late bloomer, more helpful, offered more encouragement, and were more patient when the late bloomer was having difficulty. Thus, the child performed better because the teacher expected it. The average child was not so strongly encouraged, and so did not work as hard as the late bloomer. Thus, the self-fulfilling prophecy comes true.[9]

It Works in Management, Too!

Based on this principle, McGregor developed a management model that suggested that the views that managers have of employees might bring about such a self-fulfilling prophecy. He believed that the supervisor's view of employees can be called a "working theory" about employees, and that such views can be placed on a continuum, on one end of which is the Theory-X position, with Theory-Y on the other end.

The Theory-X manager thinks employees are poorly motivated, lazy, interested only in pay, and so on. The Theory-Y manager sees employees as motivated, interested in their jobs, etc. This is shown in Figure 14.3. In other words, it is the opposite of the Theory-X view. According to McGregor, the manager who holds a Theory-X view of employees will tend to get poor performance from them and vice versa.

While this theory is generally correct, I feel that it needs clarification. It is tempting to view the leader as having unidirectional influence in the interaction with followers, whereas the influence is really *bidirectional.* That is, the follower influences the leader and is also influenced by the leader. This is shown in Figure 14.4.

No doubt the reason that the self-fulfilling prophecy works in the classroom is that the strength of the teacher's influence is greater than that of the student. In the workplace, however, the supervisor does not always have greater influence on employees

FIGURE 14.3
THEORY X, THEORY Y

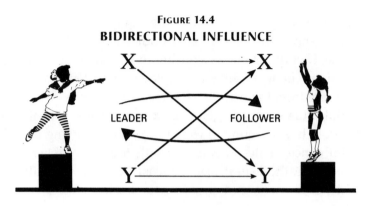

FIGURE 14.4
BIDIRECTIONAL INFLUENCE

than they have on him. For that reason, the supervisor's expectations do not always bring about the predicted result.

In my experience as a manager, I found the X-influence seemed to be a bit stronger than the Y-influence, so that the X-employee eventually causes the supervisor to lose his normal Y-outlook. However, it is a matter of degree. If the supervisor can maintain a Y-outlook in the face of an employee's X-behavior, then he or she may "turn around" that employee. Certainly, one is generally likely to get better results with the Y-outlook than its opposite.

Actions Speak Louder Than Words

As was previously mentioned, a leader who espouses one thing and then behaves inconsistently with the stated position will not be believed or trusted. For that reason, you cannot *fake* a Theory-Y outlook. You can't tell your followers that you trust and have confidence in them when you don't, because your behavior will contradict your words. For example, if you really don't trust someone, you will let them know it by looking over his or her shoulder fairly often, by asking questions that convey your distrust, and in many other ways.

Organizations tend to convey a Theory-X or Y outlook in the policies and procedures that they establish. To illustrate, consider that most adults can make major purchases on their own volition (perhaps in consultation with their spouse, of course). They do not have to obtain permission from their parents to buy a new car or house, which might amount to many thousands of dollars.

That same individual, however, finds that she cannot spend $15 of the organization's money without permission from the "powers that be." (These are our organizational parents!) Heaven forbid! She might spend that $15 unwisely, and after all, you can't expect management to meet profit objectives if every person in the company can just spend money willy-nilly.

Interestingly, managers will tell employees that they must have approval to spend $15 and in the very next breath tell them that they must all behave *responsibly!* Isn't that incredible? If you treat people as though they are irresponsible, how can you expect them to behave responsibly?

It seems to me that the way to deal with this problem would be to give every employee who might have the discretion to spend money her own individual budget. After all, the organization essentially has to create such a budget anyway. Each employee costs the company so much to support, so why not let the person have her own budget and *hold her responsible for it!* So long as she spends the money wisely, she can spend it any way she chooses, in support of her job. If she proves herself untrustworthy, then her manager should deal with her individually, rather than making a policy to tie the hands of everyone.

In Chapter 15, when motivation is discussed, it will be clear why I am advocating this. For now, suffice it to say that the best way to get people to behave responsibly is to treat them as if they are. The self-fulfilling prophecy works in all arenas of life.

CHOOSING A LEADERSHIP STYLE

Of course there must be controls. There must be accountability. Certainly a manager cannot just turn everything over to the follower. The question is, how is a manager to know just how to supervise an employee? Should the person be supervised closely? Would a participative style be best? Or could delegation be employed?

I think the answer is provided by a model of leadership developed originally by Hersey and Blanchard,[10] which I have modified, using my own terms. Their model was based on the fact that there are two primary components in the *behavior* of leaders toward their followers.[11] One is the emphasis that leaders place on getting the *task* done. The other is how they deal with their followers in terms of interpersonal or *relationship* dimensions. These are defined as follows:

Task behavior is communication on the part of a manager aimed at the task itself. When task behavior is high, the supervisor defines the follower's role, tells the person what, when, how, and where to do the job, and then closely supervises performance.

Relationship behavior is the way in which the supervisor attends to the follower at the personal level. When relationship behavior is high (strong), the supervisor listens, provides support, and involves the follower in decision making.

The two dimensions can be combined, using only high or low levels of each, into four "styles" of leader behavior. These are illustrated in Figure 14.5.

The *hand-holding* style would sound something like this: "I have a job for you to do. Here are the details (leader outlines task details). It must be done by three o'clock today. I want you to do it this way (tells follower specifically how to do the work). I'll check back in a little while, but if you run into a snag, let me know immediately, so I can help you."

The *influence* style sounds exactly like the hand-holding style, up to a point. Here it is: "I have a job for you to do. Here are the details (leader outlines task details). It must be done by three o'clock today. I want you to do it this way (tells follower specifically how to do the work). [Here it changes.] The reason I want you to do it this way is (explains rationale for procedure). I'm sure you'll do a good job. I'll check back in a little while, but if you run into a snag, let me know immediately, so I can help you."

FIGURE 14.5
MY MODEL OF LEADERSHIP

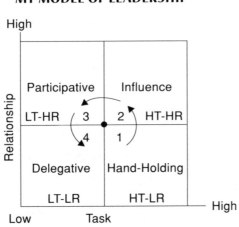

The *participative* style sounds like this: "I have a job for you. Here's what it's all about (describes the job). Let's kick around some ideas about how to do it. What do you think?"

Finally, *delegative* sounds like this in the extreme case: "I have a job for you. Here it is. You need anything from me? Any questions? Great! Drive on!"

The style that is best depends on the nature of the situation, which is a combination of the follower's skills and the difficulty of the job to be done. Note that the proper style depends on how you answer the questions:

> **Can** the person do the job?
> and
> **Will** the person take responsibility for doing it?

The dimensions of *can* and *will* combine to yield what might be called the person's job *maturity*. If the person's job maturity is very low, you need to do a lot of hand-holding. On the other hand, a high-maturity follower can be delegated to.

By combining the *can* and *will* answers, the appropriate style to use can be determined using the following guide:

Hand-holding:	Follower is unable and unwilling or insecure
Influence:	Follower is unable but willing to do the job
Participative:	Follower is able but unwilling or lacks confidence
Delegative:	Follower is both able and willing

Following this model, an interesting point can be made. As an employee's job maturity increases, the supervisor can eventually delegate to him. This frees the supervisor to attend to other matters. For that reason, it is clear that delegative management would be the ideal style, despite the strong advocacy for participative management. However, it is difficult to get all employees into quadrant four, so participative style is probably a good "average."

Nevertheless, part of a leader's responsibility is to develop people over time so that they are moved from quadrant 1 to 2, then to 3, and finally to 4. At that point, the follower can be promoted or given more responsibility. This will cause his or her job maturity to drop, so that a quadrant 2 or 3 style will have to be adopted, until the person is pulled back into quadrant 4, where the process starts again.

Over time, leaders continue to "slide" followers back and forth along the curve (as shown in Figure 14.5), until the follower arrives at the same competence level as the leader. (Hopefully, by the time that happens, the leader will have advanced, since his or her boss should be applying the same model to the leader.)

Of course, not all people want to advance beyond a certain level, so for them, this process cannot continue indefinitely. Note also that if an employee is promoted "too far, too fast," then that person may become a victim of the Peter Principle, which says, "Employees eventually rise to their level of incompetence."[12]

It is up to managers to see that employees are not promoted to a level of incompetence and then just left there. If a person is put into a position that is over his head, then the supervisor should begin pulling that person back up or remove him from that position.

In a project environment, this model can be used by a manager to decide just how much freedom members of a project team can be given. If they work for a functional manager, then that person should be practicing this model. However, if they do not know the model, the project manager can explain it and suggest to the functional manager how the person should be supervised.

If a very inexperienced person is assigned to the project and his supervisor does not provide hand-holding supervision, the project manager would have cause for alarm, and should discuss his concerns with that functional manager. If the manager is the kind of person who prefers to loosely supervise everyone, then the project manager might have to request that a more experienced person be assigned, or if possible, supervise the person himself.

Whatever the case, the model provides a practical way of deciding how to supervise people, and emphasizes that no single style is adequate.

QUESTIONS FOR REVIEW

1. What is the difference between leading and managing?

2. On what psychological premise is McGregor's Theory-X, Theory-Y model based?

3. What is the one flaw in the self-fulfilling prophecy when applied in management?

4. You have a "green" college graduate working on your project. She has never worked anywhere before. What leadership style is likely to be best for her initially?

KEY POINTS *from Chapter 14*

- A leader must practice vision, involvement, and persistence.

- People tend to behave in the way that you expect, so it pays to have high expectations for them.

- There is no single best style of supervising people—it depends on their job maturity.

- You cannot talk one line and behave in a contrary way. People will lose respect for you.

References

1. See reading list.
2. Kouzes and Posner, pp. 7–8.
3. Kouzes and Posner have instruments available to measure how closely a leader conforms to the practices that they advocate. These can be ordered from University Associates, 8517 Production Ave., San Diego, CA 92121.
4. See reading list.
5. Kouzes and Posner, p. 9.
6. McClelland, *Power, the Inner Experience* (see reading list).
7. R. L. Wing, *The Tao of Power* (Doubleday, 1986).
8. Rosenthal, R., and L. Jacobson. *Pygmalion in the Classroom* (New York: Holt, Rinehart, and Winston, 1968).
9. This description of the Rosenthal and Jacobson work has been simplified and stripped of its academic jargon, so that the person not familiar with the terminology can follow the essence of the results obtained. Those interested in a fuller exposition will find an excellent treatment in the book by Russell A. Jones, *Self-Fulfilling Prophecies*, published by Lawrence Erlbaum Associates, 1977.
10. Instruments that measure a leader's conformance to the Hersey and Blanchard model can be ordered from University Associates, 8517 Production Ave., San Diego, CA 92121.
11. The word *behavior* is very important to note. This model deals only with how a leader behaves toward a follower, not with his attitude or feelings about the follower. Blake and Mouton have a model called the GRID™, which emphasizes the leader's attitude toward task and relationship, and is based on the self-fulfilling prophecy. The two models are very different, and should not be confused. See reading list for citation of Blake and Mouton's work.
12. Dr. Lawrence J. Peter, *The Peter Principle*.

Chapter 15

HOW TO MOTIVATE
ALMOST ANYONE

When Imhotep built the great step pyramid, he probably didn't have to worry much about motivating the people who worked on it. Many of them were slaves. Their motivation was to stay alive.

However, that does not explain the accomplishments of hundreds of other project leaders who built astonishing monuments that inspire awe in us today. Through the centuries, they have been able to coordinate the efforts of thousands of people to build the henges in the British Isles, the beautiful temples of the Mayas, and others too numerous to mention. How did these project leaders motivate the people to do back-breaking work without using threats of punishment or death or the great carrot of today—money?

In my 10 years of teaching seminars throughout the United States, Canada, and the Far East, the most frequently asked question is undoubtedly, "How do you motivate people?" There seems to be almost universal concern that people are not motivated to perform those jobs that need to be done in the workplace. The consensus among managers seems to be that the only reason many people come to work is to get a paycheck. They have a somewhat Theory-X outlook, to use McGregor's terminology.

I have concluded from conversations with thousands of people that, in many cases, what they really mean by their question is, "How do we get people to want to do jobs that no one in their right mind would want to do?" When it comes to motivation, I'm afraid we have some very unrealistic attitudes. Perhaps it is because we don't really understand what motivation is all about.

In several of my classes, there have been individuals who engage in cliff climbing as a sport. In one class, someone asked the cliff climber, "What do you think about when you're up there on that cliff?"

"Do you really want to know?" he asked.

"Yes."

"I'm thinking, 'If I ever get off this thing, I'll never do this again!'"

"Really?"

"Yes. Really!"

The questioner looked puzzled. "Then I don't understand. Why do you do it again?"

The cliff climber thought for a moment, then said, "I don't know. Maybe I'm crazy, but someone tells me about another cliff somewhere that is a real challenge, and I can't wait to see if I can do it."

This example strikes me as demonstrating the essence of what we mean by motivation. The cliff climber has a built-in drive to engage in his sport, and all you have to do is tell him about a cliff that is a challenge, and he can't wait to try it. No one has to pay him. He doesn't have to be begged, threatened, or persuaded. He does it because of a drive from within himself. And that is what motivation is all about.

True motivation comes from within the individual. We call such motivation *intrinsic.* Any attempt to get someone to want to

FIGURE 15.1
HOW TO GET PEOPLE STARTED

do something by offering him external rewards is an effort to use *extrinsic* motivation.

In my own case, I have no intrinsic drive to climb cliffs. I have vertigo, so that if I get 10 feet off the ground, I get dizzy. For that reason, no one can arouse in me a desire to climb a sheer rock cliff.

"Suppose someone gave you a million dollars?" a person asked me once. "Would that motivate you to do it?"

My response was, "I might climb a cliff to get a million dollars, but I would not be motivated by the task itself, and once I had finished it and collected my million dollars, I certainly would not likely want to do it again."

This leads people to believe that you can motivate someone with money. It is an argument that probably goes back to the invention of money over 2,500 years ago, and it is a very heated argument. Those people who are adamant that they themselves are motivated by money miss a subtle point. It is not the money itself that motivates, but all the things they know they can do with the money that "turns them on."

Money is a *symbol* for many things—power, security, prestige, status, comfort, and all the other things that humans desire. So when you offer someone a lot of money to do something, they may perform admirably, because they are thinking of what the money represents—or of what they can do with it. The interesting thing is, if they were not paid again to perform that same task, they probably never would.

The cliff climber, on the other hand, continues to climb cliffs, even though no one pays him to do so. What we should learn from this is that *intrinsic* motivation is durable. *Extrinsic* motivation exists only so long as the external rewards are available. As soon as they are withdrawn, the individual no longer cares to perform the task.

In my opinion, the real conclusion to be drawn from this is that the only *real* motivation is intrinsic. The term *extrinsic*, while it is used by psychologists and other professional students of motivation, is a misnomer. For that reason, we need to adopt a realistic approach to motivation in organizations and use intrinsic factors as much as possible.

This is contrary to majority practice, and I believe it is the reason why organizations have so much difficulty with motivation. They have relied almost exclusively on extrinsic factors to motivate people, and failed to take advantage of intrinsic factors.

What this would mean is that we would try to place people in jobs that they would find intrinsically motivating, rather than giving them a job that is boring, unchallenging, or mindless, and then trying to get them turned on to it by using externals.

Another point that seems to be overlooked is that we all must do some things that virtually no one wants to do. Around our homes, for example, the toilet must be cleaned, the house must be painted, the grass must be cut, and for some people, those chores are no fun at all. Yet they do them because they are necessary. (As someone said to me, the alternatives are unacceptable!)

The thing is, we all know that while we do those tasks—such as cleaning the toilet—we are not turned on to the task, but are looking forward to finishing it, so we can do something that we really enjoy.

The same thing is true of organizations. There are, figuratively speaking, toilet-cleaning jobs at work. What we must realize is that, while someone must do those jobs, we cannot expect anyone to be turned on to the task, and it is senseless to beat our heads against the wall trying to find a way to motivate a person to clean toilets.

What we should do is to distribute the toilet-cleaning jobs as evenly as possible, so that no one person gets stuck having to do them all the time, and we should attempt to eliminate as many of them as possible.

Given that we do this, the question still remains, "How do you know what kind of work will be intrinsically motivating to a person?" and this is *the* legitimate question we should ask. If we can answer this question for most of the people who work for us—and apply it—then most of the problems with motivation in the workplace will be solved, and the remainder will not be of so much concern.

There are two theoretical models that have been taught for over 30 years in an attempt to help managers find out how to motivate people. One is Maslow's Need Hierarchy and the other is Herzberg's Motivation-Hygiene factors. Both have merits, but managers who have attempted to apply them have often had limited success.

What is needed is a method of finding out for each individual what motivates him or her, and that is something that the models do not deliver. Such a technique has been devised, and it will be presented later in this chapter. First, however, it is useful to know what Maslow and Herzberg said about motivation, because they provide a conceptual base from which to work.

MASLOW'S HIERARCHY

Human beings have a large number of needs. When those needs are active, we are motivated to satisfy them. Abraham Maslow suggested that human needs can be grouped into five general categories that vary in strength, depending on whether they have been recently satisfied. He arranged those needs in a hierarchy, because he believed that the category at the bottom of the hierarchy (the lower-level needs) must be satisfied before the upper-level needs emerge. His hierarchy is shown in Figure 15.2.

The terms have the following meanings:

- *Self-actualization:* The need to be everything one is capable of being; self-mastery

- *Esteem:* The need to be thought well of by significant others

- *Social:* The need to affiliate with other people

- *Safety:* The need to provide for unexpected happenings and to feel secure from harm

- *Physiological:* The biological needs, including food, warmth, sex, shelter, etc.

FIGURE 15.2
MASLOW'S HIERARCHY

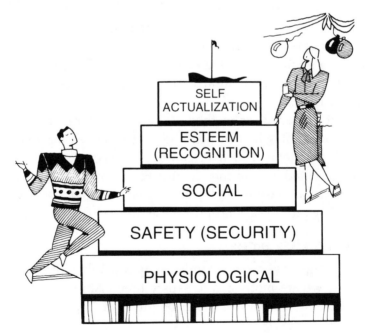

Maslow suggested that the lower three levels of his hierarchy are basic maintenance needs. The individual must have these needs met in order to experience well-being. The top two levels are those that are important in bringing about valued organizational performance. The manager's job, according to the theory, is to help individuals satisfy those basic maintenance needs so that the needs for recognition (or esteem) and self-actualization will become active.

In my experience, this is easier to say than to do. It is very difficult to know exactly where in the hierarchy an individual falls and how to help him or her satisfy basic maintenance needs.

Furthermore, there is very little research evidence that supports Maslow's theory that needs are arranged in a hierarchy. Of course, Maslow suggested that all levels of the hierarchy can be active at once, rather than progressing in an all-or-nothing manner. That is, physiological needs do not have to be satisfied completely before higher-level needs emerge. However, it seems intuitively correct to say that a starving person will not be too concerned about higher-level needs until his hunger has been satisfied.

Nevertheless, counter-examples of the hierarchy can be found. The "starving artist" is self-actualizing, despite the fact that her lower-level needs may not be met. She is so totally consumed by the drive to express herself through her art that she suppresses the lower-level needs.

This is an interesting example, which should serve as a guide to how people are actually motivated. Many people disprove the hierarchy by their actions. The athlete who submits to grueling training exercises in pursuit of excellence in his sport is an example. So is the engineer who spends long hours struggling to solve some very difficult technical problem. Likewise, the entrepreneur who works seven days a week for long periods to build a business disproves the idea that lower-level needs must be satisfied first.

Such examples actually suggest that, when people give themselves totally to something that for them is a way of fully expressing themselves (self-actualizing), they are not very concerned about the lower needs. Again, this suggests that we must change our approach to motivation in the workplace. If we can somehow help the individual become self-actualizing, then the lower-level needs become less important.

HERZBERG'S MOTIVATION-HYGIENE FACTORS

Another model of motivation that has gained widespread attention is Herzberg's motivation-hygiene theory. Unlike Maslow's model, which was largely based on theoretical construction, Herzberg's model was derived from empirical research.

Herzberg conducted a number of field studies in which he asked workers to tell what things in their jobs "turned them on" and what things "turned them off." From an extensive analysis of the data, Herzberg concluded that the things that affect motivation could be boiled down to a limited number of general factors. He called those factors that turn people off *hygiene* or *maintenance* factors, and he called the others *motivator* factors. These are shown in Table 15.1.

The hygiene factors, according to Herzberg, will turn people off to their jobs if they are not satisfied, but if they *are* satisfied, they do very little to motivate the person. That is, if they are satisfactory, they are neutral in terms of motivation, but if they are unsatisfactory, they are negative, or demotivators.

The application of Herzberg's model must take into account a characteristic of people that is well understood at the personal level, but seems to be poorly comprehended in work situations. The principle is that, when people are in pain, their pain takes precedence over pleasure. We all know how debilitating a severe headache can be. It is difficult to enjoy activities that would ordinarily be very pleasurable when one has a bad headache.

TABLE 15.1
HERZBERG'S MOTIVATION AND HYGIENE FACTORS

Motivation Factors	Hygiene Factors
• Achievement	• Company policy & administration
• Recognition	• Supervision
• Work itself	• Relationship with supervisor
• Responsibility	• Work conditions
• Advancement	• Salary
• Growth	• Relationships with peers
	• Personal life
	• Relationships with subordinates
	• Status
	• Security

In other words, a person cannot be "turned on" and "turned off" at the same time, and being turned off takes priority. Stated in more formal terms, a person cannot experience two opposite emotions simultaneously.

Given that this is true, Herzberg said that we must take care of the hygiene factors first, before we attempt to apply the motivators. That is, if the hygiene factors in an organization are unsatisfactory, they will cause people to be demotivated, and they must be "cleaned up" before the motivators can be applied.

Of course, it is not an all-or-nothing proposition. The hygiene factors can be a bit unsatisfactory and a person can still be motivated, but if the degree of "discomfort" becomes very high, then motivation will suffer.

However, in some organizations, the hygiene factors are so greatly out of line for so many employees that, if they were taken care of, those organizations would probably find that they actually have very little problem with motivation. Indeed, it is my belief that this is true for most organizations.

For example, the first item listed under hygiene factors is company policy. This is one of the most common offenders, in my experience. As Tom Peters has argued in his book, *Thriving On Chaos*, organizations have so many "Mickey Mouse" policies that it is no wonder employees are disgruntled.

Many companies have a policy that establishes a spending limit on employees.[1] The limit goes up as the level of the employee increases, but there is always a limit. There is no quarrel with such a policy in general. The quarrel is with the *level* of the limit.

Tom Peters tells about one newly hired Engineering Director who discovered that his engineers had a $25 limit. Anything that they wanted to buy for more than $25 had to be approved by someone higher in the organization. He raised the level to $200. The accounting department screamed bloody murder. "Those people will take us to the cleaners," they claimed. "You have no control over spending now." The result? Spending dropped 60%.

The reason? The engineers were so insulted at being treated like children (as they saw it) that they were playing "stick-it-to-them." Their response was, let's see how many $24.99 things we can buy—they don't have to be approved.

It might be argued that such action proves the validity of the policy. They were behaving irresponsibly. The evidence does not warrant that conclusion, however. As soon as they were treated as though they were responsible, they began to behave that way.

It is my feeling that most policies represent a "cop-out" on the part of management. Because a few employees behave badly, the organization makes a policy that is intended to limit the behavior of all employees. They do this rather than deal one-on-one with the offenders, and thereby lose the loyalty and commitment of "good" employees.

Among the hygiene factors, the word "relationship" occurs several times. When employees are in relationships at work that are disagreeable, they are turned off, and one of the most important of those is the relationship with the supervisor. This is why supervisors—in this case, project managers—must work to maintain good relationships with team members, as was discussed in Chapter 14.

This does not mean that the manager must run a popularity contest, or that all relationships will be of a highly friendly nature. It does mean that all relationships must be built on mutual respect. Where this is not possible, the employee should be transferred to another supervisor (if possible), both for the benefit of the employee and the supervisor with whom the bad relationship exists.

In support of what was said at the beginning of this chapter about salary, Herzberg found that for 80 to 90% of his respondents, pay is a hygiene factor. That is, if pay is satisfactory, it is neutral in terms of motivation, but if it is unsatisfactory, it is negative.

There are two components to whether pay is satisfactory. First, is it in line with what one's peers are making? Women in our society are sometimes victims of this. Why should a man make more for doing the same job as a woman?

Second, is the person's pay adequate to meet his needs? If not, then he will be dissatisfied, and will take steps to correct for the problem. That often means leaving the job, as it is sometimes impossible to get a larger salary.

Pay can serve as an extrinsic source of motivation when there is a direct correlation between performance and pay. That is the intention of piece-rate and commission sales jobs, and indeed, people will usually work harder under those conditions to make more money. Unfortunately, numerous stories are told about companies that change the pay or commission scale to keep employees from making more than some maximum level, thereby creating resentment, and destroying any incentive to work.

The other factors in the list are fairly straightforward. When people are made to feel like low-status individuals (by treating them as if they are not important, for example), when they feel that their job security is threatened (by automation, among other things), or when working conditions are bad, they will be demotivated.

To sum up Herzberg's "prescription," problems with the hygiene factors should be corrected before an attempt is made to apply the motivators. The problem is, most project managers have limited control over these factors. Still, that does not mean *zero* control, and every manager should do whatever is possible to correct for any hygiene factors that are a problem. If direct control is not possible, one can at least lobby with higher-level managers to have them corrected.

Assuming that the hygiene factors have been taken care of, the motivators can be applied. These are all intangibles, and correspond roughly to the top two levels of Maslow's hierarchy, as shown in Figure 15.3. The problem, however, is still the same. How do you determine which of these factors will motivate a specific individual?

FIGURE 15.3
MASLOW AND HERZBERG COMPARED

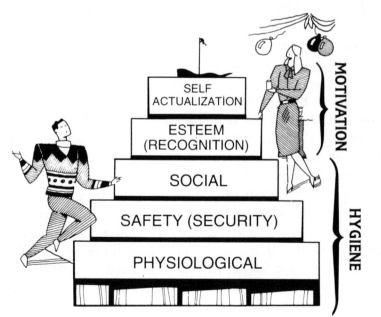

WHAT ABOUT UNRESPONSIVE AL?

What indeed? What do you do about Al, who does not respond when you take care of the hygiene factors and try to challenge him? What about Al, who seems to have less drive than a snail? "How do I motivate him?" you ask.

Well, before you go too far, you need to answer a basic question, which is, "Is it worth the effort?"

"Gee, isn't that a bit callous?" you may ask. No. We are too easily trapped into trying to "save" employees who cannot and should not be saved. In my opinion, the most respectful and kindest way to deal with another person is to expect of them the best that they can do.

If they choose not to respond to that expectation, which I cannot force on them, I can move them into a job that suits them or remove them from my organization if I have no such match. To keep someone in a slot for which they have no skills, incentive to perform, or whatever, is unfair to the person and to all other employees who are performing adequately, in my opinion.

There are two questions that must be answered before attempting to motivate Al:

- Does Al have the *potential* to perform adequately in the job?

- Does Al *want* to perform adequately in the job?

Unless you can answer yes to both questions, then you should consider transferring Al to another job or terminating him.

MOTIVATION PATTERNS: A NEW MODEL OF MOTIVATION

Suppose you decide that Al has potential and wants to do a good job, but for some reason the job doesn't challenge him. How can you determine what *would* challenge him?

You could ask him, but many people can't tell you. They have never really thought about it. For others, they don't want to tell you—for any number of reasons.

You could try giving Al a lot of different assignments, until you find one that turns him on, but that consumes a lot of time, which is something you don't have much of in a project environment. So you need a method of finding out what motivates Al that can be done fairly quickly, and that gives an accurate answer.

Such a method does exist, and I have used it throughout the United States with several thousand people, and have found only a very small number (less than a dozen) for whom the method didn't work. Here are examples of the questions I ask:

- Tell me about some job you've had, during the past six months to a year, that you really enjoyed. You looked forward to working on it, put a lot of yourself into it, perhaps thought about it on the way to work, considering what you were going to do about some particular aspect of the job. I don't need to know a lot of heavy technical detail, but I want to know the part you played in the job, what you feel you contributed to it, and so on.

Note: Don't say, "Tell me about your present job and what you like about it." The person may currently be in a job that is demotivating.

If they can't think of any job they have had during that time frame, I ask them to think back over their entire career and have them tell me about the one job that stands out in their mind.

As they tell me about the job, I pay very close attention—make notes if necessary, and probe for additional information. Next, I ask:

- Now let me ask if you have some hobbies, sports, or other outside interests that you like to spend time with. If they tell me no, I go back and ask for more job examples (or move to the final question, which I will present later). When they say they do have some outside interests, I ask them to pick one that they would spend more time doing if they had it. Activities that really motivate people cause them to want to spend more time with them, but most of us have limited time to spend on our hobbies.

The pitfall here is that someone will tell you he likes to jog, which he does because he thinks he should for health reasons, but he wouldn't spend more time doing it if the time were made available. Such activities are not motivators as such, so I avoid them, and ask the person to give me another example.
Finally, I say:

- Now tell me—is there anything you've always wanted to do but never got to do—maybe because you didn't have the time or money, or your family responsibilities prevented it? Call it a fantasy or wish list if you like. Is there anything like that? If so, tell me about it. These questions can be used as presented, or if the person cannot relate to one of them, you can use the other two. In other words, I could use jobs, hobbies, or wish-lists alone or in any combination, so long as I have at least three examples of something that motivates the person.

Now what you do is look for the common thread or pattern that runs through the three motivators, and the important thing here is that it is the *pattern of activity* that is the motivator, not the content of the activity, per se. People achieve self-actualization through engaging in a repetitive pattern of activity. Once you have determined that pattern of activity, you can then try to give the person assignments that contain that pattern.

As an example, some people are motivated by a pattern of activity that can be described as the *troubleshooter* pattern. They love to fix things. Give them a broken *anything* (within reason, of course) and they are driven to repair it.

Another pattern is the *innovator*. The person who is an innovator is always trying to come up with something new. Thomas Edison undoubtedly was motivated by innovation.

There is also the *helper*. Many helpers are found in education, nursing, counseling, and volunteer positions. They are turned on by being able to be helpful to others.

Michael Maccoby, in his book *Why Work?* lists five "types" of people, including the innovator and helper. In addition, he has the Expert, Defender, and Self-Developer. Most individuals combine two or more of these, but usually one will be dominant.

Maccoby lists only five types, however, and there are definitely more than that. He does not list the troubleshooter, for example. By using the method presented above, you can find a person's pattern no matter what it is, whether it fits Maccoby's types or not.

In fact, I prefer not to create too many labels for patterns. There is a temptation to "pigeon-hole" people into categories and miss important characteristics that do not fit a particular mold. For that reason, I encourage people to stay open to what-

ever information the person offers, and determine the pattern without attempting to label it.

It is also important to note that nearly everyone likes a challenge of some kind. However, what is a challenge for one would not be a challenge for another. The challenge of cliff-climbing would be sheer terror for me, for example. So before you conclude glibly that the person likes a challenge, you must be able to say what that means for that particular individual.

Once you know the pattern of activity that motivates a person, you can then try to assign work that will contain that pattern. If you have no such jobs, that is useful to know, because you now know why he has been unmotivated by the job he has had.

If this is the case, then transfer or termination are possible. Or—and this is always an option—you may decide that you can live with the person's level of performance. I don't recommend this very often, but there are circumstances that might justify it, such as when the individual has only another year or so until retirement and he has been with the company 25 years and in the past was an acceptable worker. For most people, however, I still prefer to see them work at full capacity (which is a value judgment on my part).

In order to learn this method, I have devised an exercise (see Table 15.2) that I use in my seminars. You can also do it yourself if you follow the instructions. I suggest that you do this with two other people, since if there is just one other person, you have to do everything yourself. It takes some practice to become comfortable with the questioning method, and also to learn to find the pattern that runs through the three examples. By practicing with two other people, you will feel more comfortable when you apply it to an employee.

TABLE 15.2
EXERCISE: ELICITING MOTIVATION PATTERNS

1. Get into groups of three people each. One person will be the interviewer, one the subject, and one the observer/timekeeper. In class, you should limit yourselves to about 15 minutes to get information from the subject and process it.

2. The interviewer asks the subject the questions outlined in the text above. The observer should pay close attention, so he or she can help the interviewer process that information when the interview is completed.

3. After all information has been obtained, the interviewer and the observer should put their heads together and see if they can find the pattern. Make sure it seems right to the subject. If the subject objects, look more closely. You probably missed something.

4. Now rotate, twice, so that all three of you "play" all three roles.

CAUTION: *Be careful not to "lead" the subject too much, or you will get your motivation pattern and not his or hers.*

QUESTIONS FOR REVIEW

1. What is motivation?

2. Why did Maslow say that lower-level needs must be met in order for a person to become self-actualizing?

3. In what way do people self-actualize?

4. If Herzberg's hygiene factors are problems for employees, what might be the result?

5. In what way are motivation and commitment related?

6. Is it possible for a manager to motivate an employee?

KEY POINTS *from Chapter 15*

- Real motivation is internal to the person, and is called intrinsic. Extrinsic motivation is an attempt to use rewards such as money or recognition to give the person incentive to do something.

- Motivation is the arousal of built-in drives. If a drive does not exist, there is nothing to arouse.

- Maslow grouped human needs into five categories and arranged them in a hierarchy. He said that the lower-level needs must be satisfied in order for the upper-level needs to emerge.

- Herzberg called hygiene factors those aspects of the work situation that are neutral if they are satisfactory, but which turn people off if they are not okay.

- The hygiene factors should be taken care of first, since a person cannot be turned on and turned off at the same time.

- A person achieves self-actualization by engaging in a repetitive pattern of activity. Once that pattern is known, the person can be given job assignments that contain the pattern.

Reference

1. This was discussed in Chapter 14. It is reiterated here with an example that demonstrates that treating employees as though they are responsible does indeed accomplish that result.

Chapter 16

A SAMPLE PROJECT PLAN

To illustrate the principles presented in this book, a sample project plan will be developed. I have tried to choose a project that a person from any discipline can follow. That is a tall order in itself, but I have found that the one described in this chapter fits the requirements fairly well—a project to develop a training program for new project managers. A general description of the project follows. The example plan will include most of the core elements from the list of contents recommended for a project plan, as presented in Chapter 2 in discussing the project notebook. Not included are a SWOT analysis, contractual requirements, or a control system.

GENERAL DESCRIPTION

This training program will be offered by Lewis Consulting & Training on both a public and in-company basis. That is, public programs will be offered that can be attended by anyone, and the class will also be offered to companies that have enough trainees to make their own class, usually in the range of 10 to 30 participants.

The class will include a participant workbook, some overhead transparencies, and a number of exercises that will help participants develop their competence in applying the skills being taught. Following are the components of the plan, together with commentary on various elements.

THE PROJECT PLAN

The first step is to develop a problem statement. Here is the one written for this project:

> *Problem Statement:* New project managers usually have no formal training in the tools and techniques of project management. They do not know how to plan, schedule, and control a project and therefore try to manage by the "seat of the pants."

▼ Are you practicing
fly-by-the-seat-of-the-pants project management?

Based on this problem statement, an overall statement of the goal of the project can be written. Following is the goal of the training program project:

Project Goal: To develop a training program for new project managers that will teach how to develop a project plan, a schedule with resources allocated realistically, and a control system. The program should be completed by August 30, 1995.

As was discussed in Chapter 2, it is a good idea at this point to list the assumptions that will govern the project plan and have those agreed upon before going further. Some of the assumptions that might govern this project include:

- The class is targeted at people who have little or no training in project management; that is, it is not an *advanced* class.

- Resources applied to the project will be available full-time for the duration of the project.

- A market exists for the training program as defined.

Next, a statement of the scope of the project might be written, to define the boundaries of the job.

Project Scope: The training program will include the essential tools of project management, including how to plan, how to schedule using either CPM or PERT methods, how to allocate resources in scheduling, and how to do variance or earned-value analysis. It will not include training in supervisory skills, as these are already available in another course. The course is also not aimed at experienced project managers, and so no advanced concepts will be presented.

A mission statement for this project follows:

> **Our mission is to develop a training program in the tools and techniques of project management for project managers who have little or no training in the discipline. This is to be achieved by benchmarking best practice throughout the world and incorporating those methods into the course.**

Although the mission statement provides a general approach to doing the project, it is helpful to spell this out more explicitly:

> **The workbook will be prepared by the instructor, using word processing combined with clip art and conventional illustrations. Desktop publishing will be used wherever possible. The camera-ready art will be provided to a printer for preparation of workbooks. Overhead transparencies that support the text will be prepared as required. The workbook will contain ample space for participants to take notes in class.**

Here are just a few of the objectives of the project, to illustrate.

OBJECTIVES:

1. To present a program that will enable a learner to put together a plan, schedule, and control system by the end of the class.

2. To develop a course that is highly practical, rather than theoretical. (No date is needed for this objective.)

3. To have the course reviewed by at least two experienced project managers by September 30, 1995.

A list of deliverables would include the following:

- A workbook to be used in the class

- Overhead transparencies to illustrate significant points covered in the class

- Handouts to be used in testing a learner's understanding of the material, and for use in class exercises

- Structured exercises to illustrate development of a Work Breakdown Structure, developing a CPM schedule (no resource allocation involved), and how to interpret a progress report using variance or earned-value measures

Specifications for a training program might be in the form of an outline.

SPECIFICATIONS:

The course content will conform to the outline that follows
(this is only a partial outline, to illustrate).

SECTION ONE	**Introduction to Project Management**
	Chapter 1. Overview of Project Management
SECTION TWO	**Project Planning**
	Chapter 2. A General Approach to Project Planning
	Chapter 3. Deciding What Must Be Done: Defining Your Mission, Goals, and Objectives
	Chapter 4. Strategic Planning in Project Management
	Chapter 5. Planning: Using the Work Breakdown Structure
SECTION THREE	**Scheduling With CPM, PERT, and Gantt**
	Chapter 6. Developing the Project Schedule
	Chapter 7. Schedule Computations
	Chapter 8. Scheduling With Resource Constraints
	Chapter 9. The PERT Statistical Approach
SECTION FOUR	**Project Control and Evaluation**
	Chapter 10. Concepts of Project Control and Evaluation
	Chapter 11. Project Cost and Schedule Control Using Variance or Earned-Value Analysis
	Chapter 12. Factors for Success and Failure
SECTION FIVE	**Organizing the Project**
	Chapter 13. Developing the Project Organization

THE WORK BREAKDOWN STRUCTURE

At this point, the planner could prepare a Work Breakdown Structure (WBS) for the project. The WBS for this one is shown in Figure 16.1.

The WBS involves three tasks. The program content must be determined, the class workbook must be developed, and so must supporting materials. The work underneath each task would be called a subtask, using the terminology from Chapter 4. For simplicity, they will be referred to as *activities* in this chapter.

FIGURE 16.1
WBS FOR TRAINING PROGRAM

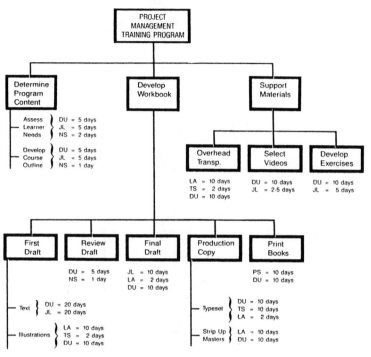

For each activity, the duration is shown in days, together with the initials of the resource(s) to be applied and their working times in days. Durations are coded as *DU* in the figure.

Preliminary Arrow Diagram

When this has been completed, a schedule can be prepared. Project Workbench™ was used to develop the schedules that follow. It is always a good idea to draw an arrow diagram on paper before entering data into the computer, since the precedence relationships will have to be entered, and these are difficult to work out on the screen. For that reason, an arrow diagram was first drawn. It is shown in Figure 16.2.

This is a fairly simple arrow diagram. It is drawn with the critical path running straight down the center, although the

FIGURE 16.2
ARROW DIAGRAM FOR PROJECT

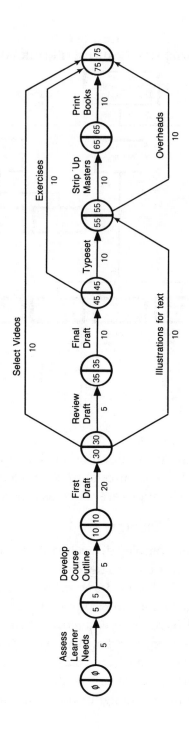

critical path location was not known when the diagram was originally drawn. The diagram is an activity-on-arrow network, and the nodes show the early and late times in working days.

The logic shown indicates that the illustrations for the text can be drawn as soon as the first draft has been completed. The selection of supporting videos could also be made at that time. Both tasks have a generous amount of float. The illustrations will be stripped in to the typeset pages to form camera-ready copy to be used in printing the books, so that arrow comes back in before the strip-up activity begins.

Overheads are not prepared until final typesetting is complete. It might be argued that they should not be done until pages are stripped up, since they may simply be copies of workbook pages. In that case, two critical paths would exist, since *print books* would be in parallel with the overheads. This would be acceptable, as the durations are small. It is also possible to overlap the overheads with the strip-up activity. That is, as soon as some of the pages have been stripped up, the overheads could be made from them.

It is also possible, however, that the overheads are being designed to stand alone. That is more or less how I viewed it, and that is why I drew the diagram as shown. I did consider that some of the material already developed might be used, so I held the overheads until this point in time for that reason. This shows that no single solution exists for scheduling project work. Other project managers would do the work in a different way.

The exercises to be used in giving participants practice with the course content can be designed only after the final draft. This activity has a lot of float, since it is in parallel with three 10-day activities.

The Initial Schedule

In Figure 16.3 is the Gantt chart for the project, as determined by standard CPM computation, that is, assuming unlimited resources. As the resource levels underneath the schedule show, overloads occur for Jim and Lea Ann Lewis and for

FIGURE 16.3

SCHEDULE WITH NO RESOURCE LEVELING

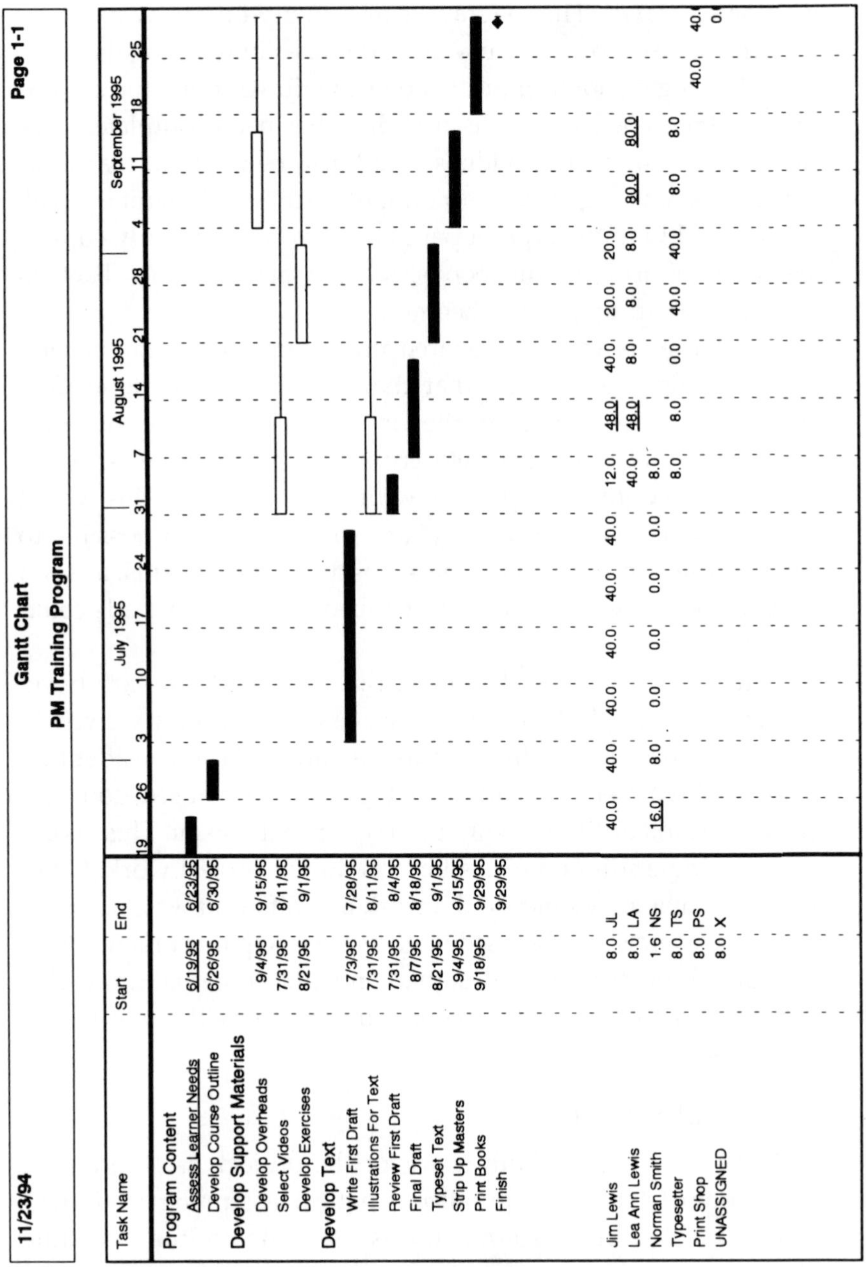

11/23/94
Gantt Chart
PM Training Program
Page 1-1
Task Name
Start
End
Program Content
Assess Learner Needs 6/19/95 6/23/95
Develop Course Outline 6/26/95 6/30/95
Develop Support Materials
Develop Overheads 9/4/95 9/15/95
Select Videos 7/31/95 8/11/95
Develop Exercises 8/21/95 9/1/95
Develop Text
Write First Draft 7/3/95 7/28/95
Illustrations For Text 7/31/95 8/11/95
Review First Draft 7/31/95 8/4/95
Final Draft 8/7/95 8/18/95
Typeset Text 8/21/95 9/1/95
Strip Up Masters 9/4/95 9/15/95
Print Books 9/18/95 9/29/95
Finish 9/29/95
July 1995
August 1995
September 1995
19 26 3 10 17 24 31 7 14 21 28 4 11 18 25
Jim Lewis 8.0 JL
Lea Ann Lewis 8.0 LA
Norman Smith 1.6 NS
Typesetter 8.0 TS
Print Shop 8.0 PS
UNASSIGNED 8.0 X
40.0 40.0 40.0 40.0 40.0 40.0 40.0 12.0 48.0 40.0 20.0 20.0
40.0 48.0 8.0 8.0 8.0 80.0 80.0
16.0 8.0 0.0 0.0 0.0 0.0 0.0 8.0
8.0 8.0 0.0 40.0 40.0 8.0 8.0
40.0 40.0
0.0

Norman Smith, as indicated by underlining the numbers. At the left side of the resource summary, the first column shows the number of hours of each resource is available on a daily basis. Except for Norman Smith, all resources are available eight hours each day. His availability, however, is only 1.6 hours each day. That is, he is available only on a part-time basis. (The resource called *unassigned* is reserved for an additional resource if one is needed.)

There are holidays shown at two points in the schedule. One is the week of July 4 (Independence Day) and the other is September 4 (Labor Day in the U.S.). These holidays cause the schedule to be extended by two days beyond what would be possible in strict working time.

If resources are allowed to be overloaded, the schedule could end on September 29, 1995. However, this cannot happen unless the resource availability is increased. This might be done by working overtime, but at this point, we do not know if that is necessary, since we do not have an end date imposed on the project, and have not yet determined how much the end will be extended if resources are leveled.

When CPM computations are made, ignoring resources, all activities are scheduled to start at the earliest possible time, reserving activity float to be used only if necessary. It might be possible to use some of that float to resolve the resource overloading.

To determine what the schedule would look like if resources were not overloaded, the *Autoschedule* routine of Workbench was run, using the contour loading heuristic, and all activity durations were treated as fixed. The solution shown in Figure 16.4 was obtained. This shows a slip of the end date to October 13, which is exactly two weeks.

Note that the overload for Norman Smith still exists, because the activity to which he is applied is a single critical-path activity, and the only way to resolve that problem is to increase his availability or reduce his required workload.

This solution shows what often happens in projects when

Figure 16.4

SCHEDULE WITH RESOURCES LEVELED

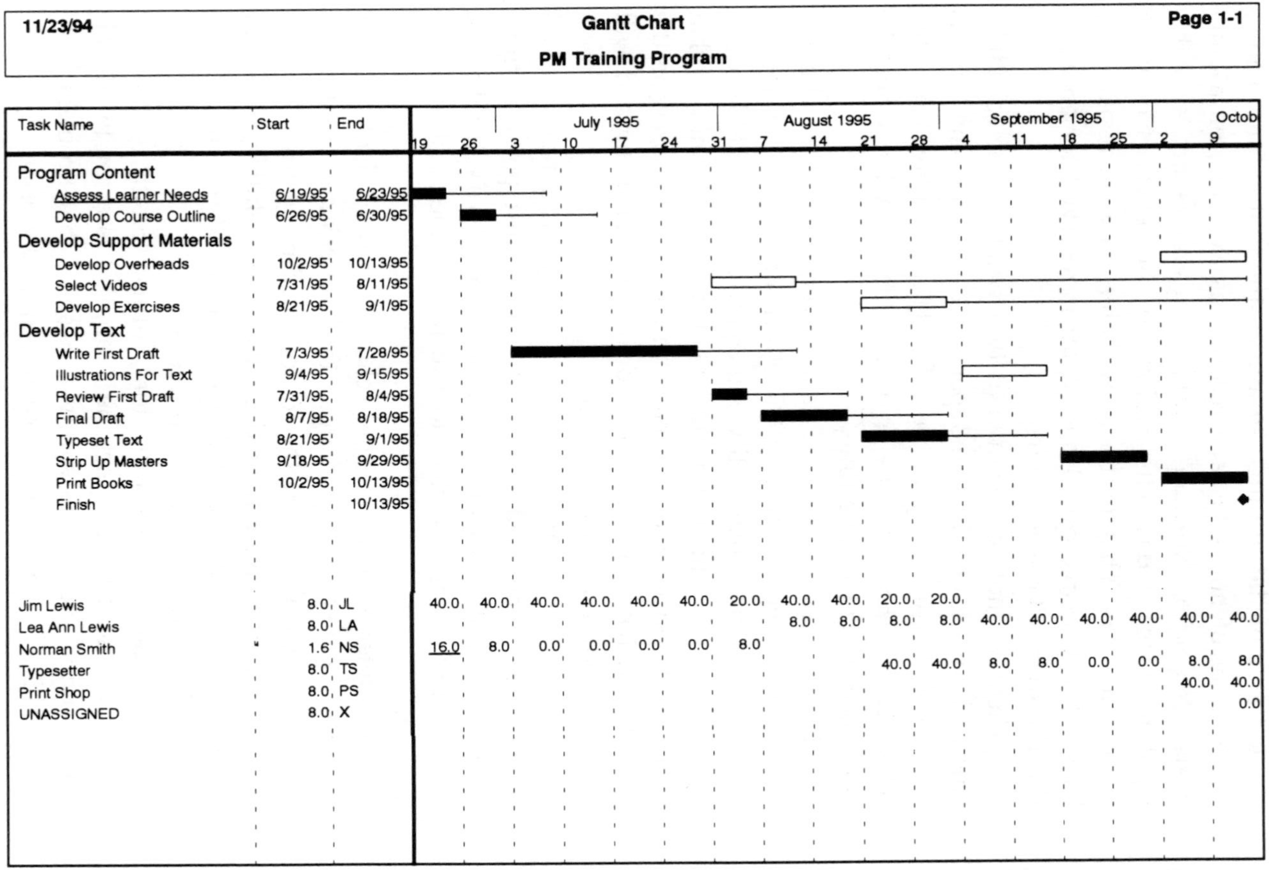

11/23/94
Gantt Chart
PM Training Program
Page 1-1
Task Name
Start
End
July 1995
August 1995
September 1995
Octob
19 26 3 10 17 24 31 7 14 21 28 4 11 18 25 2 9
Program Content
Assess Learner Needs 6/19/95 6/23/95
Develop Course Outline 6/26/95 6/30/95
Develop Support Materials
Develop Overheads 10/2/95 10/13/95
Select Videos 7/31/95 8/11/95
Develop Exercises 8/21/95 9/1/95
Develop Text
Write First Draft 7/3/95 7/28/95
Illustrations For Text 9/4/95 9/15/95
Review First Draft 7/31/95 8/4/95
Final Draft 8/7/95 8/18/95
Typeset Text 8/21/95 9/1/95
Strip Up Masters 9/18/95 9/29/95
Print Books 10/2/95 10/13/95
Finish 10/13/95
Jim Lewis 8.0 JL 40.0 40.0 40.0 40.0 40.0 40.0 20.0 40.0 40.0 20.0 20.0
Lea Ann Lewis 8.0 LA 8.0 8.0 8.0 8.0 40.0 40.0 40.0 40.0 40.0 40.0
Norman Smith 1.6 NS 16.0 8.0 0.0 0.0 0.0 0.0 8.0
Typesetter 8.0 TS 40.0 40.0 8.0 8.0 0.0 0.0 8.0 8.0
Print Shop 8.0 PS 40.0 40.0
UNASSIGNED 8.0 X 0.0

resource limitations are not considered. This would be a very real-world situation in my case, since only my wife and I would be available to do the work, and without working 80-hour weeks at some points, the program could not be completed in its shortest possible time.

In Figure 16.5 is a Task Definition report printed by Workbench. It shows the start and end dates for each activity, the duration in working days, the amount of float available, the resources applied, their planned usage, actual usage (none shown, as the project has not yet started), and the EAC (estimated at-completion cost) for each. When I entered each resource into the project database, I also entered labor rates, so that Workbench can calculate task and project costs. No cost per day was assigned to the Print Shop, since they will charge so much per book, rather than billing a labor cost.

Next, in Figure 16.6 is a printout showing the start and end dates for each task, together with the earned-value figures for each task. Since no work has started, all that is shown is the BAC (budgeted at completion) figures for each task. This report shows that the total project cost is estimated as $38,400.

Finally, in Figure 16.7 is the CPM diagram printed by Workbench. This is an activity-on-node diagram. Unfortunately, when this figure is printed on one page, the contents of the boxes are difficult to read. Each box contains the task description, its early start date, early finish date, duration in working days, and its float. Critical activities are surrounded by bold lines, and the noncritical activities by lightweight lines. Note the finish box. I put this in so that Workbench would print a final box (milestone) showing when the project ends. Note that it does not show an early start, only an early finish. (Project Workbench allows these views to be customized to show almost any combinations you wish—I have selected these as my preference.)

SCHEDULE WITH OVERLAPPING WORK

As drawn in the original diagram, the project requires that the first draft be completed before it can be reviewed. The same is

Figure 16.5
TASK LISTING SHOWING RESOURCE USE AND COST

11/23/94	Task Definition	Page 1-1
	PM Training Program	

ID	Task Name	Type	Start Date	End Date	Days	Float	Status	Resource Assignments	Total Usage	Actual Usage	EAC	Category
	Program Content	Phase										
	Assess Learner Needs	Task	6/19/95	6/23/95	5	0		Jim Lewis	5.0	0.0	2,800.0	
								Norman Smith	2.0	0.0		
	Develop Course Outline	Task	6/26/95	6/30/95	5	0		Jim Lewis	5.0	0.0	2,400.0	
								Norman Smith	1.0	0.0		
	Develop Support Materials	Phase										
	Develop Overheads	Task	10/2/95	10/13/95	10	10		Lea Ann Lewis	10.0	0.0	4,600.0	
								Typesetter	2.0	0.0		
	Select Videos	Task	7/31/95	8/11/95	10	35		Jim Lewis	2.5	0.0	1,000.0	
	Develop Exercises	Task	8/21/95	9/1/95	10	20		Jim Lewis	5.0	0.0	2,000.0	
	Develop Text	Phase										
	Write First Draft	Task	7/3/95	7/28/95	20	0		Jim Lewis	20.0	0.0	8,000.0	
	Illustrations For Text	Task	9/4/95	9/15/95	10	15		Lea Ann Lewis	10.0	0.0	4,600.0	
								Typesetter	2.0	0.0		
	Review First Draft	Task	7/31/95	8/4/95	5	0		Norman Smith	1.0	0.0	400.0	
	Final Draft	Task	8/7/95	8/18/95	10	0		Jim Lewis	10.0	0.0	4,800.0	
								Lea Ann Lewis	2.0	0.0		
	Typeset Text	Task	8/21/95	9/1/95	10	0		Typesetter	10.0	0.0	3,800.0	
								Lea Ann Lewis	2.0	0.0		
	Strip Up Masters	Task	9/18/95	9/29/95	10	0		Lea Ann Lewis	10.0	0.0	4,000.0	
	Print Books	Task	10/2/95	10/13/95	10	0		Print Shop	10.0	0.0	0.0	
	Finish	Milestone		10/13/95		0		UNASSIGNED				

FIGURE 16.6

A DETAILED ANALYSIS OF TASK COSTS

11/23/94			Detailed Analysis							Page 1
			PM Training Program							

Today's date: 11/23/94
As of date:

Name	Start	End	BCWS	BCWP	ACWP	CV	CPI	CVI	BAC	Act %
Program Content										
Assess Learner Needs	6/19/95	6/23/95	0.00	0.00	0.00	0.00	0.0	0.0	2,800.00	0.
Develop Course Outline	6/26/95	6/30/95	0.00	0.00	0.00	0.00	0.0	0.0	2,400.00	0.
Develop Support Materials										
Develop Overheads	9/4/95	9/15/95	0.00	0.00	0.00	0.00	0.0	0.0	4,600.00	0.
Select Videos	7/31/95	8/11/95	0.00	0.00	0.00	0.00	0.0	0.0	1,000.00	0.
Develop Exercises	8/21/95	9/1/95	0.00	0.00	0.00	0.00	0.0	0.0	2,000.00	0.
Develop Text										
Write First Draft	7/3/95	7/28/95	0.00	0.00	0.00	0.00	0.0	0.0	8,000.00	0.
Illustrations For Text	7/31/95	8/11/95	0.00	0.00	0.00	0.00	0.0	0.0	4,600.00	0.
Review First Draft	7/31/95	8/4/95	0.00	0.00	0.00	0.00	0.0	0.0	400.00	0.
Final Draft	8/7/95	8/18/95	0.00	0.00	0.00	0.00	0.0	0.0	4,800.00	0.
Typeset Text	8/21/95	9/1/95	0.00	0.00	0.00	0.00	0.0	0.0	3,800.00	0.
Strip Up Masters	9/4/95	9/15/95	0.00	0.00	0.00	0.00	0.0	0.0	4,000.00	0.
Print Books	9/18/95	9/29/95	0.00	0.00	0.00	0.00	0.0	0.0	0.00	0.
Finish		9/29/95								
Totals			0.00	0.00	0.00	0.00	0.0	0.0	38,400.00	0.

FIGURE 16.7
CPM DIAGRAM FOR TRAIING PROJECT

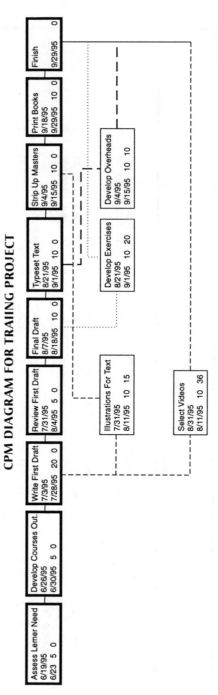

true for the reviews; they must be completed before the final draft can be done. However, if the book was reviewed on a chapter-by-chapter basis, perhaps the project duration could be reduced.

In Chapter 5 this was discussed under the heading of overlapping work. One example of such overlapping is the ladder network. Another is the use of activity splitting. Workbench allows overlapping of work so that a project can be shortened.

In Figure 16.8 is a new arrow diagram showing how activities must be connected in order to do a CPM computation. The following tasks have been overlapped, with the duration of the overlap shown, followed by the remaining task duration:

ACTIVITY DESCRIPTION	OVERLAP	REMAINING DURATION
First Draft	5	15
Reviews	4	1
Final Draft	2	8
Typesetting	2	8
Strip-up	2	8

The illustrations are also overlapped with the First Draft, but must be completed before the strip-up activity, so that arrow goes down one side of the ladder, and actually winds up on the critical path. Similarly, other parallel tasks come off at appropriate points and converge on the final event. The zero-duration dummies shown are necessary to correctly connect the activities logically. If the end points of the activities were allowed to hang out in "midair," so to speak, then they would be called "dangles," and an incorrect network computation would result.

The arrow diagram shows a possible completion time of 45 days after start, ignoring any possible resource limitations. Figure 16.9 shows the Gantt chart schedule, and the resource loading figures underneath definitely show some problems. Again, resource overloads are underlined. If the total working-days duration for the project is scaled off the Gantt chart, it turns out

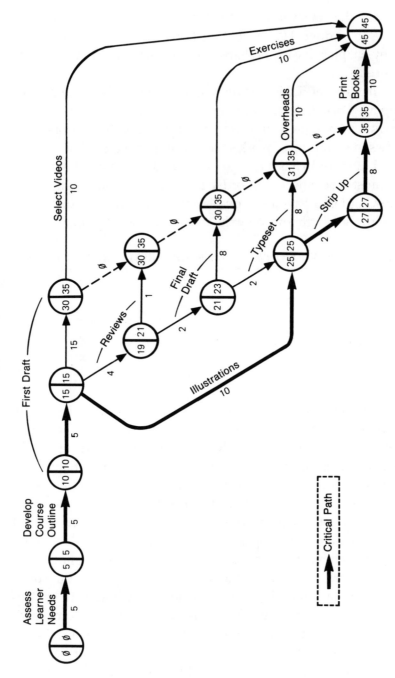

FIGURE 16.8
ARROW DIAGRAM, OVERLAPPED ACTIVITIES

FIGURE 16.9
OVERLAPPED ACTIVITIES, UNLEVELED RESOURCES

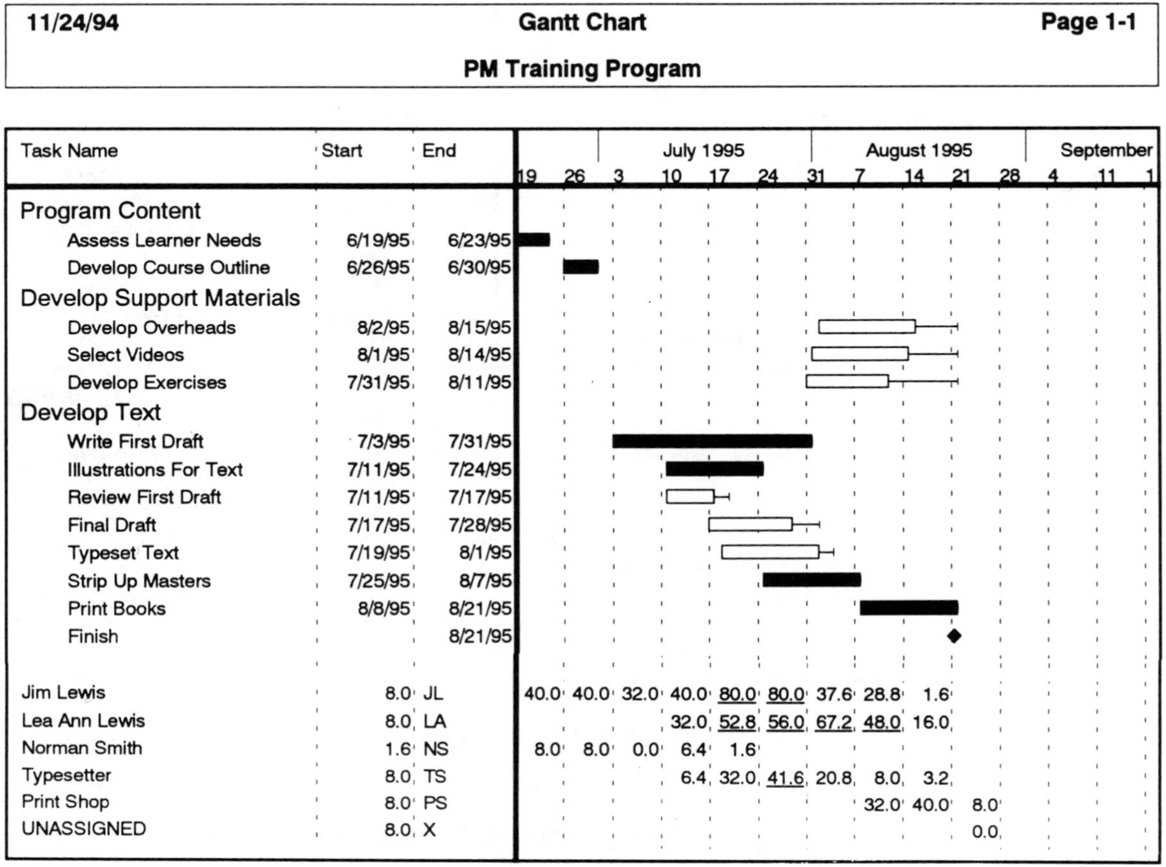

Figure 16.9 — Gantt Chart, PM Training Program, Page 1-1 (11/24/94)

FIGURE 16.10

OVERLAPPED ACTIVITIES, RESOURCES LEVELED

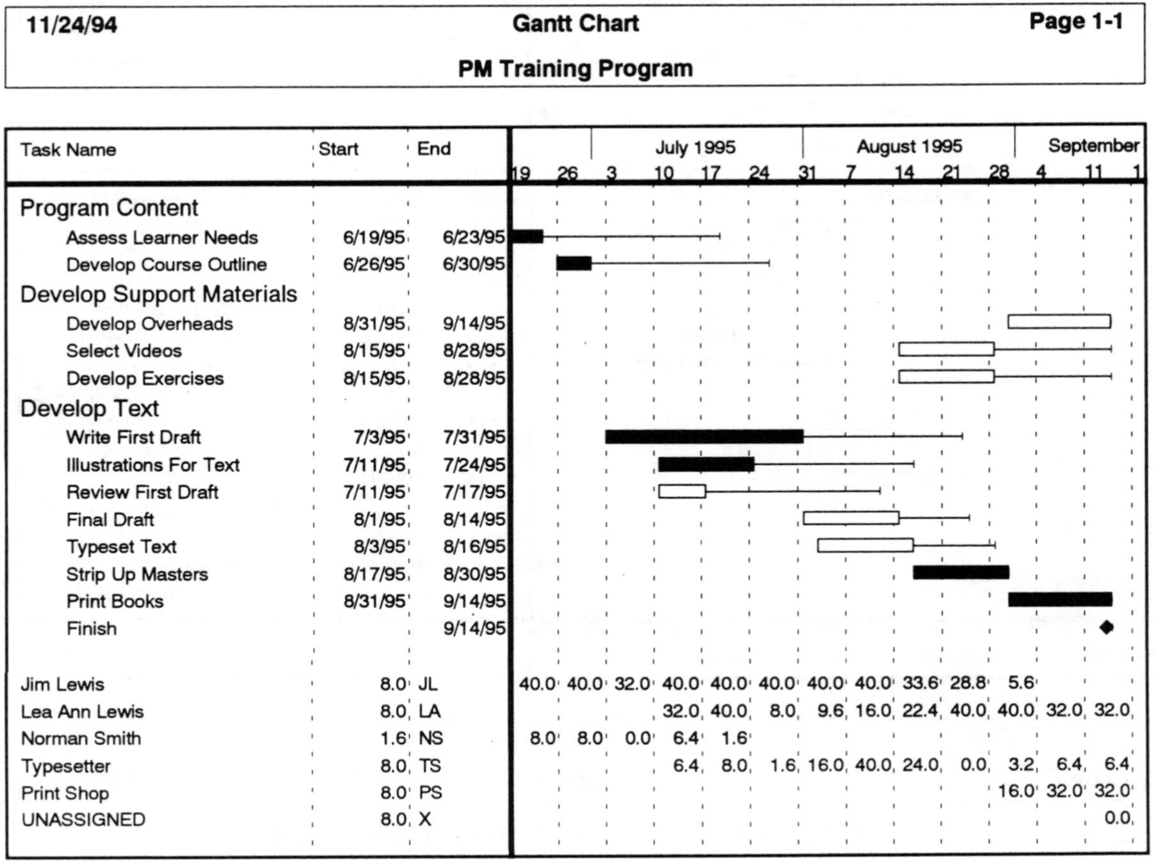
11/24/94
Gantt Chart
Page 1-1
PM Training Program
Task Name
Start
End
July 1995
August 1995
September
19 26 3 10 17 24 31 7 14 21 28 4 11 1
Program Content
Assess Learner Needs 6/19/95 6/23/95
Develop Course Outline 6/26/95 6/30/95
Develop Support Materials
Develop Overheads 8/31/95 9/14/95
Select Videos 8/15/95 8/28/95
Develop Exercises 8/15/95 8/28/95
Develop Text
Write First Draft 7/3/95 7/31/95
Illustrations For Text 7/11/95 7/24/95
Review First Draft 7/11/95 7/17/95
Final Draft 8/1/95 8/14/95
Typeset Text 8/3/95 8/16/95
Strip Up Masters 8/17/95 8/30/95
Print Books 8/31/95 9/14/95
Finish 9/14/95
Jim Lewis 8.0 JL 40.0 40.0 32.0 40.0 40.0 40.0 40.0 40.0 33.6 28.8 5.6
Lea Ann Lewis 8.0 LA 32.0 40.0 8.0 9.6 16.0 22.4 40.0 40.0 32.0 32.0
Norman Smith 1.6 NS 8.0 8.0 0.0 6.4 1.6
Typesetter 8.0 TS 6.4 8.0 1.6 16.0 40.0 24.0 0.0 3.2 6.4 6.4
Print Shop 8.0 PS 16.0 32.0 32.0
UNASSIGNED 8.0 X 0.0

to be 45, verifying that Workbench does indeed arrive at the same conclusion as the manual calculation.

This solution certainly does yield a project completion well in advance of the one with no work overlapped. The original unleveled CPM end date was September 29, whereas this one is August 21. That is a six-week gain on project completion.

However, unless resources are worked really heavy overtime, or unless more people can be put on the project to increase resource availability, the end date is not realistic. To determine the end date if no overtime is worked, *Autoschedule* was run again and the result is shown in Figure 16.10.

As the schedule shows, some of the overlaps are gone. Under limited resource conditions, it simply is not possible to do what is *logically* possible. Under resource leveling, the illustrations and reviews are overlapped with the First Draft, and the typesetting is still overlapped with the Final Draft. The end date is now September 14. This is still about two weeks earlier than the original CPM schedule yielded, thus offering a definite gain in throughput, but it is a far cry from the shortest possible schedule, because of limited resources.

The CPM printout from Workbench is shown in Figure 16.11. It looks the same as the original diagram, except that the critical path now runs along the illustrations, as was shown in the arrow diagram in Figure 16.8. The CPM printout does not capture the graphics involved in overlapping tasks.

In Figure 16.12 is a Task Definition for the project with overlapped activities. The main difference between this listing and the previous one (Figure 16.5) is the floats for the activities and the activity start and finish dates. What is significant is that activities that had float under unlimited-resource conditions now have none. It also turns out that total project costs have dropped about $400, although this figure is only shown in a Detailed Analysis report, which I have not printed.

FIGURE 16.11

CPM DIAGRAM WITH ACTIVITIES OVERLAPPED

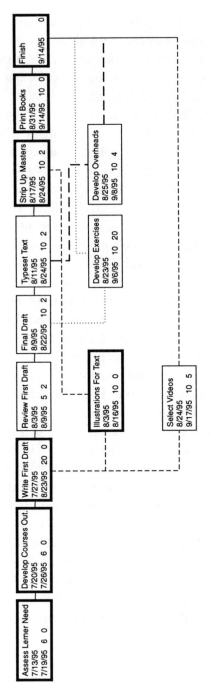

FIGURE 16.12

TASK DEFINITION FOR PROJECT WITH OVERLAPPED ACTIVITIETS

ID	Task Name	Type	Start Date	End Date	Days	Float	Status	Resource Assignments	Total Usage	Actual Usage	EAC	Category
	Program Content	Phase										
	Assess Learner Needs	Task	6/19/95	6/23/95	5	0	0	Jim Lewis	5.0	0.0	2,400.0	
								Norman Smith	1.0	0.0	0.0	
	Develop Course Outline	Task	6/26/95	6/30/95	5	0		Jim Lewis	5.0	0.0	2,400.0	
								Norman Smith	1.0	0.0	0.0	
	Develop Support Materials	Phase										
	Develop Overheads	Task	8/31/95	9/14/95	10	4		Lea Ann Lewis	10.0	0.0	4,600.0	
								Typesetter	2.0	0.0	0.0	
	Select Videos	Task	8/15/95	8/28/95	10	5		Jim Lewis	2.5	0.0	1,000.0	
	Develop Exercises	Task	8/15/95	8/28/95	10	6		Jim Lewis	5.0	0.0	2,000.0	
	Develop Text	Phase										
	Write First Draft	Task	7/3/95	7/31/95	20	0		Jim Lewis	20.0	0.0	8,000.0	
	Illustrations For Text	Task	7/11/95	7/24/95	10	0		Lea Ann Lewis	10.0	0.0	4,600.0	
								Typesetter	2.0	0.0	0.0	
	Review First Draft	Task	7/11/95	7/17/95	5	2		Norman Smith	1.0	0.0	400.0	
	Final Draft	Task	8/1/95	8/14/95	10	2		Jim Lewis	10.0	0.0	4,800.0	
								Lea Ann Lewis	2.0	0.0	0.0	
	Typeset Text	Task	8/3/95	8/16/95	10	2		Typesetter	10.0	0.0	3,800.0	
								Lea Ann Lewis	2.0	0.0	0.0	
	Strip Up Masters	Task	8/17/95	8/30/95	10	0		Lea Ann Lewis	10.0	0.0	4,000.0	
	Print Books	Task	8/31/95	9/14/95	10	0		Print Shop	10.0	0.0	0.0	
	Finish	Milestone	9/14/95			0		UNASSIGNED				

FINAL COMMENTS

This sample project illustrates the usefulness of scheduling software to solve the resource-allocation problem. Although the network is fairly simple and the total number of resources is limited, the problem is a realistic one. (I do it all the time in my training work.)

Further, it required only a few hours to enter this data into the computer and try several what-if scenarios in order to determine which would be suitable. Ten years ago this would have been virtually impossible for most project managers, simply because the software did not exist, except in huge mainframe incarnations, and even those were not nearly as user-friendly as the current personal computer software.

It seems to me, as a personal observation, that any project manager who has access to a personal computer should be able to deal with project scheduling much more effectively than was true in the past. While I have illustrated the problem using a small project, the available software is capable of handling much larger ones.

Note, however, that the software is just a tool, and no tool can correct for sloppy planning, bad estimating, factors outside the control of the manager, and so on. Nor will it help with the "people problems" that plague managers all the time. What it will do is allow you to get the most out of your skills, and that is the purpose for which this book was written.

I would welcome comments and suggestions on how the book could be improved in its next edition, and I would like to hear about your experiences in managing projects. You can write to me in care of my publisher or directly, using the following address:

James P. Lewis
302 Chestnut Mountain Drive
Vinton, VA 24179
Tel. 703-890-1560 • FAX 703-890-7470 • CompuServe 74124,2267

Best of luck to each of you.

Appendix A

CHECKLIST FOR MANAGING PROJECTS

Instructions: Check each box, as appropriate, to indicate that each activity has been completed. If the activity is not appropriate for this project, write N/A inside the box.

☐ A clear, concise statement defining the project has been prepared and reviewed by knowledgeable parties for consensus.

☐ Performance objectives have been written following guidelines in this book, and each contains an actual *calendar date for completion.*

☐ A Work Breakdown Structure has been developed to a level sufficient to prepare accurate estimates of costs, resources, and working times for all project activities.

☐ A statement of project scope clearly defines the limits of what will and will not be done.

☐ Specifications that must be met are either identified or contained in the project notebook.

☐ Tangible deliverables have been identified for specific milestones to permit progress measurements.

☐ A Linear Responsibility Chart shows involvement of key contributors to the project.

☐ A working schedule has been prepared with resources allocated so that significant planned overtime will not be required to meet project deadlines.

☐ A CPM or PERT diagram is the basis for all bar-chart working schedules, so that dependencies are known.

☐ A BCWS spending curve has been prepared to show cash flow throughout the project's duration.

☐ A SWOT analysis has been prepared, with particular attention to project risks.

☐ Where risks have been identified, contingency plans have been prepared to deal with them.

☐ If capital equipment is needed in the project, appropriate requisitions have been prepared, with cost justifications attached.

☐ The project plan was prepared with participation and/or input from individuals who must implement it.

☐ The project notebook has been signed off by stakeholders and copies distributed to contributors.

☐ A control system has been established using variance analysis to assess progress.

☐ All components of the project management system are in place, as defined by Figure 9.3 in the book.

☐ Individuals have been selected for assignment to the project whose individual needs will be met through participation, where possible.

☐ The project is planned to a manageable level of detail and no more.

☐ Work has been broken down into reasonable-duration tasks, which are not likely to be back-end loaded.

☐ A post-mortem has been done at each milestone in the project and a final one has been done for the overall project and placed in the project notebook.

☐ The controlling project notebook has been placed in a central file for use in future project planning.

☐ Members of the team have been instructed to record their working times on the project daily.

☐ A chart of accounts has been set up to track progress against the WBS.

☐ All members of the team are clear on the expectations of them in terms of authority, responsibility, and accountability.

☐ The standard operating procedure for empowering people has been applied to every member of the team.

☐ Limits have been established to determine when the project plan will be revised, such as plus or minus 10 percent budget variation, etc.

☐ The needs of customers have been carefully considered in preparing the project plan.

☐ Qualitative guides have been developed for nonquantifiable project objectives, such as project performance (the "good" component of good, fast, cheap).

☐ Checklists have been prepared for major segments of the project so that nothing is overlooked.

Appendix B

ANSWERS TO CHAPTER QUESTIONS

CHAPTER 1. AN OVERVIEW OF PROJECT MANAGEMENT

1. A project is a one-time job. A project is a problem scheduled for solution.

2. Increases in scope result in higher costs, often greater resource requirements, and perhaps a slip in the original schedule.

3. Costs decline as projects are "crashed," then rise as they are stretched out beyond a certain time because of inefficiency. This results in a minimum-cost point, or an optimum duration for the project.

4. Concurrent project management should encourage coordination of work across all functions of the organization, so that when the work is completed, everyone has had input from the beginning of the job. In this way, such things as tooling, service requirements, and manufacturability have been addressed throughout the project life cycle.

5. Problems typically occur at *concept* and *post-completion* phases of the project. At concept, the stated definition of the problem being solved is often accepted without question, leading to the right solution to the wrong problem. At post-completion, the post mortem analysis is not conducted, so that no one learns from experience with the project.

CHAPTER 2. AN INTRODUCTION TO PROJECT PLANNING

1. Control is comparing actual progress to planned progress, then taking corrective action to correct for any deviations that exist.

2. If you have no plan, you cannot exercise control.

3. Planning is answering the questions *What must be done? Who must do it? How long will it take?* and so on.

4. A signature means that, to the best of one's ability to predict, he or she will be able to meet commitments made to the project plan. For the customer, it signifies that the project, if managed as planned, will meet the customer's needs.

5. Phased planning is appropriate for research projects, which involve conditional branching, and for long-duration projects in which it is difficult to precisely predict what will take place at times exceeding a certain horizon, usually one year or greater.

6. Correct whatever about the plan is bothering the person. If the individual simply is unwilling to make a commitment, you may have to appeal to a higher authority.

CHAPTER 3. DEFINING YOUR MISSION AND DEVELOPING PROJECT STRATEGY

1. A mission statement provides all members of the project team with an overall direction, so that objectives can be set, decisions can be tested against the project mission, employees can be recruited, and so on.

2. **All** members of the project team should participate in preparing the mission statement whenever possible.

3. Exit criteria are used to tell everyone whether they are ready to leave the present phase of work and move on to the next one.

4. Strategy is the overall approach to the project, such as building a ship upside-down rather than with the keel down. Tactics are the specific steps taken to actually build the ship upside-down once that decision has been made.

5. If you are going about the project in the wrong way (wrong strategy), then no amount of attention to tactics, logistics, or other means will be likely to give you a desired outcome. Adopting a good strategy usually provides its users with a competitive advantage.

6. Any of the strategies listed by Coxon are candidates for this question. A few are: Construction-oriented, Finance-based, Design, Technology, etc. Other examples of strategy are: JIT, concurrent engineering, and cross-function management.

7. SWOT stands for Strengths, Weaknesses, Opportunities, and Threats. A SWOT analysis is the identification of these areas, with the objective of managing them to make the project successful.

8. One danger is that if there are a lot of risks facing a project, people become demoralized. Another is that the group might go into *analysis paralysis*, so that no work gets done.

9. By identifying contingencies after risks have been listed, you keep the team focused on *solutions*, rather than problems.

CHAPTER 4. DEVELOPING AN IMPLEMENTATION PLAN

1. A WBS is used to allow more-accurate estimates to be made of project cost, duration, and resource requirements than would be possible if such estimates were made at the project level.

2. The probability of an average is 50%.

3. Factors outside the person's control. These are sometimes called *system noise*.

4. A chart-of-accounts provides a numerical code that can be used to track actual work applied back to a project.

5. Because most individuals can only *guess* at how long they worked if more than a few days have passed. Future estimates based on such guesses are clearly going to be biased.

CHAPTER 5. DEVELOPING THE PROJECT SCHEDULE: GENERAL GUIDELINES

1. An event takes place at a momet in time. It is therefore *binary*—it has either occurred or it has not. An activity, on the other hand, is spread over time. It can be partially complete.

2. The hidden assumption that the organization has unlimited resources.

CHAPTER 6. SCHEDULE COMPUTATIONS

1. A forward-pass computation determines the earliest times on which activities can be completed, whereas a backward-pass computation determines the latest times for the activities.

2. The final event late date is set equal to the earliest date determined by the initial forward-pass calculation.

3. Shortening duration with planned overtime is undesirable, as it leaves no room for solving unforeseen problems and productivity tends to drop quickly. Sacrificing quality is also very undesirable.

4. Customers should approve the reduction in scope beforehand.

5. The *real finish* for an activity **must** be its *earliest finish!* The reason is that whatever float an activity has should be held in reserve in the event that unforeseen problems develop with the work. If we assume that the latest finish is acceptable, there is a tendency to allow all activity float to be used up. Then when a problem develops, it may not be possible to resolve and still meet the latest date, thus causing the end date for the project to be impacted.

6. Network solution is shown in the following diagram:

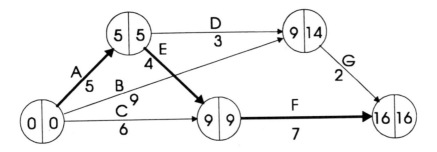

A. Activities A, E, and F are on the critical path.
B. The maximum float for activity D is six days.
C. The minimum float for activity D is one day.

CHAPTER 7. SCHEDULING WITH RESOURCE CONSTRAINTS

1. A fixed-duration activity is one that is assumed to take a fixed amount of time to complete. A variable-duration activity is one in which the duration can be changed by the computer by changing the resource levels applied. By adding resources, the duration can be reduced, and conversely.

2. Two people might take about five hours. Four people might take about three hours. You reach the *point of diminishing returns* as you continue adding people.

3. A *knowledge work* task might not be shortened by adding people. Only labor-intensive tasks can be shortened by adding people.

4. Every person must take breaks, answer the phone, and attend to other nonproject tasks. Assuming that a person is available to work on a project 100% of the time is certain to lead to trouble.

CHAPTER 8. THE PERT STATISTICAL APPROACH

1. The probability of completion in the range of 14 to 16 days is 68%. This is called a 68% *confidence interval*.

2. The probability is approximately 84%. This is determined as follows:

$$s_{cp} = \sqrt{s_A^2 + s_B^2 + s_C^2}$$

Inserting the standard deviations for each activity into the formula, we have:

$$s_{cp} = \sqrt{(0.7)^2 + (1.1)^2 + (0.4)^2}$$

which calculates to be 1.36 days. Referring to the normal distribution curve, if we add 1.36 to the 20-day critical path duration, we know that this places the upper limit one standard deviation above the mean, so there is an 84% probability that the project will end by that time.

CHAPTER 9. CONCEPTS OF PROJECT CONTROL AND EVALUATION

1. Control is exercised by comparing progress against the plan, so that steps can be taken to correct for any deviations that may exist.

2. Empowerment makes it possible for each employee to be in control of his or her own work, which is the only way in which a project manager can achieve overall project control.

3. If you have no plan, you cannot have control. This applies at *both* the project and individual level.

4. An attitude of blame and punishment on the part of an auditor will likely cause defensiveness on the part of team members and render an audit ineffective.

5. Audits should be conducted at major project milestones.

CHAPTER 10. PROJECT CONTROL USING EARNED-VALUE ANALYSIS

1. Earned value is the *dollar value* of work accomplished. If 1,000 hours were estimated to be required to do a job and only 80% of it has been completed, we say that the project team has *earned* 800 hours of work. In other words, they should have been able to do what they have done in 800 hours. If that number is multiplied by the budgeted labor rate for the work, you have BCWP, or the *value* of the work accomplished.

2. Work is ahead of schedule.

3. Because ACWP does not provide a measure of what has actually been *accomplished*. ACWP only tells what labor has cost the project. Only by including BCWP can you really tell what has been accomplished and whether the money spent has been worthwhile.

4. A summary or aggregate analysis of a project's status can be very misleading. One part of the project can have a very high negative variance that is offset by a very high positive variance, making it look as if the project is doing very well. A lower level of analysis is necessary to spot problems before they become serious.

5. The critical ratio is a composite schedule and cost index. If it has a value greater than 1, the project is doing better than plan, and conversely. By establishing limits for the critical ratio values, the project manager can establish rules for intervention.

6. Progress is *estimated* by examining the work.

CHAPTER 11. DEVELOPING THE PROJECT ORGANIZATION

1. One of the major problems is the difficulty a project manager has in keeping resources assigned to the project. There is a tendency for other project managers to "steal" them because they have emergencies.

2. Cross-functional management can be a multidisciplinary project team. The project is managing a cross-functional team in that case. Cross-function management, on the other hand, is an attempt to coordinate across functions by looking at the processes by which work gets done and optimizing those.

3. It is vital to work on *relationships* with other members of the organization.

CHAPTER 12. STAFFING A PROJECT

1. The first step in staffing is to determine what work must be done.

2. The WBS is always the starting point, as it identifies all of the tasks involved in the project.

3. In a pure-project organization, the project manager often selects those people who will be on the team. In a matrix, the members are usually assigned by functional managers.

4. Ask *open-ended* questions as much as possible. An open-ended question requires an answer beyond a simple yes or no.

Chapter 13. The Role of the Project Manager

1. It is very important to be *proactive,* as opposed to *reactive.* Further, a project manager seldom has a lot of authority, so he or she must use influence to get things done.

2. A common way to reduce the flexibility of a group is to impose lots of prohibitions on them. These are called *policies.* They are the "thou shalt nots" of the organization. This is **not** the way to reduce variability. The way to reduce variability is to insist that each team member have an individual working plan, which she or he follows. This is the only way that each member will be in control, and similarly, the only way that the project manager will achieve control.

Chapter 14. Leadership in Project Management

1. *To manage* means "to handle." *To lead* means "to influence others to go in the same direction in which you are going." I see managing as dealing with the administrative aspects of managing a project—the budgeting, scheduling, controlling. Leading has to do with dealing with people, to keep them committed, motivated, and so on.

2. The self-fulfilling prophecy.

3. It is based on the assumption of linear causality, whereas in human interaction, most causality is *circular.* That is, influence is *reciprocal!*

4. The hand-holding style. She needs guidance, structure, and nurturing until she can begin to work more independently.

Chapter 15. How to Motivate *Almost* Anyone

1. Motivation is the internal drive to satisfy needs.

2. If a person is hungry, cold, insecure, or cut off from society, he or she is not likely to try to self-actualize. Those lower-level needs must be minimally met in order for a person to move up the hierarchy (according to Maslow).

3. By engaging in certain *patterns of activity.* For some it is innovation. For others it may be trouble-shooting. There are a number of fairly common patterns, and some that are not seen very often.

4. They may become *demotivated.* Herzberg suggested that you cannot be motivated and demotivated at the same time, and that being demotivated often takes priority.

5. It is hard to imagine someone being motivated to do a job unless she or he is first committed to it. Commitment comes from seeing

the value of doing something. Motivation comes from having one's needs met through engaging in the activity.

6. All motivation comes from *within* a person. All a manager can do is try to place the employee in a job that contains his or her motivation pattern, and the rest is up to the employee.

SPECIAL NOTES:

_____

_____

_____

_____

_____

_____

_____

_____

_____

_____

_____

_____

_____

_____

_____

_____

_____

_____

_____

Glossary

PROJECT MANAGEMENT TERMS

Activity The work or effort needed to achieve a result. It consumes time and usually consumes resources.

Activity Description A statement specifying what must be done to achieve a desired result.

Activity-on-Arrow A network diagram showing sequence of activities, in which each activity is represented by an arrow, with a circle representing a node or event at each end.

Activity-on-Node A network diagram showing sequence of activities, in which each activity is represented by a box or circle (that is, a *node*) and these are interconnected with arrows to show precedence of work.

Authority The legitimate power given to a person in an organization to use resources to reach an objective and to exercise discipline.

Backward-Pass Calculation A calculation made working backward through a network from the latest event to the beginning event to calculate event late times. A forward-pass calculation determines early times.

Calendars The arrangement of normal working days, together with nonworking days, such as holidays and vacations, as well as special workdays (overtime periods) used to determine dates on which project work will be completed.

Change Order A document that authorizes a change in some aspect of a project.

Control The practice of monitoring progress against a plan so that corrective steps can be taken when a deviation from plan occurs.

CPM An acronym for Critical Path Method. A network diagramming method which shows the longest series of activities in a project, thereby determining the earliest completion for the project.

Crashing An attempt to reduce activity or total project duration, usually by adding resources.

Critical Path The longest sequential path of activities which are absolutely essential for completion of the project.

Dependency The next task or group of tasks cannot begin until preceding work has been completed, thus the word *dependent* or *dependency.*

Deviation Any variation from planned performance. The deviation can be in terms of schedule, cost, performance, or scope of work. Deviation analysis is the heart of exercising project control.

Dummy Activity A zero-duration element in a network showing a logic linkage. A dummy does not consume time or resources, but simply indicates precedence.

Duration The time it takes to complete an activity.

Earliest Finish The earliest time that an activity can be completed.

Earliest Start The earliest time that an activity can be started.

Estimate A forecast or guess about how long an activity will take, how many resources might be required, or how much it will cost.

Event A point in time. An event is binary. It is either achieved or not, whereas an activity can be partially complete. An event can be the start or finish of an activity.

Feedback Information derived from observation of project activities, which is used to analyze the status of the job and take corrective action if necessary.

Float A measure of how much an activity can be delayed before it begins to impact the project finish date.

Forward-Pass Method The method used to calculate the Earliest Start time for each activity in a network diagram.

Free Float The amount of time that an activity can be delayed without affecting succeeding activities.

Gantt Chart A bar chart that indicates the time required to complete each activity in a project. It is named for Henry L. Gantt, who first developed a complete notational system for displaying progress with bar charts.

Hammock Activity A single activity that actually represents a group of activities. It "hangs" between two events and is used to report progress on the composite that it represents.

Histogram A vertical bar chart showing (usually) resource allocation levels over time in a project.

i-j notation A system of numbering nodes in an activity-on-arrow network. The i-node is always the beginning of an activity, while the j-node is always the finish.

Inexcusable Delays Project delays that are attributable to negligence on the part of the contractor, which lead in many cases to penalty payments.

Latest Finish The latest time that an activity can be finished without extending the end date for a project.

Latest Start The latest time that an activity can start without extending the end date for a project.

Learning Curve The time it takes humans to learn an activity well enough to achieve optimum performance can be displayed by curves, which must be factored into estimates of activity durations in order to achieve planned completion dates.

Leveling An attempt to smooth the use of resources, whether people, materials, or equipment, to avoid large peaks and valleys in their usage.

Life Cycle The phases that a project goes through from concept through completion. The nature of the project changes during each phase.

Matrix Organization A method of drawing people from functional departments within an organization for assignment to a project team, but without removing them from their physical location. The project manager in such a structure is said to have *dotted-line* authority over team members.

Milestone An event of special importance, usually representing the completion of a major phase of project work. Reviews are often scheduled at milestones.

Most Likely Time The most realistic time estimate for completing an activity under normal conditions.

Negative Float or Slack A condition in a network in which the *earliest time* for an event is actually later than its *latest time*. This happens when the project has a constrained end date that is earlier than can be achieved, or when an activity uses up its float and is still delayed.

Node A point in a network connected to other points by one or more arrows. In activity-on-arrow notation, the node contains at least one event. In activity-on-node notation, the node represents an activity, and the arrows show the sequence in which they must be performed.

PERT An acronym that stands for Program Evaluation and Review Technique. PERT makes use of network diagrams as does CPM, but in addition applies statistics to activities to try and estimate the probabilities of completion of project work.

Pessimistic Time Roughly speaking, this is the *worst-case* time to complete an activity. The term has a more precise meaning, which is defined in the PERT literature.

Phase A major component or segment of a project.

Precedence Diagram An activity-on-node diagram.

Queue Waiting time.

Resource Allocation The assignment of people, equipment, facilities, or materials to a project. Unless adequate resources are provided, project work cannot be completed on schedule, and resource allocation is a significant component of project scheduling.

Resource Pool A group of people who can generally do the same work, so that they can be chosen randomly for assignment to a project.

Risk The possibility that something can go wrong and interfere with the completion of project work.

Scope The magnitude of work that must be done to complete a project.

Subproject A small project within a larger one.

Statement of Work A description of work to be performed.

Time Now The current calendar date from which a network analysis, report, or update is being made.

Time Standard The time allowed for the completion of a task.

Variance Any deviation of project work from what was planned. Variance can be around costs, time, performance, or project scope.

Work Breakdown Structure A method of subdividing work into smaller and smaller increments to permit accurate estimates of durations, resource requirements, and costs.

FURTHER READING

Aaker, David A. *Developing Business Strategies*. New York: Wiley, 1984.

Adams, James L. *Conceptual Blockbusting: A Guide to Better Ideas*. 2d ed. New York: W.W. Norton, 1979.

Adams, John, ed. *Transforming Leadership: From Vision to Results*. Alexandria, VA: Miles River Press, 1986.

Adams, John, ed. *Transforming Work*. Alexandria, VA: Miles River Press, 1984.

Akao, Yoji, ed. *Quality Function Deployment: Integrating Customer Requirements Into Product Design*. Cambridge, MA: Productivity Press, 1990.

Albrecht, K. *The Northbound Train*. New York: AMACOM Books, 1994.

Argyris, Chris. *Overcoming Organizational Defenses*. Boston: Allyn and Bacon, 1990.

Blake, Robert R., and Mouton, Jane S. *The Managerial Grid*. Houston, TX: Gulf Publishing, 1964.

Block, Peter. *The Empowered Manager: Positive Political Skills at Work*. San Francisco: Jossey-Bass, 1987.

Bolles, Richard N. *What Color Is Your Parachute?* Berkeley, CA: Ten Speed Press, 1987.

de Bono, Edward. *Serious Creativity*. New York: HarperCollins, 1992.

de Bono, Edward. *Six Thinking Hats*. Boston: Little, Brown & Co., 1985.

Bramson, Robert M. *Coping With Difficult People*. New York: Dell, 1981.

Burns, James MacGregor. *Leadership*. New York: Harper and Row, 1978.

Burrill, C.W., and Ellsworth, L.W. *Modern Project Management*. Tenafly, NJ: Burrill-Ellsworth Associates, 1980.

Calero, Henry H., and Bob Oskam. *Negotiate the Deal You Want*. New York: Dodd, Mead & Company, 1983.

Carlzon, Jan. *Moments of Truth*. New York: Perennial Library, 1989.

Cleland, David I., and King, William R., Editors *Project Management Handbook.* New York:Van Nostrand, 1983.

Coxon, R. "How Strategy Can Make Major Projects Prosper." *Management Today.* (April 1983).

Davis, Stanley M., and Paul R. Lawrence. *Matrix.* Reading, MA: Addison-Wesley, 1977.

Dimancescu, Dan. *The Seamless Enterprise: Making Cross-Functional Management Work.* New York: Harper, 1992.

Drucker, Peter F. *Management: Tasks, Responsibilities, Practices.* New York: Harper & Row, 1973, 1974.

Dyer, William G. *Team Building: Issues and Alternatives.* 2d ed. Reading, MA: Addison-Wesley, 1987.

Fleming, Q. W. *Cost/Schedule Control Systems Criteria.* Chicago: Probus, 1988.

Fleming, Q. W.; J. W. Bronn, and Gary C. Humphreys. *Project and Production Scheduling.* Chicago: Probus, 1987.

Fournies, Ferdinand F. *Coaching for Improved Work Performance.* New York: Van Nostrand, 1978.

Hackman, J. Richard, and Greg R. Oldham. *Work Redesign.* Reading, MA: Addison-Wesley, 1980.

Harvey, Jerry. *The Abilene Paradox: And Other Meditations on Management.* San Diego: University Associates, 1988.

Hersey, Paul. *The Situational Leader.* New York: Warner Books, 1984.

Hersey, Paul, and Kenneth Blanchard. *Management of Organizational Behavior: Utilizing Human Resources.* 4th ed. Englewood Cliffs, NJ: Prentice Hall, 1981.

House, Charles H., and Raymond L. Price. "The Return Map: Tracking Product Teams." *Harvard Business Review,* Vol. 69, No. 1, pp. 92-100. HBR reprint number 91106.

Juran, J. M. *Leadership for Quality.* New York: Free Press, 1989.

Kouzes, James M., and Barry Z. Posner. *The Leadership Challenge.* San Francisco: Jossey-Bass, 1987.

Kram, Kathy E. *Mentoring at Work.* New York: University Press of America, 1988.

Lewis, James P. *The Project Manager's Desk Reference*. Chicago: Probus, 1993.

Lewis, James P. *How to Build and Manage a Winning Project Team*. New York: AMACOM, 1993.

Maccoby, Michael. *Why Work: Leading the New Generation*. New York: Simon and Schuster, 1988.

March, James G., and Herbert A. Simon. *Organizations*. New York: Wiley, 1958.

McClelland, David C. *Power: The Inner Experience*. New York: Irvington, 1975.

Mendelssohn, Kurt. *The Riddle of the Pyramids*. New York: Irvington, 1975.

Miller, William C. *The Creative Edge: Fostering Innovation Where You Work*. Reading, MA: Addison-Wesley, 1986.

Moder, Joseph J., Cecil R. Phillips, and Edward W. Davis. *Project Management With CPM, PERT, and Precedence Diagramming* 3d ed. New York: Van Nostrand, 1983.

von Oech, Roger. *A Whack on the Side of the Head*. New York: Warner, 1983.

von Oech, Roger. *A Kick in the Seat of the Pants*. New York: Warner, 1986.

Oncken, William, Jr. *Managing Management Time*. Englewood Cliffs, NJ: Prentice-Hall, 1984.

Packard, Vance. *The Pyramid Climbers*. New York: McGraw-Hill, 1962.

Patterson, M. *Accelerating Innovation: Improving the Process of Product Development*. New York: Van Nostrand, 1993.

Peters, Tom. *Thriving on Chaos: Handbook for a Management Revolution*. New York: Knopf, 1987.

Peters, Tom. *Liberation Management: Necessary Disorganization for the Nanosecond Nineties*. New York: Knopf, 1992.

Ray, M., and R. Myers. *Creativity in Business*. Garden City, NY: Doubleday, 1986.

Reddy, W. and K. Jamison. *Team Building: Blueprints for Productivity and Satisfaction*. San Diego: University Associates, 1988.

Rickards, Tudor. *Problem Solving Through Creative Analysis*. Epping, Essex, England: Gower Press, 1975.

Rifkin, Jeremy. *Time Wars*. New York: Touchstone, 1987.

Ritvo, Roger, and Alice Sargent, eds. *The NTL Managers' Handbook*. Arlington, VA: NTL Institute, 1983.

Ritz, George J. *Total Engineering Project Management*. New York: McGraw-Hill, 1990.

Schumacher, E. F. *Small Is Beautiful*. New York: Perennial Library, 1973.

Senge, Peter M. *The Fifth Discipline: The Art and Practice of the Learning Organization*. New York: Doubleday Currency, 1990.

Steinmetz, Lawrence L. *Managing the Marginal & Unsatisfactory Performer*. 2d ed. Reading, Mass.: Addison-Wesley, 1985.

Stewart, Rodney D. *Cost Estimating*. 2d ed. New York: Wiley, 1991.

Uris, Auren. *The Executive Deskbook*. 3d ed. New York: Van Nostrand Reinhold, 1988.

Ray, M., and R. Myers. *Creativity in Business*. Garden City, NY: Doubleday, 1986.

Walpole, Ronald E. *Introduction to Statistics, Second Edition*. New York: Macmillan, 1974.

Walton, Mary. *The Deming Management Method*. New York: Dodd, Mead & Company, 1986.

Walton, Richard E. *Interpersonal Peacemaking: Confrontations and Third-Party Consultation*. Reading, MA: Addison-Wesley, 1969.

Watzlawick, P., J. Beavin, and D. Jackson. *Pragmatics of Human Communication*. New York: Norton, 1967.

Wheelwright, S., and K. Clark. *Revolutionizing Product Development: Quantum Leaps in Speed, Efficiency, and Quality*. New York: Free Press, 1992.

Winner, Robert I., James P. Pennell, Harold E. Bertrand, and Marko M. G. Slusarczuk. *The Role of Concurrent Engineering in Weapons System Acquisition*. Alexandria, VA: Institute for Defense Analysis, 1988.

RESOURCES FOR PROJECT MANAGERS

Following is a list of sources of information, books, and professional associations which may be helpful in managing projects. Not all are specifically aimed at project management, but you may find them helpful anyway.

The Business Reader: This is a mail-order bookstore specializing in business books. If it's on business, the chances are they have it! P.O. Box 41268 • Brecksville, OH 44141 • Tel. (216) 838-8653 • FAX: (216) 838-8104

CRM Films: A good source of films for training, including *Mining Group Gold, The Abilene Paradox,* and many others. 2215 Faraday Avenue • Carlsbad, CA 92008 • Tel. (800) 421-0833

Lewis Consulting & Training: In 1995 LCT will be offering a certificate series in project management, consisting of six courses. These will include Team Building, Finance and Accounting for Project Managers, Total Quality Management and QFD Analysis, Tools, Principles & Practices, Advanced Project Management, and Negotiating Skills. 302 Chestnut Mountain Dr. • Vinton, VA 24179 • Tel. (540) 890-1560 • FAX: (540) 890-7470 • CompuServe 74124,2267

MindWare: The store for the other 90% of your brain. A source of tools, books and other materials for helping enhance learning and creativity in organizations. They have a nice catalog listing their materials. 6142 Olson Mem. Hwy. • Golden Valley, MN. 55422 • Tel. (800) 999-0398 • FAX: (612) 595-8852

Morasco, Vincent: A newspaper clipping service that operates on a pay-per-use basis. You pay only for the clippings you actually make use of. A good source of up-to-the-minute information. Vincent Morasco • 3 Cedar Street • Batavia, NY 14020 • (716) 343-2544

Pegasus Communications: Publishers of *The Systems Thinker,* a monthly newsletter. They also have videos by Russell Ackoff and Peter Senge, among others. P.O. Box 943 • Oxford, OH 45056-0943 • Tel. (800) 636-3796 • FAX: (905) 764-7983

Pfeiffer & Company: A source of training programs, training materials, instruments, and books on management. 8517 Production Avenue • San Diego, CA 92121-2280 • Tel (800) 274-4434 • FAX: (800) 569-0443

Pimsleur International: The most effective way to learn a language on your own is with cassettes, using a method developed by Dr. Paul Pimsleur. Learning is virtually painless. 30 Monument Square, Suite 135 • Concord, MA 01742 • Tel. (800) 222-5860 • FAX: (508) 371-2935

Project Management Institute: The professional association for project managers. Over 10,000 members nationwide. They have local chapters in most major U.S. cities. 130 S. State Road • Upper Darby, PA 19082 • Tel. (610) 734-3330 • FAX: (610) 734-3266

ABOUT THE AUTHOR

James P. Lewis, Ph.D., is the founder of Lewis Consulting & Training, an association of professionals providing project management and behavioral consulting and training throughout the United States, England, and the Far East. This includes team building, project management, engineering management, and problem solving to several Fortune 500 companies in the United States. He has also conducted team training workshops for organizations in Bintulu, Sarawak, and Surabaya, Indonesia.

An outstanding workshop leader, he has trained more than 15,000 managers and supervisors since 1981, drawing on his many years of firsthand experience as a manager with ITT Telecommunications and Aerotron, Inc., where he held positions including Product Engineering Manager, Chief Engineer, and Project Manager. He also served as Quality Manager for ITT Telecom during the last two years of his industrial career. During his 15 years as an electrical engineer, Jim designed and developed a variety of communications equipment for application in land, sea, and mobile environments. He holds a joint patent on a programmable memory for a transceiver.

He has published numerous articles on managing as well as four books on project management: *How to Build and Manage an Effective Project Team*, *Fundamentals of Project Management*, both published by the American Management Association; *Project Planning, Scheduling and Control*, and *The Project Manager's Desk Reference*, published by Probus Publishing. He holds a B.S. in Electrical Engineering and both M.S. and Ph.D. degrees in Organizational Psychology, all from North Carolina State University.

Jim is married to the former Lea Ann McDowell, and they live in Vinton, Virginia, in the Blue Ridge Mountains. Although they have no children of their own, they have three exchange-student "daughters," Yukiko Bono of Japan, Katarina Sigerud of Sweden, and Susi Mraz of Austria. He can be reached at (540) 890-1560 or by fax at (540) 890-7470.

INDEX